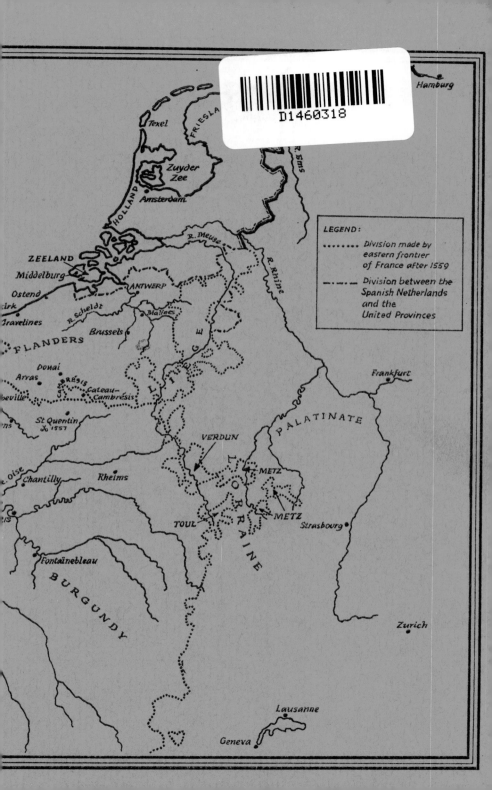

THE DEBATABLE LAND

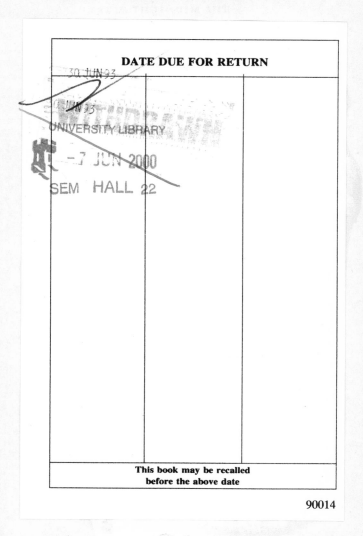

SIR NICHOLAS THROCKMORTON

MICHAEL BURN

The Debatable Land

A STUDY OF THE MOTIVES
OF SPIES IN TWO AGES

HAMISH HAMILTON
LONDON

First Published in Great Britain, 1970
by Hamish Hamilton Ltd.
90 Great Russell Street London W.C.1
Printed in Great Britain by
Western Printing Services Ltd, Bristol

© 1970 *by Michael Burn*

SBN 241 01778 5

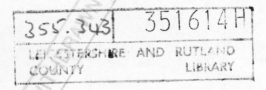

TO FREDA AND JOHN BRIDGMAN

Contents

Illustrations

Maps

(by Patrick Leeson)

Genealogical Tables

Prologue

QUESTIONS ARISING

THE main purpose of this book is to examine the motives of spies. No classic History of Espionage has yet been published. The subject is a vast one. Here I have confined myself to studying a limited number of people, patriots and traitors, who engaged in international or domestic espionage during the Tudor (principally Elizabethan) period. This study occupies most of the book, and at the end I have set these 16th-century spies against some from our own day; the circumstances are vastly different, but the motives I believe to be the same.

Many subsidiary questions have occurred, and are bound to occur to anyone who tries to go at all deeply into the nature of espionage. First of all, what is a spy?

In England the word has no legal definition. In most countries men and women thought of and written about as spies have been tried, or would have been tried if caught, and not killed outright, for specific offences against the security of the State; and these offences have varied enormously from country to country and from age to age. The *Encyclopaedia Britannica*, proposing a general definition, calls espionage 'the attempt to obtain, by clandestine means, for communication to a foreign Government, information concerning another Government which is likely to be injurious to that Government'. This definition leaves large gaps. It does not cover spying against spies, which forms part of the apparatus of any large well-run State. It does not cover the secret surveillance a Government practises over its own citizens, nor the secret surveillance practised against a Government by hostile citizens who wish to overthrow it. Domestic spying for or against the Government proliferates on the fear or hope of interference from abroad or revolt at home. Most modern countries engage in domestic spying, and so did England and most of Europe during the first Elizabethan age.

For the purposes of this book I define a spy as possessing four essential characteristics:

1. He is deliberately involved in the conveying of information about people or things recently observed.

2. He acquires or sends it secretly. Those ordered to observe the Earl of Essex during his fatal Irish campaign could obtain the facts quite openly; but they had to pass them back to London secretly. It is unusual for intelligence obtained secretly to be passed on openly.

3. The information he seeks or conveys is for the use of people hostile to or suspicious of those it is about, and usually for and about people in Government positions, or thought to be threatening to a Government.

4. He is consciously a deceiver. This excludes people, of whom there have been many, who are drawn into spying unaware. A diplomatic courier often carries secret and hostile intelligence. This he knows, but so do the enemy; he is not a spy. But a man certainly involves himself in espionage who conveys or collects intelligence while pretending to be doing something else.

Deception will usually, though not necessarily, extend to the betrayal of some allegiance which on the surface the spy maintains. All men, whether they like it or not, are born into certain allegiances, some with and others without the force of law. There have been allegiances to a tribe, a clan, a family, a feudal lord, a Church, a nation. Allegiances may be acquired to a wife, a family of one's own, to friends. More is heard now of allegiances to a view of history, or a class, or democracy, or peace, or liberty, than of the allegiance to God which mattered profoundly in 16th-century Europe and savagely divided it. Spies reject allegiances in secret, while outwardly appearing still to hold them; often they will of set purpose assume some public allegiance in order the better to go about their work. Whether it is a book he has sworn on, or a paper he has signed, or a clan whose badge he wears, or a bed he sleeps in, or only an unwritten and unspoken confidence reposed in him, sooner or later a spy's activities are likely to have the taint of a betrayal; employed on a sufficient scale, spies destroy all trust.

Many spies do not of course think of themselves as breaking faith; their faith is hidden in their secret heart and mind. But they can rarely avoid the exterior assumption of some role or the profession of some loyalty, which role is not their true one, which loyalty they calculate continually to violate. The firmer the pledges and deeper the trust, the greater the breach and probably the more brilliant the success.

Thus the study of espionage becomes a study of the validity of loyalties and causes us to weigh the relative importance to ourselves of things we seldom trouble to put into the scales. It exposes in the story of spies an initial crisis of choice which may have been more searching than the subsequent risks and thrills, and by asking us how we ourselves would have chosen, and why, drills to the foundation of our own constancies. In particular it challenges those alike who unhesitatingly follow the national flag ('My country, right or wrong') and those who tend to scoff at it ('Patriotism means nothing to me'), inquiring of the former at what point it might cease to influence them, and of the latter at what point it might begin. For though people spied long before they became members of a nation, and though patriotism was little cherished in the Middle Ages and may during this century pass into a wider allegiance, it is nonetheless the breach of national loyalty with which people still most commonly reproach the spy, and obedience to it for which they praise him.

Within this limit we observe the following categories:

1. The espionage one Government practises against another.
2. The espionage used to defeat this.
3. The secret watch a Government keeps on its own people.
4. The secret watch some of its people keep upon the Government.

All involve the secret passing of information. All have a hostile or a suspicious motive, and all sooner or later involve deception.

Most novels about spies depict men and women who do little else but spy. Most spy stories purporting to be true depict men and women whom spying, and spying alone, distinguishes. A convention has developed among historians, according to which the Gentlemen are called 'secret agents' and only the Players spies, the difference depending upon whether or not a person does it for a livelihood. (Professional spies, however, writing about themselves, speak of themselves as 'agents'.) There seems to be a wish to avoid the stench of what is still a nasty word. Professionals have their protocol; as for the part-timers, what they did was in their own eyes anything but nasty, and historians show them a differentiating courtesy. Yet many people must be booked as spies who were (and doubtless are) better known for something else.

Benedict Arnold turned from a brilliant soldier into a spy. Beaumarchais, author of *The Marriage of Figaro*, was deeply and profitably involved. So was the great financier, Sir Thomas Gresham.

Christopher Marlowe probably spied. Lawrence of Arabia spied. The eminent Irish barrister, Leonard Macnally, sold the Irish patriots he defended to the English. Père Joseph, Capuchin mystic, was that same Grey Eminence who headed Richelieu's secret service. We know, though it is not openly made too much of to Boy Scouts, that Lord Baden-Powell spied. So did the author of *Robinson Crusoe*. A man who really is a respected merchant, or banker, priest, civil servant, writer, doctor, or professor, has ready a genuine cover. Certain professions, notably those which demand dispassionate research, train people from youth in the attitude of mind necessary for secret service. The roll-call of spies famous for something else would be a long one; according to the definition given above, many illustrious people spied at some time or another during their lives, whether or not they did it part-time or all for love, whether or not the cause for which they spied succeeded and is therefore said to have been 'justified by history'.

It has been difficult to decide how the material should be presented. A study of Elizabethan espionage, offered as a mere inventory of Elizabethan spies, might have been of value as research, but also dull and narrow in the extreme, failing to depict them as part of a living Intelligence service, itself a part of much larger operations. Intelligence involves many people reporting from many places. It needs to be seen on a great canvas, like a mighty policy or a war. Those who take part include not only men and women who plunged dagger or assumed cloak, nor only those who sat in dungeons as stool-pigeons, who listened at keyholes or behind screens or down tubes. We should not forget the secret couriers, nor those who sent out spies, ciphered what they carried, deciphered what they brought, paid them and analysed the results. Most spy stories throw the spotlight on the exciting activities of one or two individuals. This is not *Hamlet* without the Prince of Denmark. It is *Hamlet* with almost no one else.

I have started therefore by telling the story of Intelligence during one great Elizabethan conspiracy, and only one, in which the figures take their places under a more dispersed illumination. The reign abounds in conspiracies: Ridolfi plot, rising of the Northern Earls, the Duke of Norfolk's plot, Throckmorton plot, Parry plot, Babington plot, Lopez plot, and the final intrigue to ease James VI of Scotland peacefully on to the English throne, to name only a few. Exciting though they all are and dominated, some of them, by the seductive personality of the Queen of Scots, they have been well worked over and the truth about several remains in doubt. I have chosen the conspiracy of 1559–60, which ended in a brief war and resulted in the final expulsion of the French from Scotland and the triumph of the Scottish Reformation.

The conspiracy in Scotland possesses a chronological advantage in that it took place almost immediately after Elizabeth's accession. It had lasting consequences of first importance to England, Scotland and Christianity. The facts are not in serious dispute. It affords incidentally an opportunity to examine the vast difference between espionage in capital cities and espionage across a wild Borderland. Above all it displays in a fairly simple form that recurrent conflict between a man's allegiance to the Government of his country and his allegiance to a faith which his Government opposes and persecutes; English Catholics were beginning to intrigue and spy against the Protestant State re-established by Elizabeth, while in France and Scotland Huguenots and Calvinists spied against a Catholic Government. The intellectual and spiritual transgression by spies of frontiers within which they continue to live is an ingredient present in all the later conspiracies of the reign and in countless others until our own time.

This account of international Intelligence occupies the first part of this book. The second is principally concerned with domestic Intelligence, and emerges from the first. Scotland was a powder-barrel connected to two fuses leading into England, one Franco-Catholic, the other Scottish-Calvinist. If in 1559–60 the French fuse was allowed to run on unchecked, Elizabeth stood to lose her throne to Mary Stuart and the English Catholics; if the Scottish, she might find herself compelled to submit to extreme English Reformers sympathetic to John Knox and flocking home from exile in Germany and Geneva. Checked both fuses were, and ran on more slowly, the Catholic cause passing into the control of Spain rather than of a France crippled by civil war. It was not until some twenty years later that Elizabeth felt the internal security of the realm to be threatened critically and simultaneously by both the Catholics and the Puritan allies of Scottish Presbyterianism. I have followed therefore with some account of the Intelligence conducted against both during the 1580s. 'Penetration' and 'infiltration' are part of the vocabulary of contemporary secret service. Some of the Elizabethan Puritans were penetrators and infiltrators, counter-penetrated and counter-infiltrated by Richard Bancroft. In this part of the story I have aimed to bring out the climate of parochial spite and animosity, which any Intelligence service can so easily exacerbate and exploit. Many Governments have been more than ready to supervise a people through the green eyes of private jealousies, and a big shark can be raised in quite a small puddle. But neither in the story of the Scottish conspiracy, nor in that of the Puritans, is there any nameable spy out of whom to make a sensation, no individual to compare with Yevko Azev, who penetrated the Russian Social-Revolutionaries at the end of the last century, no Richard Sorge, no Colonel Abel, no Philby.

The Roman Catholic story is immense, intricate, and in parts still obscured by controversy. It offers dozens of well-documented professional spies, some of them well enough known already. I have been content with only a few and concentrated on one or two aspects of that story, which were relevant to my general purpose.

Intelligence is given its place and no more than its place within the background and necessities of State. Out of background men emerge, or are forced or coaxed, and start to spy. Some full-time spider will be waiting for them somewhere. Spiders spin from nests. Intelligence, in order to succeed for any length of time, must be conducted from a nest or centre. Such a centre existed in England unbroken during a longer period of the 16th century than of the 17th or of course the 15th. When Elizabeth came to the throne the feudal fabric had long been in decay and within a year the temporal power of the Papacy in England had been destroyed. Throughout most of her reign, until her declining years, she continued to consolidate her hold. A number of her courtiers (the Earls of Leicester and Essex, for example) entertained personal Intelligence services; but without the centralized and settled Government there could not have been such flourishing signs of a national Secret Service as we now know it. The most distinguished spy-masters and State detectives were William Cecil, later Lord Burghley; Sir Francis Walsingham; Richard Bancroft, Bishop of London and later Archbishop of Canterbury; and outside the limits of this book Robert Cecil, later Earl of Salisbury. Behind them all sat the Queen.

General-Lieutenant Gorny, one of the judges at the trial of the Russian spy Oleg Penkovsky, warned the Russian people that an English Intelligence Service had been at work for some 300 years. He had miscalculated by some 150 years. The 'old fox', as he called it, can be traced back with ease to the reign of King Henry VII, who came to the throne in 1485, and reached one of its hey-days during the reign of Queen Elizabeth I. Yet the bibliography of the Tudor period, a catalogue of several thousand books and articles, which offers copious references concerning (apart from more obvious needs) such matters as madrigals and landscape architecture, does not mention espionage at all. The subject, as a whole, has scarcely been approached for that or indeed for several other periods. Evidence must be ferreted out of State Papers, contemporary correspondence, histories, biographies, and books primarily about something else, as if even in the dust the spies wished to lie concealed; so many secrets, too, were never put into writing and remain secrets for ever.[1]

*

I have never myself been engaged in espionage, although war and journalism occasionally brought me to its fringes. Immediately after the war *The Times* sent me to Vienna, Hungary and Jugoslavia. My wife and I lived for some time in Budapest. Things became more difficult as Stalinism neared its height, and by 1949 the Communist-dominated Government of Hungary seemed to suspect me as a British spy. Our telephone was tapped, and children from a neighbouring house informed us that our house was being watched.

My work took me regularly to Vienna and Belgrade, and when Jugoslavia broke with Russia and left the Cominform these journeys made me feel as if I was travelling along a smouldering tightrope. I reported the trials of Cardinal Mindszenthy, General Mihailovich and Laszlo Rajk, the Communist Foreign Secretary of Hungary, all of whom were sentenced for treason or espionage or both. People I had known as devoted Communists or loyal Left-wing supporters of the revolutionary regime began to disappear; later I learned that they had been accused of spying. Later still some of them, or their memories, were rehabilitated. Some had died in prison or been executed. Others escaped or were allowed to leave. Others vanished without trace, and some took office.

During 1947 I reported chiefly from Vienna, then occupied by the four Great Powers. It was that eager time when western diplomats and journalists were bent on 'getting to know' the Russians and the Russians reputed inaccessible. I thought the inaccessibility exaggerated, found it so, and became friendly with a fairly influential little group. We visited one another's offices and lodgings, and I spent a fortnight with them touring the Russian zone in Austria. I liked

them greatly. One evening, after some months, one of them asked
me to his flat. I was asked alone. He had a companion whom I knew.
After we had talked as usual about people, books, history, the war,
their conversation suddenly took a new direction; and it struck me
that without putting it too bluntly they were on the way to inviting
me to work for them. In retrospect this episode provided a partner
question to be answered at the end of this book. The first had always
been: why do some people become spies? I well remember Guy
Burgess, Donald Maclean and Kim Philby; their background and
education had been much the same as my own, and the revelation of
what they had been doing partly stimulated this first question. The
second question, stimulated by my own experience, became: why, if
they accepted, have other people refused?

I was thus no longer content to confine myself to the Elizabethan
age. Indeed while I was reporting events from central and eastern
Europe, I used to have the impression that I had heard it all before,
although it was not until I had read Professor Conyers Read's
Mr. Secretary Walsingham that recognition stirred and recollections
focused. What I had witnessed abroad then began to take on a vivid
likeness to events in England and Europe 400 years ago: similar
political passions, similarly divided loyalties, similar dedication,
similar fears, accusations, cruelties, hopes, betrayals, similarly opposite meanings given to the same sacred or accursed word.

The resemblance between the religious wars of the 16th century
and the ideological wars of the 20th is by now a commonplace. In
contemporary England extensions of political liberty have provided
outlets for opposition which formerly could only find expression in
conspiracy; and Englishmen today agitate publicly in politics or
journalism who in the 16th century might have had no alternative
but to rebel violently and, as part of their rebellion, spy. Advances in
technical skill and knowledge have transformed methods of spying
and of detecting spies. William Cecil could not have the Spanish
ports raked from space for photographs of the Armada, nor could
agents of Mary Queen of Scots plant microphones behind the wains-
coting or hidden in an hour-glass in the study of Sir Francis Walsingham. But spies still thrive in England and throughout Europe. All
the paraphernalia of sophisticated modern spying must somewhere
have hands, eyes, ears and brains controlling it, which are themselves
controlled by human motives; and no new human motive has been
invented since the Renaissance, nor has any old one disappeared.

It seemed therefore that my memories of recent events might illumine the far-off past, and my reading about the far-off past help to clarify the present. Historical parallels are a notorious pitfall, and I am aware of Professor G. R. Elton's dictum that 'the historian studying the past is concerned with the later event only in so far as it throws light on that part of the past he is studying. It is the cardinal error to reverse the process and study the past for the light it throws upon the present.'[2] Nonetheless I shall be found committing Professor Elton's 'cardinal error' throughout this book, and especially at the end. Most eras have resemblances to our own which can, and sometimes ought to be used as a light, though not as a revelation, and for me this Elizabethan study has greatly helped to loosen and clarify my thoughts about patriotism today.

People deeply read in that period will discover little here with which they are not familiar, though they may find familiar things looked at from an unfamiliar angle. I hope that professional historians will treat this story with indulgence, and that it may stimulate one of them one day to undertake a full account of the Rise of the English Secret Service or even, if he is prepared to give most of his life to it, of Espionage in general. Such a work is all the more needed at this time, when millions are constantly reading about spies in newspapers and hundreds of thousands in books. Such writings excite, astonish, bewilder and alarm. Lack of time, lack of knowledge, admiration for some spy's sustained adroitness in deceit, envy of the thrills, dissociation from an existence so bizarre, all tend to put judgment of the moral nature of his acts to sleep, and this is dangerous. Spying, like war, is one of the most odious instruments of power. It violates one of the most profoundly felt of human longings, the desire to trust. Such a monstrosity deserves its classic.

Part One

INTERNATIONAL INTELLIGENCE

Chapter One

'IN THIS CHANGE . . .' 1558-9

ON October 25, 1555 the Emperor Charles V, attended in unconscious premonition of a divided Europe by his son Philip and the
young Prince William of Orange, advanced through the crowded
Hall of the Golden Fleece in Brussels, took his throne there for the
last time, and abdicated a great part of the vast dominions he had
fought over, striven vainly to retain as a single Catholic Empire and
after a fashion ruled for the past forty years. The following year he
abdicated the remainder and in 1557 withdrew to the Gerolamite
monastery at Yuste in Estremadura, where on September 21, 1558 he
died.

The last of the old lions—Charles, François I of France, Henry
VIII of England—had departed, leaving a chaotic Europe to be
ruled at once or very soon by some mediocre sovereigns, some fierce
or astute subjects, and a handful of extraordinary women. Philip,
now King of Spain as well as of England, and his wife Mary Tudor
were never, even at their best, more than shadows of their fathers at
their best and as tormented, cruel and obsessed as their fathers at
their worst. Henri II of France was a younger son who had not
expected to succeed the dazzling François on the throne. This
sombre, loyal and retarded Valois had now reigned for eleven years,
the constants in his life being his devotion to Diane de Poitiers, his
passion for hunting, and his determination to suppress the Huguenots. 'Act,' the Cardinal of Lorraine had cried at his coronation, 'act,
so that posterity may say of you that, had you not reigned, the Church
of Rome would have been shattered. This you will do, if you ponder
that nothing will be more pleasing to God. And you will be not only
King of France, but also what a King only of France can be—the
priest and, as it were, public servant and chancellor of God Almighty.'

Henri had so acted ever since. In the same year he issued decrees
against blasphemers which sentenced them at their seventh offence
to have their upper lip so severed as to show their teeth and at the

eighth to have their tongues cut out. A little later he set up the notorious Chambre Ardente, which made five hundred arrests for heresy in three years. Diane had been his mistress for twenty years and Queen in all but name since his accession, while Catherine de' Medici, Queen in name alone, stayed demurely in the background with her six children, biding a time that might never come. Should it come, and remembering the fate of previous royal mistresses, Diane had taken out some sensible insurances: material in the form of châteaux, jewels, and the lands of attainted Huguenots, human in the marriage of one of her bastards and the daughter of another into the two prolific families which, for more than a generation, had disputed the favour of the French throne.

One family was dominated by the ageing Constable Duke de Montmorency, the other by the soldier Duke de Guise and his brother Charles, Cardinal of Lorraine. The Constable was an able diplomat, an almost legendary and ruthless warrior, and at home that kind of sternly patriotic and Catholic disciplinarian whom the French have more than once made their heroes. His foreign policy had at moments appeared to favour England, even—if in the interests of France—the Protestant England of Edward VI. 'He was born, lived and died for the King of France and the Catholic Church.' The Guises give the impression of having put themselves first, the Catholic Church second, and the King of France as it suited them. Lorrainers by birth, in the eyes of their enemies at Court half-foreigners, they claimed descent from Charlemagne and had designs on the thrones of Sicily, Denmark, Scotland, England, and France itself; at one time the Cardinal had dreamed of becoming Pope. Only the Popes and Philip of Spain were to take precedence of the Guises among the enemies of England.

Their spearheads against England were two women scarcely less ambitious or vigorous than the men. Their sister Marie, widow of James V of Scotland, had ruled alone there since 1554 with French advisers, French captains and French troops, as Regent for her daughter. It was an almost impossible assignment. In many parts of Europe at that time, or at an earlier time in Scotland, she might have been a great and successful ruler. She showed striking administrative ability and the same militant devotion to Roman Catholicism as all her family, but she had married into the wrong country. Things in Scotland had gone too far for Reformation to occur of its own momentum within the Catholic fold, and France had been too far

away, too unconcerned and too troubled to enforce it. She seems to
have missed her rendezvous with Time.

Nonetheless she continued courageously to do her best. Henry
VIII had once had his eye on her, and she would have been equal to
him. She led her own troops and on at least one occasion had narrowly
escaped death in battle. Henri II told the Constable that no one knew
better than she how to manage Scotland. On the whole she had been
respected as a ruler and liked as a human being. Although the spy
Ninian Cockburn could complain of her imperiousness—'She has
played me ane pleasure because I would not come at the answer of
her bell'—someone else at the Scottish Court said, 'I have lost the
power of laughter till she comes'. In youth a great beauty, she had
now grown somewhat stout. John Knox, who had no love for her,
had compared her coronation as Regent to the saddling of an unruly
cow; she herself took it as a fair joke when her soldiers likened her to
the largest cannon on Castle Hill.

Her daughter, Mary Queen of Scots, was sixteen in 1558 and
renowned so far only for her beauty and her prospects. She had
lived and been educated at the Court of France since being smuggled
thither from Dumbarton Rock ten years earlier, and had married the
Dauphin in the spring; one day, if she survived—and her health
gave cause to fear that she might not—she would be Queen of France
as well as of Scotland. Her uncles had brought her up to believe
herself the rightful heir to England.

The third of these Catholic Marys, Mary Tudor, reigned at
Westminster. She had no child. Her Spanish marriage, arranged as
an arc in the encirclement of France, and her persecution of the
Protestants had lost her nearly all the good-will which had helped to
set her on the throne; by 1558 it seems almost to have been taken for
granted that she had nothing left to do but die and, if she would not
die, to be assassinated or deposed. In the spring, during the second
of her phantom pregnancies, she made a will. In October, no longer
even under the deluded hope of death in childbirth, she made another
and all in England who had sails to set were busy setting them
towards her sister. For some while Elizabeth had been in communication with William Cecil; it was generally assumed that once she
came to the throne she would appoint him Secretary.

In 1558 England, France and Spain had certain important
characteristics in common. Monarchy was established. Feudal over-
lords, until recently kings in their own domains, no longer seriously

threatened disruption. Power had left the peripheries and resided at
the centre. It was the last year in history that all three countries
would be Catholic. All of them desperately needed money.

*

Elizabeth, waiting at Hatfield in discreet withdrawal, and Cecil,
retired into semi-private life in Lincolnshire for the last three years,
had lately enjoyed much leisure, though less security, to consider the
European and domestic scene; and Cecil could only conclude from
such a survey that if this Aurora was indeed to rise, he would have
to shepherd her across a challenging and gloomy landscape. The
fortune amassed by Henry VII had been dissipated. Since the summer of 1557, in part following the commercial and political tradition
of a Burgundian alliance, in part dragged in by Mary's Spanish
marriage, England had been unprofitably at war with France. The
battle of St. Quentin, won that year for Philip by Emmanuel
Philibert of Savoy, had brought the King of Spain's English subjects
little advantage. Montmorency, now in his middle sixties, had once
again, and not even for the last time, allowed himself to be taken
prisoner, and the Anglophobe Duke de Guise had avenged the
French defeat, to England's special ignominy, by taking Calais.
Fortresses at home were in disrepair and essential munitions only
obtainable by favour of the Spanish Netherlands. In Scotland Marie
de Guise had fortified the little port of Eyemouth as a direct
and deliberate threat to Berwick, and though the Scottish nobles
had refused to follow her across the Border and she had been
compelled to postpone an invasion of England 'in great choler',
the two neighbours and ancient enemies were again officially at
war.

French reinforcements were to be expected in Scotland as soon as
they could be released from fighting against Spain; and many an
Englishman feared that Berwick and the North could be France's
almost for the taking. For the time being, however, France was not
ready. Both France and Spain needed a respite from the war which,
under various aspects and in various theatres and with few intervals,
had ravaged vast areas of western Europe for half a century. The
soldiers' pay on both sides was even more than usually in arrears.
The Spanish lords wanted to go home. The Constable yearned for
Paris and power from his prison apartments in Flanders, and Henri
and Diane needed him as a counterpoise to the Guises. But the voice

which most urgently summoned Valois and Habsburg to a truce was
not intended to achieve that purpose; it did not come from favourites
awaiting ransom, prisoners, despoiled peasants, merchants whose
trade was interrupted, bankers who could not get their interest, or
mutinous soldiers who could not get their wages, but from Calvin in
Geneva. Heresy had been creeping and was now sweeping across
France, whence he had been driven and where he had been born.
Even without bankruptcy, heresy might have driven the Catholic
sovereigns to make peace.

For England peace in Europe would mean a welcome breathing-
space. Yet many Englishmen had misgivings about a peace from
which might spring an even worse evil than the present war: namely,
that alliance between two major European powers which it had
already become, and was to remain, almost the first article of English
foreign policy to prevent. Henri II was showing a sinister readiness
to abandon all France's ancient claims in Italy to the Spaniards. No
more southern loot, or not for the present; no more dreams of a
Mediterranean Empire, or not for the present; no more of those
heroic days when a King of Naples and the Two Sicilies could be put
into such a panic that 'in the night he would cry out he heard the
French and the stones and the trees sounded, "France, France!"'.
Were the French about to turn their horses' heads towards the
North? Were London and Edinburgh to become the prizes instead
of Rome and Milan? Were the new Alps to be the Cheviots and the
English Channel, and heretic English, instead of infidel Turks, to
become the object of the next Catholic crusade?

On November 17, 1558 Mary Tudor died and Philip of Spain
ceased to be King of England. A note of foreboding accompanied the
chimes that rang in Elizabeth. The accession of a young woman known
at the very least to have Protestant sympathies strengthened the
religious motives and pretexts behind French military ambition in
the North, and embarrassed Spanish readiness to resist it. On the
same day Cecil wrote himself a memorandum, of which the first
heading reads: ' . . . to make a stay of passages to all the ports until
a certain day, and to consider the safety of all places dangerous in the realm towards France and Scotland, specially in this
change.'

The dangers were visible, and imminent. There were advantages
too, but hazy, difficult to grasp, and most of them counterbalanced
with a liability. The most valuable was the growth of Protestantism,

moderate or extreme, in France and Scotland. But the new Queen, however exuberant the Reforming temper of some of those already near her and many of those hurrying back from exile, was at that moment about the last person prepared to undermine even a Catholic throne; she felt far too uncertain of her own. Peace would restore the *politique* Constable to France, but not necessarily to power; the Guises were well-entrenched. The dilemma in which Spain now found herself offered a powerful lever, if the English could only seize and operate it. Philip, although as implacable against religious Reformation in Scotland as in any other quarter, had no desire, by standing by while France destroyed it, to see Scotland transformed into a province of the French crown—another Brittany—and thereby a pathway into England. Religion warred with strategy, his conscience with his commonsense, and the hesitation which this conflict of interests imposed on him could be played upon to great purpose. For the time being strategy and commonsense had the upper hand and he could be depended upon to give his little ally cautious support against the French. Elizabeth did all she could to avoid provoking him and he thought of making her his third wife.

These were all vague and impalpable resources, lacking the solid merit of a bulging exchequer, a well-equipped and weathered army, or even a few impregnable frontier posts; yet in skilled hands straw out of which to make substantial bricks. Money, arms, repairs, all could be arranged in time. Time, that was what was needed; and to cajole time statesmen and diplomats of the highest order; and to assist such men a well-spread network of Intelligence at the points of danger.

The personnel were there, beginning at the top. Both the Queen and Cecil had lived at or near the centres of conspiracy for years. During the past decade both had been compelled to learn for their personal survival most of the tricks that had now become necessary for the survival of the realm, and now that she was at last Queen Elizabeth could really begin to enjoy dissimulation. Danger at home or in exile had taught similar lessons to several courtiers. Two particularly concern us here, Sir Nicholas Throckmorton and Sir James Croft, since the places to which they were soon to be appointed became the conduits and outposts of a great conspiracy, perhaps the most triumphant single operation of the entire forty-five-year reign. Through them were now to pass nearly all the principal spies, couriers, committers of secret treasons, agents, instigators high and low, possible heirs to thrones, statesmen, preachers, soldiers, sometimes under assumed names, sometimes in disguise, who plotted for a variety of reasons to drive the French from Scotland and succeeded in saving the northern frontier from being overrun.

Chapter Two

RETROSPECT

i. Sir Nicholas and Sir James

BOTH Croft and Throckmorton came of old-established shire families (which survive in the same homes in Herefordshire and Warwickshire to this day). Throckmorton had been born in 1515, Croft a few years later, and they were related to one another through the Herberts and the Parrs, whose powerful households helped their rise. Both had fought in the French and Scottish wars of Henry VIII and Edward VI. Both became friendly with Elizabeth during the threatened years of her youth; a short while before her accession Throckmorton even took it upon himself to advise her how she should conduct herself and whom she should appoint to which great offices when she became Queen.

But two very different characters look from the splendid portraits we have of them. Sir Nicholas glitters, almost glowers; he is unmistakably of the Renaissance, a man not to be watched by but to watch. Sir James appears peaceable and mild, like a dignified and handsome sheep, and though renowned as a soldier has more the air of an administrator. It was at Court principally that Sir Nicholas found his fortune, while Sir James's appointments suggest either that people at Court wanted to get rid of him or else that, born and bred on the Welsh Marches, he had acquired a special aptitude for outposts. He became Governor of beleaguered Haddington. In 1551 he held some post in the Pale of Calais, but almost at once was made Privy Councillor and packed off to Ireland with £1,000 'to his relief'. His career is marked from the beginning by an exceptional need for money and by faint hints, later in life to become strident, of too close familiarity with the enemy.

Nicholas had entered the household of his kinswoman Queen Catherine Parr, a great patroness of Reformers, and it was there he first came to know Elizabeth. He warned her first love, the Lord

Admiral Seymour, against trying to match with her: 'I trusted he had no such Desuyre in his head, but rather he soulde have . . . it were better he weare buryed.' The warning went unheeded, and Seymour was executed; but perhaps Nicholas had really meant to warn the young Princess, who would have forfeited the crown under her father's will, had she married without the consent of the Privy Council.[3] On Catherine's death he had himself transferred to the Privy Chamber of Edward VI and became the boy King's favourite. He possessed the intuition of the crevasse. The next one he avoided engulfed Seymour's brother, the Protector Duke of Somerset. Turning aside in time towards Somerset's victorious rival, John Dudley, Duke of Northumberland, he was rewarded with land in Northamptonshire, a seat for the shire in Edward's last Parliament, an annuity of £100 and the Treasurership of the Mint.

On July 6, 1553 the blow fell that pole-axed many and for a time incapacitated both Sir Nicholas and Sir James. Edward VI died. Northumberland kept the King's death secret and next day moved the whole Council into the Tower in order to have them under his control while he disinherited Mary Tudor and proclaimed his puppet Lady Jane Grey Queen. Sir Nicholas (so it is said) warned Mary in time for her to escape capture, and simultaneously drew up the Proclamation of 'Queen Jane'; William Cecil had refused and conveniently 'turned the labour to Mr. Throckmorton, whose conscience I saw was troubled therein, misliking the matter'. Within days both Sir Nicholas and Sir James had abandoned Northumberland and Jane like everybody else, and Sir Nicholas was guarding Mary on her triumphant way to London within the week. She pardoned them both, but her clemency made no odds; within six months they were prisoners in the Tower.

They had turned against her marriage and deeply implicated themselves in the anti-Spanish rebellion of Sir Thomas Wyatt. Sir Nicholas had opened his mouth too wide, uttering at friends' houses and in the gossip market of St. Paul's what most of the country thought about Philip. Sir James had actually gone off to the Welsh Marches to gather troops. The Council put Hereford and Ludlow in a state of alarm, but there is no evidence that he did anything effective, and he was captured at home in bed. Yet Wyatt declared at his trial that Sir James had been the real leader of the rising. He had certainly been in close touch with the French Ambassador, Antoine de Noailles, and with d'Oysel, French Ambassador in Scotland, who had come to London to encourage the rebels, and had asked them for French arms, money and munitions.

The lives of both knights seemed doomed, but not at once. They were minnows only, dangled to catch the carp. It was Elizabeth the Government were after. Simon Renard, Charles V's Ambassador in London, informed the Emperor that Croft had written his deposition incriminating the French Ambassador. On the nightmare Palm Sunday of March 18, 1554 Mary had her sister brought through Traitor's Gate. At Elizabeth's second examination Sir James Croft, 'marvellously tossed and examined', was led out to confront her. The Government expected him to put it past doubt that he had sought French aid to depose the Queen and crown the young Princess. Renard was insisting hourly that Elizabeth must have had foreknowledge of the rising and demanded her execution. A letter of hers had been intercepted, folded into a dispatch of the French Ambassador's. Why had she refused Mary's demand that she must come to Court? She had pleaded illness, but had there not been another reason? She was known to have had a private conversation with Sir James in her house at Ashridge; had its purpose not been to arrange her removal, on Wyatt's orders, to her house at Donnington, away from London and the clutches of the Privy Council?

'At first she was somewhat amazed . . . but having recollected herself she said "as touching my remove to Donnington, my officers and you, Sir James Croft, being there present, can well testifie whether any rash or unbeseeming word did at that time passe my lippes, which might not have well become a faithfull and loyal subject . . ." Sir James Croft kneeled unto her, being heartily sorry that ever hee should see that day to bee a witnesse against her, taking God to witnesse that hee never knew anything by her working of the least suspicion.'[4] The ruse had failed. It is possible that by refusing the desired confession Sir James had saved her life. He had certainly risked his own, and his ordeal was not yet ended.

He and Sir Nicholas were arraigned for treason at Guildhall on April 17. The trial of Sir Nicholas began soon after dawn. The judges had assumed the customary quick process, at which the accused man would plead guilty and throw himself on the Queen's mercy. Instead, hour after hour during the spring morning, he dominated the thronged court, rending the threadbare case at every seam, lecturing the judges on their duty, quoting against them St. Paul, St. Jerome, and Parliamentary and historical precedent, never disrespectful of Mary herself but vehement against her marriage, insisting that he had committed no overt act of treason and only said what had been said by many others not on trial, some of the judges among them. They refused to let him consult the Statutes in court, but he recited them from memory; perhaps some friend in authority had slipped them into the Tower. He spoke with eloquence, courage and erudition for the liberties of England, and he merits a high place among the heroes of the political dock. He himself became the prosecutor, and his prosecutors the accused. 'I was never interrupted thus in my life,' ejaculated Edward Griffin, the Attorney-General, 'nor I never knewe any thus suffered to talke, as this Prisoner is suffered: some of us will come no more at the Barre, an we be thus handled.'

Once again the Government involved Sir James Croft. 'There is Croftes Confession,' alleged Serjeant Dyer for the Crown, 'who sayeth that he and you and your Accomplices, did manye times devise about the whole Mattere, and made you privie to all his Determinations, and you showed him that you woulde goe into the West Countrey . . .', the insinuation being, to raise troops against the Queen. 'Mr. Croftes is yet living,' Sir Nicholas retorted, 'and is here this daye; how hapneth it he is not brought Face to Face to justifie this matter . . .?' He gave them the reply himself. 'Will you knowe the Truth? either he sayd not so, or he will not abide by it, but honestly hath reformed himself . . .'

The court adjourned till three in the afternoon. The same day Sir Thomas Wyatt's head was stolen from its spike. The jury returned at five and found Sir Nicholas not guilty. He was discharged of treason, but at once rearrested by a discomfited and angry Bench, 'for there are other matter to charge him with'. The jury were let out on bail of £500 apiece, and afterwards imprisoned and heavily fined. No time was left that day to try Sir James Croft. On the 28th he too nearly got off; but the jury was packed and found him guilty.

Mary again treated both knights leniently. Sir James was bound over for £500 to a 'good abearynge', taken back into service in the North, and held a commission in the Army when war broke out against France and Scotland in 1557. Sir Nicholas was bound over in the sum of £2,000. Sir James's release occurred a week before John Rodgers, the first Protestant martyr, went to the stake. The Queen was just beginning the religious persecutions; if Sir James's Protestantism had been as serious as his patriotism, his opposition to the

Mass as fervent as his opposition to the marriage, it is likely that he would have stayed where he was.

Sir Nicholas now engaged in certain secret activities in France, but stepped back into the limelight immediately the curtains were drawn about Mary Tudor. He it was whom Elizabeth sent from Hatfield to bring the black enamelled ring, Philip's wedding-gift, which would never leave Mary's hand till death. He discussed the order of the Coronation with William Cecil; issued directives at the new Queen's command to stop all sailings; was one of those sent to sequester the house and goods of Cardinal Pole, who had received England's submission to the Pope and died within twenty-four hours of Mary; and he became a member of Elizabeth's first Parliament. He was certainly a Protestant, and Sir James Croft appeared to be one also, though in the light of later intimations we must remain in doubt. Two of the chief posts that must have been in Cecil's mind on the first day of the reign as 'dangerous . . . towards France and Scotland' seemed to be waiting for this hopeful and seasoned pair. The new Secretary did not want either of them at Court. Throckmorton was ambitious, fiery and a possible rival, Croft a protégé of the Queen's thrusting young favourite Lord Robert Dudley; and men who had been traitors once, in whatever cause, might become so again. What better choice then for the soldier-administrator Sir James than Berwick, or for sophisticated Sir Nicholas than the Embassy in Paris?

The two men's contrasting gifts were well matched by the contrast offered by the brilliant French Court and the bleak Border fortress. In both places they could expect to have their fill of spies. On the one hand there would be espionage conducted in a capital city between two States at a similarly high level of organization; on the other, espionage between one such State, England, and a second, Scotland, at a lower level. The former is the kind we hear most about today, but the latter has continued across countless other borders into other wild areas not yet settled into nationhood. Great Britain practised it all over the Orient throughout the 19th century. America, China, Russia are at it hourly, the situation given them to exploit being not at all unlike the situation along the Scottish Border during Elizabethan times.

ii. Espionage at Court: the Ambassador as Spy

By the middle of the 16th century the species Ambassador, in earlier times a bird of a few weeks' passage on special mission, had settled into less roving habits and become more of a bird of residence. It began to acquire nests at foreign Courts, where it remained two or three years and occasionally very much longer before it homed. The Ambassador was a sacred bird; according to some authorities any who laid violent hands upon it committed sacrilege and could be excommunicated.

In theory a dove of peace that bore the olive-branch through fire and slaughter, in reality it had two faces; one pacified, while the other plotted. It was expected to possess as many eyes as a peacock, the percipience of a hawk, the nocturnal habits of an owl, and the grandeur of a swan, which last usually had to be maintained on a purse more suited to a sparrow. During the last few decades it has seemed to be declining into something little better than a carrier-pigeon, but in the 16th century it soared in the splendid and suspect plumage of its youth. Although known in one form or another in all ages, its rise to power and glory was contemporaneous with the rise of nations. It is a fowl sprung from the Renaissance. The Papacy and the City States of Italy, the great State of Venice especially, were the first to nurture and develop it. By the time Cardinal Wolsey resolved that England should have her own aviary, France, Spain and the Empire had been sending brilliant specimens abroad for many years.

Abraham de Wicquefort, a voluminous chronicler of 16th- and 17th-century diplomacy, quotes the instructions Elizabeth gave to Walsingham, setting out for Paris in 1570, as containing the pith of diplomatic duties. They were twofold. First, the Ambassador was to appear as a messenger of peace. He must erase misunderstandings that might have occurred in the past and combat men of ill-will who might provoke them in the future. He had been sent, he must explain, to preserve and fortify the treaties which enshrined the love and respect his own sovereign protested always to have felt for the sovereign to whom he was accredited. But in the second part of her instructions the Queen exhorted Walsingham to other duties, which de Wicquefort defined as those of an honourable spy. 'You will take note of the [French] King and Queen's actions, both public and private, that may be harmful to us or our State, and are to inform us of them with all the necessary speed and secrecy. To help you ... you will learn from your predecessor the means by which to discover those matters we ought to know of . . .' It is these functions with which we are concerned here.

The 16th century, which marks the youth of organized diplomacy, marks also the infant stage of organized Intelligence; or rather, the embryonic, since the Intelligence service was still one and the same as the ambassadorial, lying as it were concealed within it and not yet separated into a bureaucracy with an establishment of its own. The multiplication of resident Ambassadors brought not only a multiplication of spies, but also of learned discussion about both; and it was much pondered at what point spying ceased to be honourable and an envoy, who spied or suborned others to spy for him, should forfeit his inviolability. These writings exhibit a similar conflict as do others, on other subjects, at this period of transition between the idealism (whether or not practised) of the Middle Ages and the brutal and candid expediency of the Renaissance; between what an Ambassador ought to be, and what in fact he was; between the demands of the new national monarchies and those of a moral law superior to nations.

As early as the 1490s the humanist Ermolao Barbaro, who had represented Venice at the Papal Court, wrote in his *De Officio Legati*: 'Remember you are an Ambassador, not a spy.' Yet he defined the first duty of an Ambassador as identical with that of any other State servant, '. . . to do, say, advise, and think whatever may best serve the preservation and aggrandisement of his own State.' Bishop Juan de Fonseca, Ferdinand of Aragon's Ambassador to the Emperor Maximilian, frankly resolved any apparent contradiction between the claims of altar and crown; instructed to inveigle Austria into war against France in gross violation of treaty obligations, he replied that he placed this aim of Ferdinand's 'higher than the safety of my immortal soul'. But Alberico Gentili, the Italian Protestant exile who, thanks to Walsingham's influence, became Regius Professor of the Civil Law at Oxford, thought otherwise. An Ambassador, he declared in his *De Legationibus* (1585), was not bound to obedience if a Prince's wishes contravened the moral law. Soul was superior to State. But 'I know very well,' he added, 'how much I depart from the common code . . . I paint ambassadors not as they are, but as they ought to be.' Some writers tried to solve the dilemma by suggesting that the dirty work should be left to subordinates. An Ambassador ought to employ one cautious servant (wrote Etienne Dolet in 1541) whose job it would be to wander about the town, insinuate himself into people's confidence, and bribe them to reveal State secrets. Juan Antonio de Vera, whose *El Embaxador* came out in 1620, rejected spying, lying, and conspiracy in principle, but qualified the principle away by arguing that diplomacy was a kind of permanent warfare, and deception permissible in war.

One French historian thought that Ambassadors must have emerged at the opening of Pandora's box, which released the seeds of all evil upon the world. Philippe de Comines interrupted his famous history to write of them at length, because 'I have known so many intrigues and so much mischief carried on under that colour'. As one of Louis XI's close confidants, he had conducted many such intrigues himself and heartily approved them, 'for there is no spy so good and safe, nor can have such liberty to pry . . .' He commended the prince who, for every Ambassador sent to him, sent back two or more than two (advice which Sir Nicholas Throckmorton later quoted) and refused no proposal from a foreign court that might give him a pretext to send yet more. Ambassadors from hostile sovereigns should be honourably received, but have experienced men attached in order to observe the people they conversed with and prevent them from getting in touch with malcontents; a secret watch must be set upon them day and night and they must be sent home as soon as possible.

Most writers agreed that to give and receive presents was not necessarily dishonourable. Pages could be filled with lists of the pensions which princes, usually through their Ambassadors, doled out to foreign princes and ministers.[5] One must know too where to give, and how, and how much. To thrust a gleaming object into an Ambassador's lap, without warning, in the darkness of a Venetian church, might be a mistake. The Cardinal of Amboise preferred a Mantegna to ten thousand ducats; but ten thousand was the sum the Venetian Council of Ten authorized their envoy to pay Chièvres for Charles V's support in Lombardy, with a thousand apiece for the grandees. After the death of Louis XII of France the Venetians sent his widow jewels worth five thousand ducats. 'Frankly,' their Ambassador wrote home, 'you should have sent them to the new Queen. She won't think much of anything left over for her, after you've satisfied the Dowager, and besides she hasn't any of her own.'

Contemporary writers on diplomacy tried to set limits to such favours, and the modern historian of Renaissance diplomacy believed that, though Ambassadors often possessed secrets worth a fortune, very few of them turned out to be corruptible.[6] Jean Hotman declared that an Ambassador should never accept a gift until he had his foot in the stirrup to depart. The Spanish Ambassador to Charles VIII of France actually refused some silver goblets on the ground that his embassy had not yet come to a successful end, and Venice had forbidden its Ambassadors to solicit presents since the 13th century. The Ambassador of Louis XII of France signed an undertaking before he went to Rome that he would neither solicit nor receive any benefices, money, plate, rings, or anything else except a bishopric the King had promised to ask from His Holiness for his brother; 'and if I am caught doing any such thing, I wish and agree to have my head cut off.'

All writers agreed (in principle) that no Ambassador ought to engage in treason. According to de Wicquefort, this meant that they must not attempt the life of the Prince to whom they were accredited, conspire against the peace of his State, or give its enemies advice that might disturb it; but he claimed universal consent that an Ambassador who managed to corrupt a foreign minister was not violating international law. A year before Alberico Gentili published his *De Legationibus* the Spanish Ambassador in London was caught conspiring with Mary Queen of Scots; and both Gentili and Jean Hotman were called in to advise the Privy Council on the law. Gentili decided that though conspiracy deprived the Ambassador of his inviolability he ought not to be punished with death; and proud Mendoza, who had put himself in no hurry to leave, was lucky merely to be sent home.

Were all these qualifications mere words, camouflage, pretences aimed vainly at keeping the disreputable necessities of state within decent bounds, like the millions of other words poured out then and since in the attempt to set limits upon war—or indeed upon business, politics, and every other manifestation of power? It may not be entirely true that 'current diplomacy pursued its course guided by no moral considerations whatsoever, and the only tribute which statesmen paid to contemporary writers' view of international obligations was perpetually to express the most lofty principles with the most transparent insincerity'.[7] As we have seen, there was a degree of pitch a few Ambassadors would not touch, and not all took easily, or as of obligation, to espionage. Their practice seems to have varied not according to any law, or generally accepted code, but to the situations they found themselves in, their own characters, sympathies, ambitions and wish to please their Princes, and their estimate of what they could get away with.

One of the most gigantic cases of diplomatic espionage in recent times had come from the country to which Sir Nicholas Throckmorton was now to be accredited; Europe had rung with it less than twenty years ago.

In 1539 François I had appointed, as his Ambassador in Venice, Guillaume Pellicier, Bishop of Montpellier, one of the most cultured men of the century. In a short while Pellicier had recruited the Cavazza brothers, of whom one was secretary to the Council of Ten and the other to the Senate. He employed among his chief gobetweens a certain Augustin Abondio and a high-born lady, Camilla Pallavicino, who called on him under cover of religious devotion. Soon he had enlisted agents by the score, to whom he referred in his dispatches to François as *'bons serviteurs du Roi'*: one, for example, pleasantly sited on Lake Garda on the route through the Brenner into Germany, and another highly placed in the Imperial Court, who helped him to win the German nobility over to the French. His information and intrigues covered most of Italy, and spread to Hungary, Algiers and Turkey. This tireless prelate, who wrote a commentary on Pliny, studied natural history, and had an antirrhinum named after him, is today honoured as the scholar who supplied François with the marvellous collection of Greek, Hebrew and Syriac manuscripts which are one of the glories of the Bibliothèque Nationale; but that was only one, and at the time among the least, of the functions the King demanded of him.

Seconded by men we would now call military attachés, except that their mission was 'to act rather than to observe', the Bishop rapidly became the paymaster and supervisor of the Italian princelings and *condottieri* he mobilized in the cause of France. He organized expeditions, recruited armies, plotted the seizure of Imperial towns, and planned to close Imperial communications with Italy through the Valtelline and Brenner passes. He guided his secret service with the erudition and wit to be expected from a correspondent of Aretino and Rabelais and a friend of Paolo Manuzio. His link with Constantinople put presents of unusual splendour at his disposal; 'I am sending you some wine and furs,' he informed his agent on Lake Garda, '—not ordinary ones, but real *marroquins de Turquie*.' Aretino wrote to him, 'Is it on diplomacy or the pursuit of learning

that you lavish every hour of your day ? It is really extraordinary, and
takes my breath away, to see you supplying His Majesty with books
and soldiers, Greek manuscripts and Italian captains, all in the same
delivery.' The Bishop even became astonished at himself. When
certain prophecies his intelligence service had permitted him came
true, he asked whether God had not endowed Ambassadors with
special gifts of prescience, 'like vultures sniffing out a battlefield'.

It had to end. The whole stunning network was blown in the most
humdrum way. A certain Martolosso became the lover of Abondio's
wife, and found the letters of one of the Cavazzas in a drawer in
Abondio's house. He informed the Senate. One Cavazza was caught,
the other fled. Abondio took refuge in the Ambassador's palace.
Troops and menacing crowds surrounded it by lagoon and land.
Pellicier meditated strangling Abondio in order to save the rest of his
'*bons serviteurs*', but in the end surrendered him. The wretched
agent was alternately tortured and offered bribes of liberty and
money. Having disclosed everything he knew, which led incidentally to the unmasking of the Imperial Secret Service as well as
the French, he was hanged between the columns of St. Mark. The
Venetian Government gave Martolosso a huge reward, and the
Bishop of Montpellier was sent back to France.

By the time Sir Nicholas Throckmorton arrived in Paris, French
intelligence had achieved a formidable reputation. Even the secrecy
of a papal election did not defeat them. In 1549–50 when the
Cardinals were immured in the Castle of St. Angelo to choose a
successor to Pope Paul III, the French Ambassador put a ladder
against a wall, climbed across roofs, and received news and passed
instructions to the Cardinal of Guise through a hole bored in the cell
of the Cardinal of Bourbon, who had not yet arrived. These were the
kind of people against whom, and in the midst of whom, Sir Nicholas
would have to work. His occupation, he well knew, would probably
ruin him financially if he was left at his post too long, and certainly be
dangerous and disagreeable. All manner of tricks would be played
upon him. Pietro de' Medici had hidden the Milanese Ambassador
in a cupboard, so that he could eavesdrop on the Ambassador of
France. Louis XI, sitting close to a screen and pretending to be deaf,
encouraged the envoys of the Constable of St. Pol to speak ill of the
Duke of Burgundy (supposedly their ally) at the top of their voices,
and to do mocking imitations of him. Behind the screen the King had
placed the Burgundian Ambassador, as a result of whose subsequent

report the Duke broke with the Constable and surrendered him to the King, who had him executed.

The English Foreign Service could not yet boast of any deception so hugely successful as that conducted by the Bishop of Montpellier. But even Comines, who was often rather contemptuous of English diplomacy, could not have described Throckmorton's immediate predecessor in the Paris Embassy as naïf.

*

Born about the turn of the century, the last of England's great cleric-Ambassadors, Nicholas Wotton, Dean of Canterbury, was one of those practitioners of secret Intelligence who have also been scholars and display an air of innocent and unworldly mildness. He was extremely short. For someone so frail and bookish he had survived a surprising amount of buffeting. Henry VIII, who left him £300 and made him an executor of his will, had entrusted him with some harassing missions. He had been one of those delegated to probe the foreign universities about the divorce from Catherine of Aragon. He had accompanied Anne of Cleves to England and later been sent back to tell her brother that Henry did not fancy her. Instructed to cajole Charles V into an attack on France, he had several times felt the edge of the Imperial tongue; and though he managed to negotiate the 1554 alliance between Emperor and King he failed to save Henry from being left in the lurch. Both his Embassies in Paris ended in war. He knew about everyone of importance on the European stage, and had dealt personally with many of them. His dispatches ranged with a light though worried eye over the whole of Europe as far as Turkey and took the disputes between the German and Italian princelings with an easy stride. His patience and experience were vast.

At home his politics had been cautious and flexible enough for him to occupy high office under four Tudor sovereigns. He at first opposed Queen Mary's marriage to Philip of Spain and asked to be recalled, although on the political ground that it was certain to cause war with France. But three months later he was writing to her of his devotion to 'her constant mind . . . to the true religion and Catholic faith', and almost begging her to restore England to the Pope. He compromised in order to survive; when Elizabeth, who had done the same, came to the throne, rumour had it she offered him the Archbishopric of Canterbury. Perhaps the key is to be found in

Cecil's comment on him that he 'is very wise, but loveth quietness'.

In 1547 the Constable's spies managed to acquire the English plans for the defence of Boulogne; but the Dean's network had given him the French plans to attack it. '*Petit homme instruit et fin*', a French historian has called him; the Constable respected him and thought, years before they did, that the English ought to appoint him Secretary. His dispatches, notched with classical quotations and donnish little jokes, are lightened by an engaging pose of inadequacy and diffidence; in 1559, for example, '. . . my long babbling . . . my simple wit—always simple but by age and travel so decayed as to be not only simple but most simple'. He belonged to the school—and perhaps his Kentish origin had something to do with it—who believed that the last people in the world to be trusted were the French.

His second embassy, under Mary, lasted from 1553 to 1557. The French were doing their utmost to encourage and exploit English opposition to the Spanish marriage; *ex officio*, as it were, head of the Secret Service in France, Wotton had it as one of his tasks to discover their English accomplices and where and when they might be plotting to invade. He enjoyed exceptional chances for enlisting spies among the scores of Englishmen who left the country in the early part of the reign. Not all went in fear of religious persecution. Far from all betook themselves to the Lutheran and Calvinist colonies in Germany, Geneva, and the Swiss cantons, there to read their Bibles, squabble about liturgies and theologies, and wait as patiently as they could for Mary to die. Many, Protestant chiefly in their dislike of Philip, had taken part in the Wyatt rising of 1554 and Henry Dudley's conspiracy of 1556. These worldly activist groups sought refuge in France, hoping that France would help them; when they became bored, Dean Wotton was waiting. He knew quite a number of them and was kin to several.

iii. Spies in Exile

Refugees have always offered promising fishing for Intelligence services. There are obvious appeals to be made to lack of money; to disillusion with the hostess country; to homesickness; to self-importance, embittered by loss of status; and perhaps most of all to jealousy and dislike of other refugees. Dean Wotton asked for pardons for some, no doubt purely from the kindness of his heart; others, Sir Nicholas Throckmorton among them, he also enlisted as informers.

Sir Nicholas first went into exile in the summer of 1554, six months after his release from the Tower, and more than a year after his trial. He had no means of livelihood and, if the Queen would not grant him a pardon, told Wotton he would have to enlist in the French army. Wotton reported him determined not to serve with the other English rebels in French pay and successfully interceded for him. He went home, became involved in Henry Dudley's conspiracy to rob the exchequer and again fled, breaking his bond for £2,000. He arrived at St. Malo in July 1556 and again made straight for the Ambassador. On the way to Paris his horse fell on him and he had to send a messenger, Thomas Middlemore, who promised on his behalf, yet again, that he would have nothing to do with rebels and wished only to see Wotton. This time the Ambassador was less friendly and suggested that Sir Nicholas would do best to disappear into Germany for a while. He obviously expected Sir Nicholas to offer himself as an agent, but no longer trusted him. He added a warning that if Sir Nicholas did have dealings with the other rebels, it 'would so damage his business, that I will never thereafter have anything to do with it'. Middlemore replied that Sir Nicholas would certainly wish to act as Wotton advised; unfortunately he was injured and could not anyhow afford a journey into Germany.

A few days later he arrived in Paris and sent another message, asking for a secret meeting. Wotton would not consent, and became even more suspicious when one of his servants caught a glimpse of Sir Nicholas in the street, going towards the Louvre of all places. By the autumn, however, he had been prevailed upon to give Sir Nicholas several appointments, and was beginning to think he might be used. 'He tells me all that he hears.' Sir Nicholas was hearing a good deal. In spring of the following year he brought the Ambassador details of a French plan to seize the English fortress of Guisnes in the Pale of Calais. His information began to come not only from the French. The ban on mixing with the other English exiles had evidently been lifted, on Wotton's terms; for a few days later Sir Nicholas sent in a warning that Thomas Stafford was buying arms to invade England and an extremely accurate hint that one of the objectives might be Scarborough. This was immediately followed by news that Stafford had set sail with a small Anglo-French force in well-armed and well-manned ships. Wotton had already sent the

Queen similar warnings derived from other agents. The 'invasion' succeeded in capturing Scarborough Castle and then collapsed; a month later Thomas Stafford was executed. Throckmorton's intelligence had arrived a little late, but it had been correct and shown goodwill towards the Queen, and in the same year she received him back into allegiance.

The Paris Embassy discovered two more profitable expatriates in the brothers Thomas and Edward Randolph, sons of Avery Randolph of Badlesmere in Kent. Thomas was to become celebrated, and here surely we are in the presence of one of the arch-intriguers of the time. Born in 1523, he had entered Christ Church, Oxford, at its foundation, taken his B.A. in 1545 and his B.C.L. soon afterwards. In 1549 he became a public notary and was Principal of Broadgates Hall, soon to be merged in the new Pembroke College, until 1553. A fervent Protestant, he formed a close friendship at the University with John Jewel, the future Bishop and apologist of the Elizabethan religious settlement, and gave him refuge at the beginning of Mary's reign. Jewel described them then as 'subsisting wretchedly enough, yet better perhaps than they desire to whom our being alive is a vexation'. Soon both had to flee abroad. Randolph came to know some of the leading Continental Reformers and also established connexions with the exiled Scots which both sides turned to good use later. Sir Nicholas Throckmorton knew him in France and, in the letter he wrote to Elizabeth just before her accession, recommended that he should be appointed a Clerk to the Privy Council.[8]

In Paris Randolph attended the University and studied under the great Scottish humanist George Buchanan, whom long afterwards he still corresponded with and spoke of affectionately as 'my master'. He was a learned man and one of the greatest of Elizabethan historians has called him 'loveable'.[9] His dispatches are certainly most readable and often witty, and he played a leading if secret part in helping the Scottish Reformation to victory during 1559–60, but in later years the intrigues he conducted on behalf of the English Government caused him to be much less beloved north of the Tweed. James Melville, who had once worked with him, ended by comparing him to the Emperor Nero watching the burning of Rome: 'sa Mester Randolphe delyted to se sic fyre kendlit in Scotland . . . and glorified himself to have brocht it till pass.' Sir Nicholas Throckmorton also ended by detesting both him and Cecil.

Randolph spied on the other English exiles for Dean Wotton. He it was, in 1557, who brought the first advance news of Thomas Stafford's ludicrous raid on Scarborough. A most curious reference to him two years later seizes the attention. It occurs in a passage of autobiography written long afterwards by Sir Henry Killigrew, where, listing a lifetime of services to the Queen, Killigrew recalled that he had gone to Germany at the outbreak of war between France and England (June 1557), 'at the beginning whereof . . . Maister Randall was sent thither out of England unto me; and in Her Majesty's name, beinge then Lady Elizabeth, willed me to make a journey into France, to discover theire Intents there against this Realme; which I did, with the apparent Daunger and Venture of my Life; and came back again to Vavghbourgh's [Strasbourg], unto Maister Randall, who sent the Advertisement into England, being tenne sheets of Paper, at my owne chardges . . .'[10] Mary was then still Queen. Did Elizabeth possess some secret intelligence system of her own, even during her sister's reign? Was her life during those bleak days perhaps not quite so withdrawn as it has sometimes been made out to be? Cecil had been Surveyor of her Household, and she had been accused of 'secret intelligence' with him. Certainly they both had a number of men in useful positions very soon after her accession. Randolph was reporting from the wings in Germany at that time. Within a few months he emerged upon a dazzling career as diplomat and confidential agent that took him as far afield as Moscow and lasted nearly three-quarters of the reign.

His brother Edward had been an associate of Wyatt's and fled to France as soon as Wyatt's rising failed. Like Throckmorton, he at once got in touch with the Ambassador. He had only fled, he too explained, to save his life and would on no account take service with the French. At the moment it was a little difficult to shake off his fellow-exiles, but Wotton could depend on him to report their movements. By the end of May Wotton had persuaded Mary to pardon Edward Randolph on condition that he spied. None of the other exiles knew so much about military affairs, and he provided some most helpful intelligence by attaching himself to the French army. In August Wotton sent him home, forgiven for his part in Wyatt's rebellion, and with a strong recommendation to Queen Mary. No sooner was he back in London than he offered his services to the French Ambassador, even moving into the next-door house, and began to urge the invasion of England. He must have been at that time a very plausible double agent, and managed to obtain a captaincy in the English artillery from Philip, whose Ambassadors remembered this in years to come, when Philip needed agents.

Sir William Pickering, another of Wyatt's lieutenants, seemed likely to prove a special embarrassment as a refugee in Paris. He had actually been Ambassador there during Edward VI's reign. Tall, jovial and attractive to women, he knew the King, the Constable and the Guises quite well, and had been a guest at the château Philibert de L'Orme had built for Diane de Poitiers at Anet. He also knew the Embassy cipher; and when Mary invoked the Anglo-French treaties to make Henry extradite the exiles, Wotton had to tell her that Pickering held the official copies. The other exiles entertained high hopes of him. So did the French; if they really wanted to invade England and turn Mary off the throne, here was an obvious leader. They were disillusioned almost at once. Sir William arrived at Caen towards the end of March. Within a month he had approached one of Wotton's agents and informed him that the French had intercepted at least one of Wotton's letters to the Queen; he was risking his neck, he said, but he wished after all to serve Mary, not the French.

In April the Court set out on its springtime trek to the châteaux. Hungry for pensions, eager for active service—raids on the English coast, or piracy against English shipping, or invasions, anything to keep going—Sir Peter Carew and others of the exiled rebels followed in its train. Sir William Pickering stayed behind in Paris. So did Dean Wotton. On April 24 Pickering again got in touch with an agent of Wotton's and informed him that Sir Peter had persuaded Henri to land two groups of exiles at Lee in Essex and on the Isle of Wight; also that Sir Peter had an English spy travelling between London and Paris; also that a French spy in London had arranged for all the Queen's letters to the Emperor to be opened. Next day Sir William fled, hoping that his fellows would not find out till he had left France. An accident brought them the news at once. Terrified that Wotton had sent him home to betray their secrets, they decided to have him followed post-haste and murdered. Dean Wotton doubted if Sir William could escape; when he did, he hoped the Queen would pardon him. Sir William reached the Low Countries destitute, and the Queen and Philip, who badly needed men of his calibre, decided to forget his views about their marriage. In 1556 we hear of him buying arms for England in the Netherlands and employed on a mission in Germany to hire 3,000 mercenaries. Four years later this ebullient Lothario was back home, seriously considered as a suitor to

Queen Elizabeth, holding mysterious private conversations with her, and demanding special meals at Court, a nine days' wonder of a rival to Lord Robert Dudley.

But Sir Peter Carew is the most spectacular of this ruffling crew. As a child he had been such a terror that his father coupled him to one of his hounds 'and so continued him for some time'. He refused all schooling, went off to France at the age of ten, fought at the battle of Pavia at the age of eleven and changed sides when he saw the French were getting the worst of it. He was all but arrested as a spy in Constantinople and all but died of the bloody flux in Vienna. His experience as soldier and sailor, his gift for singing, vaulting, and riding, and his gossip about the French Court, endeared him to Henry VIII, who sent him against the Emperor in 1543 and next year gave him command of a 700-ton ship at the capture of Boulogne.

The Carews had planned to start a rising in Devon at the same time as Wyatt's in Kent. When the county failed to follow them, Sir Peter escaped in a boat belonging to the pirate Killigrews, and piloted by Sir Walter Raleigh's father. Pickering and other rebel gentry joined him in Normandy. Within a couple of months English agents had the whole lot under close supervision. Carew was attainted of high treason *in absentia*, and a large part of his estate confiscated.

Dean Wotton, whose sister had married Sir Peter's uncle and fellow conspirator, Sir Gawen, went swiftly to work, and managed to coax a reluctant promise of pardon from the Queen on condition that Sir Peter repented and proved his repentance by betraying all he knew. Edward Randolph was set to watch him. He learnt that Carew had promised Henri II not to leave France without permission, but early in July had made up his mind to go. Unable simply to disappear and either too ashamed or too scared to face the King himself, he sent Henry Killigrew to tell the Constable. It must have been a peppery interview. Montmorency kept Killigrew four days before giving angry consent, and complained much, Wotton heard, 'of the inconstancy of the English, who ever showed how little they were to be trusted'.

The Constable's permit reached Sir Peter on July 10. At midnight he took horse for Venice. Wotton wrote to Mary that he had barely enough money for the journey and without a pardon and 'some order for his entertainment . . . is like to lead a most miserable life'.

He moved on to the Low Countries, and that autumn Mary gave his wife permission to send him 'material relief'. Not enough, apparently; for in April 1555 he slipped across to Lincolnshire, where she had estates, and begged some of the local gentry and nobility for more. In July he was in Brussels, still writing 'lamentable letters . . . of unfeigned repentance' to Mary's Ambassador, Sir John Mason. Sir John, who had some personal knowledge of the suppleness it cost to keep in favour, risked an opinion that Sir Peter had worn the hair-shirt long enough and might be useful, and on December 9 Sir Peter's pardon was finally enrolled.

But recent research has suggested he had more to pay, and not all in money. On May 15 next year he and Sir John Cheke were suddenly kidnapped near Brussels, hurried home, and thrown into the Tower. Sir John is known to us as the centre of a brilliant set at Cambridge, the tutor of Edward VI, the pioneer of education in Greek, and the friend and brother-in-law of William Cecil. To save his life and his family, he recanted the Protestant convictions he held so deeply and had spread among so many others, and died in misery and remorse soon afterwards. No comparable humiliation befell Sir Peter Carew. He was forced to acknowledge a debt to the Crown of £2,000, but only part seems to have been paid. He was released from the Tower. In September he recovered his land in Devon, either directly or in reversion. The attainder had already been lifted by his pardon. Some years ago Miss Christina Garrett examined the whole case. She came to the conclusion (not challenged since) that Sir Peter had betrayed Cheke as a kind of final instalment for his pardon and an advance payment on the return of his estates.[11]

Dean Wotton had his duty to the Queen and his own reputation to consider, and experience had taught him to drive hard bargains in human lives. He did the best he could for men he thought to have made fools of themselves, but intercession for misguided relatives was not an Ambassador's chief task. The French were the enemy; without French help the exiled rebels could do nothing. And every year, every month almost of the four years between his appointment and the renewal of war, reports were reaching him of French designs on Calais. Calais must not be allowed to fall. Calais was all that remained of Edward III's and Henry V's conquests and the last English foothold on the Continent. Though its value as the staple of the wool trade had greatly diminished, the Spanish marriage had given it new strategic importance as a protective outpost to the

Spanish Netherlands, and the French, for the same reasons of prestige and strategy, had set their hearts on it.

In the autumn of 1556 Wotton had reported a Frenchman called Nicholas Devisat in Calais, ostensibly to teach the children of the English Comptroller. This man had lately received money from Henri II. Wotton believed that Devisat had been compelled to flee from England for forgery and ought to be examined . . . 'a crafty child . . . he left not such a *mignonne dame* as his wife in Paris to teach children in Calais'. This particular warning went unheeded, and Devisat, during a general alarm, escaped by jumping off the walls. About the same time Wotton warned the Queen to be prepared for a certain M. Chesnes, '. . . the same who by subtlety took the town of Merano from the King of Bohemia fourteen years ago'; he was now off to Calais, disguised as a French or Flemish merchant. That November an Englishman at Rouen asked him to send someone to hear 'matters of great importance'; he dispatched his confidential secretary, John Somer, with instructions to proceed straight on to England. The same evening, another of the exiles informed him that troops were massing at Rouen to deliver Calais to the French. Wotton sent a second messenger to the town at once. This time he was listened to, and the Privy Council landed reinforcements. In the spring of 1557 the warning about Calais came from Sir Nicholas Throckmorton. War was declared in mid-June and Wotton was in tears when he took leave of Henri II. On the 14th Lord Grey of Wilton surveyed the town's defences and found them 'utterly useless'. That winter it surrendered. No wonder Wotton felt bitter, and dreaded the same fate for Berwick.

Secret service was in the Wotton blood. Two of the Ambassador's great-nephews became notable intelligencers; to one of them, the poet-diplomat Sir Henry, also celibate, a scholar, and a lover of quiet, we owe the well-known definition of an ambassador as 'an honest man sent to lie abroad for the good of his country'. The Dead had handed Mary an admirable warren of spies in France. Under Elizabeth Sir Nicholas Throckmorton proved worthy of such a patron, and years later it was to Sir Henry Wotton that Arthur Throckmorton bequeathed his father's papers.

*

Ambassadors have to communicate; without couriers 16th-century Ambassadors would have been little more than ornaments plastered on to a main purpose, like the exquisite excrescences of rococo churches, conveying nothing except fantasy and style. It is worth inquiring, before we come to the more barbaric mission of Sir James Croft at Berwick, by what means Ambassadors at sophisticated Courts managed to keep in touch with their sovereigns, and what security their mail enjoyed in tiny boats on pirate-infested seas and in a Europe still part forest and part swamp and everywhere beset by war.

Neither the Tudors nor their contemporaries made much use of pigeons. A certain Freiherr in Franconia employed a tame stag that carried the mail in a sack tied round its neck; and Sir John Harington's 'rare dogge Bungey' took letters to Elizabeth from its owner in Bath, 'nor was it ever told our ladie Queene that this messenger did ever blab ought concerning his high truste, as others have done in more special matters'.[12] But on the whole all secret couriers had to travel like any others, on horseback or by ship. 'The written word abides', and sometimes the most secret part of their message was delivered verbally; they would have been glad of those legendary 'hyena's claws bound up in a linen bag', of which it was believed that 'the wearer would never forget whatsoever he hath heard or knoweth'.

In the previous century the spy-King Louis XI had set up a system of guides and post-horses in France well in advance of any other State, linking the King in Paris with his armies in Brittany, Burgundy and Provence. His couriers, the *chevaucheurs*, whose widows succeeded to their many privileges and exemptions, blazoned the Royal arms on their shoulders, and signed or made their mark on a contract which a priest and, significantly, one other had to witness. At one time over two hundred couriers kept him in constant touch with his provincial governors and contributed to his hold on France; there were as many as five services a week between Paris and Poitiers. The Post of the Hanseatic League covered eighty-five towns. In the Low Countries no one could become a member of the Butchers' Guild until he had first bound himself, each in his turn, to provide a courier service. Thronged with students from the entire western world, who wanted money and news from home, or wanted to send home, the great Universities, Paris especially, elected messengers who made rounds once or twice a year. The Parisians enjoyed the protection of the King. The messengers of the commune of Toulouse sported a livery and a badge and enjoyed the protection of the Archangel Gabriel. All were ill-paid, if paid at all, though their blazons are said to have been of the best workmanship; but they enjoyed favours and prestige and for a livelihood took such private mail as private folk could write.

It was the Thurn und Taxis family, in the territories of the Holy Roman Empire, who had first organized the Post as a successful business, meeting a need that became more urgent with every mile westward the Turks advanced. Gabriels, Rogers, Lamorals, Leonards, Simons, Johann Battistas, children, cousins, uncles, even aunts, found employment in the vast network. They threw out branches to Naples, Sicily and Spain, issued timetables of arrival and departure, and gained a reputation for sticking to them. During the first quarter of the 16th century the Thurn und Taxis Post scheduled: Brussels–Paris, 36 hours in summer, 40 in winter; Brussels–Burgos in Spain, 7 days (8 in winter); Brussels–Innsbruck, 5 days (6 in winter); Brussels–Rome, 10½ (12); Brussels–Naples, 14 days in winter. After the Thirty Years War the family employed more than 20,000 messengers. They were soon tycoons, and became counts and princes. Prince Albrecht, the last of them active in their original profession, remained Hereditary Master of Bavarian Posts until 1918. Their horses wore a badger's skin on their foreheads (*tasso* means badger, and they came from a mountain near Bergamo renowned for badgers). Their livery was blue and silver.

The risks couriers ran more than matched their privileges. Little was yet known about flood control; bridges were swept away, the Post fell in. The Earl of Sussex took a month from Antwerp to Vienna; the Rhine had no charms for him, 'forced every day to be in the wagon or the boat by dawn, and travel till dark', and all the bridges were down across the Danube. Highwaymen at Gadshill and Shooters Hill threatened Throckmorton's couriers on their last lap home. As for the sea! . . . 'horrible vomitings' were the common lot. Storms blew back fugitives into watched harbours, and thence to prisons. 'Lusty footman as I am,' wrote Dean Wotton, pursued by pirates and dumped on the Flemish coast at night without a guide, 'I am sure that of those ii myles I made a-foote vi myles ere I came to Dunkirke: the which journey, I assure you, was more paynefull to me than you cowde well beleeve and my gowtye toes and feete are the worse for it yet.'

Martin Luther had once warned the Duke of Saxony that to violate the secrecy of the mail was 'a mortal sin, which will bring with it the loss of divine mercy'. Nevertheless a great number of

Lutheran monarchs risked this loss, and Catholics had been opening other people's letters for generations. Vaillé, historian of the French Post Office, unearthed many orders issued by the Popes and the French Kings to stop couriers and steal their dispatches long before the 16th century, and English writs to search suspect travellers are in existence from the 14th. William Cecil did not hesitate to purloin diplomatic mail. When he became suspicious of the Spanish Ambassador, he ordered two agents to dress up as highwaymen, waylay the Ambassador's courier, and detain him while his letters were deciphered and copied. When the Ambassador protested to the Queen, Elizabeth replied that she would halt the Posts and examine what she pleased, if she had heard of anything plotted to her harm.

It suited the French Kings that the Thurn und Taxis Posts between Spain and the Empire should be allowed to pass through France; since this made them the easier to examine. The bankers Balbani, who farmed the carriage of mail from Lyons, complained that François I had set up a special office charged with opening it. Most sovereigns understood by the 16th century that a secret service must have plenty of eyes in Post Offices, though it was not until the 17th that Richelieu and the Austrian Habsburg Lodges brought this prying to an art and a sort of clandestine black peacock spread its giant fantail across all western Europe.

One would like to believe that the French post-boy was always proud of his status, always carried a beautifully wrought badge and post-bag, and see him always arrive, as a contemporary described him, 'at the Red Rose at the bottom of the Rue St. Jacques, and there shut himself up in his little office, and through a half-barred window hand to one man his *sac de procès*, to another his packet of letters, to another butter, capons and smoked ham'. A German engraving shows a footman with his long pike (one of those older Posts that survived beside the horse-posts of the Thurn und Taxis), sauntering through a serene landscape; the rhyme beneath tells how he hears the birds sing, and thinks of the wineglasses clinking in the inn, and the stories he will invent there. It may often have been so. But the city of Basle knew enough of the dark side to put up a statue to a faithful courier. Jean Second, the poet, found an inscription on the tomb of another at Arras, honouring his *esprit de sacrifice*, and wrote him an epitaph in verse. The lives of couriers were dangerous, their journeys often critical. They linked plots and broke them, and carried life and death in their post-bags. They saw the heads withering on the spikes, the chained limbs bleaching on the gallows, and some knew that at any hour their own might join them.

iv. Espionage on a Frontier

The office allotted to Sir James Croft presents a picture quite different from Paris. Berwick, though infinitely drearier, was probably less perilous. Sir James had no diplomatic immunity; on the other hand, he did not have to operate, like Sir Nicholas, in the very heart of the enemy citadel, but in a fortress on its fringes. As an intelligencer, he had other advantages. The English were poorer than the French, but the Scots much poorer than the English and that much the easier to bribe. The Border had been like a sieve to spies for generations. The Scots in relation to the English were as untutored in dissembling their emotions as—according to Comines—the English in relation to the French. Finally, a State divided is a ready prey to spies.

In the mid-16th century Scotland was divided indeed. Spasmodically ignited and welded into patriotic unity by foreign threats, it broke more often into warring sectors which the magnet of bribes could draw wholly out of the circumference. Where the King lodged had not yet become the heart, nor where the Court lay the hearth, to which all must repair who wished to make their fortunes. Of the first Jameses of the Stuart line who reigned between 1424 and 1542 two had been murdered by their nobles and two killed in wars with England; and though James V was absent from the field of Solway Moss, the defeat brought on his death. The first James spent twenty years a prisoner in England; the next four succeeded to the throne at an average age of eight. In 1542 the crown fell once more to an infant; James V heard of Mary Stuart's birth on his death-bed.

The great warrior-nobles followed sometimes their own interests, sometimes an alloy of their own and the interests of France or England, and lived obsessed by hereditary feuds, spied on and enflamed by foreign powers. The struggle of four people to control Mary's destiny dominated the years after Solway Moss: first, the Earl of Angus, seeking his family's advancement and the independence of Scotland by means, at first, of the English alliance and Mary's marriage to the young Protestant Prince Edward; second, Marie de Guise, seeking ultimately the annexation of Scotland to Catholic France by means of Mary's marriage to the Dauphin; third,

Cardinal Beaton, seeking his own advancement and the independence of Scotland by means of the French alliance and her marriage now here, now there; and lastly the Governor, James Hamilton, second Earl of Arran, and next heir to the throne, seeking it is hard to know what, except the advancement of his own family by means of her marriage to his son. Like all other royal children, she was a pawn from the beginning.

Centralized national government collapsed under the tugging not only of a centrifugal feudalism, rapidly losing its disruptive force in France and England, but also under the vertical fissions of the clan; particularly along the Border, the region most vulnerable to invasion and intelligence. The name itself, and even more the name given to that lost domain between Sark Water and the river Esk (the Debatable Land), claimed by both countries and the refuge of men from broken clans who no longer had a chieftain, are symbolic of the psychological regions spies inhabit.

The Scottish Border Lands exercised upon those who rode, reived and raided there, and still exercise upon those who read about them, the appeal which lawlessness will always have. Their tumultuous anarchism and fierce contempt of institutions have in an extreme and savage form something in common with certain moods in western societies at the present moment. The Borderers were constantly suborned as spies. The motive can only exceptionally have been religious. Many of them believed at least as much in the superstitions which Catholicism had taken over, or fabricated, as in a Catholic faith sluggishly taught and selfishly and ignorantly practised. Ghosts, elves, brownies were as real to them as the saints, and the Queen of Faeryland as the Virgin Mary; and they armed and mounted not when a Church, and not always when a King, called them, but when a wife put stirrups on the table in place of meat, or a kinsman lay chained in Carlisle or Newcastle jail.

All the English Wardens employed spies. Wharton at Carlisle, only half an hour's gallop from the Border, entertained dozens. Already in September 1557, after the French defeat at St. Quentin, one of them had reported that the Scots wanted peace with England, and the Privy Council ordered Wharton 'to have continual spies in Scotland . . . to understand . . . the Scots assemblies . . . what purposes and enterprises they mind to take in hand, against what time, who shall have the charge'. At Berwick Lord Eure had 'espiall money' of £6 13s. 4d. a year, about one-fifth of his salary. Up at the

river Tay's mouth, in the English foothold at Broughty Craig, Sir
Andrew Dudley received £100 'for men, spies, and timber for the
fleet'. But countless are the bonds, oaths, commitments to serve,
wear the red cross, even undertake murders, by which lords and
lairds manœuvred to safeguard themselves, their kin and their
possessions, from English interference, and secure themselves
advancement if the English won. Cecil, while one of Edward VI's
secretaries, held lists of over a thousand Scotsmen 'sworn to serve
the King of England'. The practice of treason had grown so common
and so commonly accepted that, when Governor Arran proclaimed
a traitor's death for any 'Scotsman born' found serving the Duke of
Somerset in the English army, Somerset took it as an outrage
'contrary to justice and usage of Christian realms'.

These bonds seldom lasted. Over and over again English intelligence was warned that Scottish patriotism could be reconciled but
not tyrannized. All Scotsmen had come to believe, his Scottish agents
advised Sir Ralph Sadler, who passed on the advice to Henry VIII,
that England 'seeketh nothing else but to bring them to subjection
. . . which universally they do so detest and abhor . . . that they will
never be brought unto it but by force'. But King Henry was ageing,
and perhaps a little mad, and had to have his way at once. At the end
of the 1540s, but for the countervailing insolence of the 'auld ally'
across the Channel, the 'auld enmity' across the Cheviots seemed
likely to last for ever. The neglect of the advice the King was
repeatedly given is a classic example of the disasters that follow,
when accurate intelligence is ignored.

A mutual code of conduct to be observed in time of war prohibited
all intercourse with the enemy. English laws forbade Englishmen to
aid or abet any Scotsman in robbing, burning or stealing within the
realm of England; in time of war to give Scotsmen any information
of exploits intended against them; and even to communicate with
Scots, or marry a Scottish woman, or play football matches, then a
ferocious pastime, against the Scots. Custom brought laws and codes to
very little. 'For seven years past there has been as great familiarity and
conventions and making of merchandise . . . between Englishmen
and Scottish men, both in peace and war, as Scottish men use among
themselves within the realm of Scotland: and this familiarity has
been the cause that the King of England got intelligence with diverse
gentlemen of Scotland.'[13]

The English Borderers claimed that the handkerchiefs they wore

round their arms in battle and the letters embroidered in their caps
were signs of recognition, so that they could come the more quickly
to one another's aid; others in the English army believed them to be
secret signals to the Scottish Borderers 'each to spare other or gently
each to take other'. It was alleged that the English Borderers sewed
on their red crosses so lightly that a puff of wind could blow them
off. In the middle of a battle they would hold confabulations with
the Scots; when observed, they made a great show of running at one
another, as if in a game where people 'strike few strokes but by assent
and appointment'.

So long as Scotland remained the cockpit between England and
France, so long the greater rivals on their thrones continued to
exploit and embitter the lesser rivals in their castles, keeps and dales.
Some of the lesser spies appear merely as 'my espialls' in a letter
from an English Warden or commander to the Privy Council, and
seem to have been engaged in little more than minor military
reconnaissance. Many have no names. None has a portrait. Faceless
and anonymous, they ride out of a forest or a mist, say something or
hand over something, and into a forest or a mist return. A few are
known and possess even the shadow of a personality. We can follow
their perilous journeys, see and hear what they did and said on their
arrivals, read their long and valuable reports, and make reasonable
guesses at their motives.

A certain Patrick Kincaid bore a grudge against the Governor
Arran, who had expelled his master from the Captaincy of Edinburgh
Castle and deprived a kinsman of the post of Constable. So off he
galloped to the Border in a vengeful fit and offered to deliver the
castle to the English. Patrick Graeme was a spy who crept right to
the heart of power. He belonged to the Graemes of Esk and Leven, in
Wharton's jurisdiction, an incendiary marauding clan, 'stark moss-
troopers and arrant thieves both to England and Scotland, outlawed
yet sometimes connived at because they gave intelligence forth from
Scotland . . .' During the forties they operated into the Debatable
Land. The English found Patrick a 'witty fellow' and in the winter
of 1544–5 sent him north with letters to the Earl of Angus, whose
devotion to England was in doubt. He rode out of Carlisle in the
company of Robin Scott, laird of Waynfray. Leaving him at Peebles,
the laird rode on to Edinburgh and sent him back a passport that
admitted him close enough to see 'the Queene [Marie de Guise]
knelynge to here Masse, the Governour, the Cardinall, therles of

Monnterosse Argyle Glenkerne . . . with other lordes standyng by.
. . . And the said Patrick went to therle of Glenkerne and asked hym
in his eare, whether he wolde be a true man or a false?—who
answered hym, he wolde be true, and said he never made promes to
the Kynges majestie [of England], but he wolde kepe it . . .' Patrick
learnt much more both there and riding back to Dumfries and told
it all to the English at Darlington eight days after he had left
Carlisle.

The Pringles, another violently unruly clan who contributed a spy
to England, came from Teviotdale the other side. In the summer of
1543 they raided across the Border and Jock Pringle was taken
prisoner—'a very rank rider and attemptour', Lord Parr called him,
who deserved to be hanged at once. However, he had great influence
in Teviotdale and might be useful, and Parr waited to hear Henry
VIII's pleasure. While he was waiting, Sandy Pringle arrived to beg
his kinsman's life, promising in return, and in writing too, to bind
himself and twelve 'of the best of his name' to serve Henry all their
lives. Parr thought the offer worth submitting to the Privy Council;
'there had been no like sute for any other man'. The King accepted
it and Sandy Pringle proceeded to pay amply for Jock's pardon. He
felt no qualms. He was a Borderer; to him there was nothing in the
Scots 'but fraude, supteltie, and blandysshing promyses'. Next year
he was reporting direct to Somerset, who paid him the compliment
that he had 'not hitherto advertised us otherwise than we found it to
be true'. His treason soon became known. Marie de Guise heard that
'a Scottish man called Sanders Pringle' was betraying all the men of
the south-eastern Lowlands to the English. Donaldson, a follower of
Lord Home's, met him riding towards the English camp and
threatened to denounce him. Pringle replied that he would regret his
words, and next night a company of English burst into Donaldson's
house and killed him and his son.

These were men of whom violent personal impulses made spies,
and the State papers are scarred and slimy with their tracks. Several
were anything but contemptible. Alexander Crichton, laird of
Brunstane near Penicuik, and John Cockburn, laird of Ormiston a
few miles to the east, spied first and foremost for a cause. They were
both pro-English Calvinists, all the more important because their
fields and houses lay on strategic territory straddling the English
approaches to Edinburgh from Berwick and the Border passes, and
the French from their fortified landing-places at Dunbar and

Eyemouth. Ravaged repeatedly, it brings to mind the Low Countries and the flat fertile entrances from north-eastern Europe into France.

The laird of Ormiston had been an early convert to Calvinism and John Knox tutored his son. The laird of Brunstane first took to spying when in the service of Cardinal Beaton. In 1539 he was entrusted with letters to Rome asking Pope Paul III to make Beaton a Cardinal *a latere*. Either wrecked or (perhaps willingly) forced ashore on the Northumbrian coast, he had the letters taken from him by the captain of Bamburgh Castle, who sent them to Henry VIII.[14] The King was exerting pressure on James V of Scotland at the time to follow his own example, expropriate the Roman Catholic clergy, and ally himself with England, and thought the letters might assist. He therefore passed them to his envoy in Scotland, Sir Ralph Sadler, to be used as evidence that Beaton (like Wolsey) was seeking to exalt himself above his sovereign. The trick did not work and James remained loyal to the Cardinal. Not so Brunstane. It is from this time that he clearly passed into the service of England, in which he and Ormiston were to thrive and suffer for at least fifteen years.

Leaving the Cardinal's household, he joined that of the Governor Arran, about the time the latter was abandoning his first Protestant phase and veering towards the Cardinal and France. He proceeded to hoodwink both Governor and Cardinal without at first, apparently, becoming suspect or losing the favour of James V. In June 1542 he received £100 for journeying to France at James's command with four horses; and in November the King, a week before the disaster at Solway Moss and a month before his own death, issued Brunstane and his son John Crichton a grant of land at Gilberton. After the battle Brunstane warned Sadler that the Cardinal, despite his protestations to the contrary, had set his heart on a war of revenge. Sadler was his spy-master at this stage and he was already sufficiently trusted to have the use of a cipher.

In March 1544 he reported Henry's enemies to be putting it about in Scotland that the King intended to lay the country waste and received instructions to emphasize the royal streak of magnanimity; the Duke of Somerset, who was to command one punitive invasion, promised Brunstane personally that his own lands would be spared if he would join the English army. In May this army disembarked at Leith and seized and pillaged Edinburgh, but either because he had no chance to desert, or lacked the inclination, Brunstane found himself still in the Scots camp. Leaving the tents at nightfall, he was detected by an archer of the English watch who, unapprised of his role, drew a bow and wounded him in the thigh. He reappeared at dawn, however, and this time got safely through the lines, hale enough to give Somerset and the English captains a résumé of Scottish public opinion.

Ormiston too had offered himself to Somerset, and one of his first services had been a list of all his neighbour gentlemen of Lothian hostile to England, who thereupon had their lands burnt and their cattle seized. His own crops suffered from the English bands; but in compensation he obtained permission to import wine and certain necessities across the Border. By the mid-forties both lairds were working for union of the two countries, considered the Cardinal the foremost enemy of Scotland and had become fully pledged to the Reformed religion.

It was Brunstane who sent Henry the names of certain Scotsmen willing, in return for asylum in England, to assassinate the Cardinal. The King accepted the offer, but the Cardinal got wind of the plot and most of the conspirators were arrested. By now Brunstane was under suspicion. The governor sent him two summonses during 1544, and in January 1545 the Lords of the Council demanded his presence immediately in Edinburgh. Nonetheless he and Ormiston took the preacher George Wishart under their protection and had the courage to attend at Inveresk on the third Sunday of that December, when Wishart publicly challenged the Cardinal and conducted a Reformed service in the parish church. Early next year Wishart supped with them at Ormiston. Knowing that his time had come, and perhaps theirs too, he discoursed to them on the deaths of martyrs and sang John Wedderburn's metrical version of the fifty-first psalm, 'Have mercy on me, God of might'. At midnight they heard that the Earl of Bothwell was approaching with soldiers sent jointly by the Governor and Cardinal. The house was surrounded. Brunstane got away, but Wishart and Ormiston were taken as prisoners to Edinburgh Castle, whence Ormiston escaped by climbing over a wall. The Governor handed Wishart over to the Cardinal, who had him burnt at the stake.

Brunstane fled across the Border, but soon was back again, back in the Scottish army, back even in the Governor's confidence, and all the time equipped with a cipher, reporting on the Scottish fleet and

urging Henry to invade before the French arrived. They did invade
and in 1545 suffered a shattering defeat at Ancrum Moor. And there
was Brunstane on the wrong side again. A precious spy must always
run the risk of being caught with the armies he is betraying at the
moment they go into battle. It is a risk he and his employers should
avoid; he may be killed, and his talents are rarer than those of mere
soldiers. Things become even more awkward for him if the army he
is with happens to be victorious. Brunstane found a way out. The
night before the battle he contrived to have his horse fall on
him, damaging his arm; and the Governor, either from doubts
of his loyalty or from gullibility, allowed him to be absent from
the fight.

In May 1546 the Cardinal was assassinated in his castle of St.
Andrews. Neither Brunstane nor Ormiston had to do directly with
the murder, but Ormiston and his sons subsequently joined the
assassins, John Knox, and other leading Scottish Reformers and
were besieged. In the same month a summons for treason was issued
against Brunstane. Next year both lairds were ordered to have their
oxen ready to haul the Scottish artillery and in September the
Governor again demanded their attendance. No wonder, and no
wonder he demanded in vain. Throughout 1547 they had been
constantly in touch with England, and had planned to take part in
Patrick Kincaid's assault on Edinburgh Castle, with Sandy Pringle
as their guide.

In September 1548 the English took their revenge for Ancrum
Moor at Pinkie; it was Ormiston who guided them from Berwick.
Brunstane was dissatisfied with the victory. Only the 'ungodly
spurring of the French', he wrote, kept the Scottish in the field, and
he called for an even larger English army 'to make an end'. But the
time had passed. That winter Henry VIII died and though Ormiston
wrote direct to Somerset, now Lord Protector, 'to forward your
godly wish for union of the realmes', the French landed at Leith in
strength and Somerset soon had troubles of his own at home. The
pressure from the south lost impetus. Arran surprised Ormiston, and
killed ten of his men. The lairds were accused of putting the houses
of Ormiston, Salton and Gilberton 'in our auld ynemeis hands' and
orders sent from Edinburgh to pull them down 'so that no habitation
salbe had in ony of the saidis places to our saidis auld ynemeis fra
thyme forth in ony tymes to cum'.[15]

Ormiston's home was burnt with many of Brunstane's and his

own possessions inside. 'The more patiently he takes it,' Lord Grey wrote to Somerset of Brunstane, 'the more worthy he is of recompense.' He had much cause for patience and at the moment little hope of recompense at home. Scotland was sick of war and ready to settle for the French. The Lowlands had been so devastated '. . . there is nothing to destroy. The bareness, want of lodging, scarcity, wet and cold, makes war here more painful than elsewhere, wastes men and horses, brings men out of heart, causing even them to forswear war who cannot live without it.' Brunstane's home was razed to the ground. The work went on throughout the spring of 1548. Gunners with ten culverins were hired to protect the demolition squad. Eight pioneers came from Leith 'to cart the great timber and fell the same'. All the corn was borne away, Brunstane's other goods seized from Penicuik, a slater paid 22 shillings to rip off the slates, and the stones transported to build some enemy a house in Edinburgh. A summons for treason was issued and hue and cry raised against both lairds. Brunstane escaped to the Continent. Ormiston, declared a banished man and his estates forfeit, received some 60,000 acres in Northumberland and Durham from Edward VI by way of compensation for his 'trusty and acceptable service . . . as well as . . . the great burdens and damage which he has sustained'.[16] He returned home in time to share in the victory of the Scottish Reformation.

*

The multitude of Scottish treasons belong to a period before any concept of national loyalty had taken lasting root. In practice there was neither unity of government nor unity of law. As to Government, enough has been said here about the Lowlands; elsewhere, great lords like Huntly and Argyll ruled almost as independent sovereigns in their mountainous domains. As to laws, we have the celebrated *mot* that there were many, and only one was lacking, which would ensure the enforcement of the rest. Individual patriotism, reflecting the oscillations at the centre and helping to produce them, was mostly a weathercock. The prelates had a vested interest in Catholicism and in that, if in little else, were constant. Marie de Guise, despite many reefings and tackings, never seriously altered her French course. But the majority were two-faced, because politically the country still faced two ways. All the less powerful and less settled countries of the world have been in such a state. Their citizens know that a decision must be made, if they are not to remain in a condition of division bordering on civil war. The passion for liberty, whether innate, or derived from memory, or from some myth or fact of liberties long departed, makes the ease of total subservience impossible. They seem to be waiting for a leader, or for some exile to return, who will give them the direction they are to take for generations, even centuries. Until this happens they waver and are unsure; and when almost an entire nation is in such a mood, individuals are the more readily found to act as spies.

In 1550, when peace was signed between England, France and Scotland, it seemed that the direction of Scotland was to be Catholic and French. Marie de Guise felt herself secure enough to leave for home for the first time since her marriage; there she visited her daughter and had many discussions with Henri II and her warrior and Cardinal brothers. In 1554, as a result of this visit, she gained her first ambition; Arran yielded up his Governorship in return for the French dukedom of Châtellerault[17] and a considerable pension, and she was crowned Queen-Regent. In 1558 she achieved her second; Mary Stuart married the Dauphin François in Notre Dame and the Dauphin was granted the crown-matrimonial of Scotland. The daughter's future seemed assured; one day, if she lived, she would govern both kingdoms and her descendants reign over a Franco-Scottish union. If she did not live, in secret clauses to the marriage contract she had signed Scotland away to the King of France. In Edinburgh, supported by French soldiers and advisers, the mother seemed supreme.

It was all illusion. Scottish patriotism burnt on, of whatever religion, and the French committed the same atrocities and errors as had the English. Alongside patriotism smouldered the fire of Reformation, each throwing sparks upon the other. In order to counterbalance the ambitions of the Hamiltons, Marie was driven to perform so many acts of conciliation and apparent tolerance towards the preachers and Reforming nobility, that she sowed the seeds of her own undoing. She pardoned the Cardinal's murderers.[18] In 1556 she rescinded the decree of treason and forfeiture against Ormiston and Brunstane. On all sides she smiled, forgave, and seemed to rule. That she was only Regent on sufferance was made clear to her that day in 1557, when nearly all the Scots nobility refused to follow her for France's sake across the Border. But next year the victory of Calais and the capture of the Constable made her brothers all-powerful with Henri II and Diane de Poitiers. An era of increasing authority seemed to lie ahead. The accession of Elizabeth and the establishment of the Protestant religion by law in England altered everything. 'This change . . .' as William Cecil had written to himself.

Chapter Three

A GREAT CONSPIRACY

i. The Border: Winter–early Spring 1558–9

AT the moment of Elizabeth's accession Sir James Croft, though in the North, did not yet hold one of the chief commands. Thomas Percy, seventh Earl of Northumberland, was warden of the East and Middle Marches, and Lord Dacre Warden of the West; both of them were suspected of being Catholics and therefore distrusted by the new regime. In January 1559 Lord Eure received letters-patent as Captain of the castle and town of Berwick. Sir Henry Percy, Northumberland's brother and heir, was Constable of Norham and Tynemouth; he was a Protestant and Cecil had confidence in him. Ancient family trees always attracted the Secretary's rising eye and three years later he married his son Thomas to Percy's Neville sister-in-law.

Ever since Marie de Guise had refortified Eyemouth and (although in vain) mustered her army on the Border, these men had been sending the Privy Council messages of alarm. The garrisons were not up to strength. Berwick was short of guns and ammunition, and the repairs begun during Mary's reign urgently needed to be finished. The footbands were described as 'clean decayed' and the horsemen scarcely better, because the captains had been playing Falstaff's trick with the muster-rolls, like so many captains, and taking Crown pay for men either dead or absent. The Wardens reported the soldiers on the other side to be disturbingly disciplined and well armed. Just before Christmas a Franco-Scottish foray galloped across the Tweed at sunrise, killed the commander of the Cornhill garrison and took all his men prisoner; 'like beasts . . . they never sought stroke for it after the captain was slain.' Francis Chesylden wrote one midnight from Berwick to Sir John Thynne that the Scots rode even as far as Morpeth unhindered, ten or twelve in a company, '. . . and call men by their names "I am Jok of the Hare Well or Hob a Gilchrist or Tom of the Covis or a Davison or a

QUEEN ELIZABETH

MARY QUEEN OF SCOTS

Young . . . rise, the great host of Scotland is coming, all your town shall be burnt. If thou wilt be my prisoner, I will save thy horse, corn and cattle"'. Even as Chesylden was writing he could see villages burning within cannon-shot.

Through such flames there arrived overtures for peace: a message to Sir Henry Percy from d'Oysel, the same who had plotted with Sir James Croft in Mary Tudor's reign and was now Marie de Guise's Lieutenant of the Realm. According to one English spy Marie could not afford to maintain the Scots in arms the rest of the winter; according to three others, she expected a great French army in the spring. A truce would give her time; Sir Henry therefore advised against it, and the raids continued. Elizabeth decided to levy 1,000 men in Yorkshire and the Bishopric of Durham, and summoned Sir James to Court, perhaps their first meeting since their confrontation in the Tower. She gave him letters to act as Deputy-Captain in Lord Eure's 'absence', and sent him hurriedly back to instruct Northumberland where to place the new levies and the old Bishop of Durham which captains were to command them. He reached Berwick on the afternoon of January 23, and at once found himself in the heart of a conspiracy.

The day before there had again been overtures for peace,[19] but this time from neither d'Oysel nor the Regent. Angered and dismayed by the aggressive change in Marie's policy, the Reforming party had decided to court Elizabeth on their own. Sir Henry Percy had been summoned to a secret rendezvous somewhere near Norham, and no less a person had slipped out of Edinburgh to meet him than the one-time Governor, formerly known as Earl of Arran, but now as Duke of Châtellerault. This wily and wavering old bird, the despair of whichever side he happened to be taking at the moment, never abandoned one thought—he was heir to the Scottish throne—and never varied one ambition—either he or one of his family should wear the crown. Though ousted from the Regency by Marie de Guise, he still ruled the Hamiltons and possessed great power. He was jealous of her, but remained in the background, ostensibly Catholic and a pensioner of France.

He had been in touch with Percy before by messenger, but this was the first time they had met. He now wished Elizabeth to be informed that he pledged the whole support of his family and following to prevent a French attack on Berwick or invasion of England. They would also assist her, if she herself decided to invade

Scotland to expel the French, and he professed his desire to maintain 'the Word of God which he supposed shall by the Queen be set forth'. In other words, he was changing sides again. Further he would not go: as heir, any conspiracy to oust the lawful and Catholic Queen of Scots would be disastrous to him. He would put nothing into writing. Sixteen years earlier Sir Ralph Sadler, trying to commit him to Henry VIII, had met the same evasiveness. He would promise verbally, and 'earnestly desire', but later deny what he had promised and desire the opposite. Then he had pleaded circumstance. This time he excused himself to Percy on the grounds that he lacked 'uniform calligraphy' and had never before corresponded with 'any so high and mighty princess'.

It was unlikely that such a man would have dared to break with Marie de Guise without pressure from some new persuader. In a letter to Cecil and Sir Thomas Parry two days later, Sir Henry Percy disclosed this hidden influence. 'The young Laird of Lethington [William Maitland] being Chief Secretary to the Dowager of Scotland, and one of her Privy Council and in great estimation with her,' wanted a one-month truce 'to the end that he might but once talk with the Council of England and specially with you, Sir William Cecil, whom he is most desirous to speak withal. This man is as much my lawful friend as can be, and a man both godly true in his doings and of a good religion . . .', in other words, a Protestant.

On February 11 William Kirkcaldy of Grange also crossed to Norham to treat openly with Sir Henry Percy about peace. Asked if he spoke for Marie de Guise, Kirkcaldy replied that Maitland had instructed him, which he would surely not have done without Marie's consent. He added that Maitland would wish to travel to London, giving a peace treaty as the reason; almost certainly Kirkcaldy knew there was more to it than that, but at this meeting he did not say more. The Border thus became the scene for two separate sets of negotiations, one open and serving as a cover for the other, which was secret. This intricate quadrille continued for some time. On the English side, the Earl of Northumberland took charge of the official talks, and M. Sarlabos and the Earl of Bothwell on the Franco-Scottish. Cecil told Northumberland nothing of the secret talks; neither Marie de Guise nor d'Oysel could tell their delegates anything, since they knew nothing about them. They were conducted by Maitland and Kirkcaldy for Scotland; and for England, by Percy and Sir James Croft, now fully restored in blood and favour and appointed Captain of Berwick. The secret group were attached to the official group; sometimes, inevitably, they all met together, and dissembling had to be practised in rather difficult circumstances. Croft and Maitland had to draw one another aside to discuss matters Northumberland must not overhear; on one occasion Maitland became aggressively Scots, and Croft had to whisper to the eager young conspirator that he was overplaying his official act.

Maitland advised Croft that Marie would probably choose him as her representative for the peace talks in London, of which he had made sure by persuading her that Elizabeth sincerely desired a reconciliation. Dispatched ostensibly on matters 'tending to the quietness, wealth and commodity of both the realms', and with a safe-conduct signed by Northumberland, he set off south on March 6, 1559. Sir James rode a little of the way with him. Maitland confided that he intended to speak frankly to Elizabeth, and if his offers did not go far enough he would do all he could to meet her. He mentioned Mary Stuart's claim to the throne of England and said that it had 'never entered into any wise man's head', since it could only prevail by conquest. Sir James felt he could report that Maitland would handle the whole matter with secrecy and tact. Maitland reached London on March 19, saw the Queen and Cecil, and went on to Fontainebleau to pay his duty to the Queen of Scots. A few days later a Frenchman set out from Fontainebleau in the reverse direction. This was M. de Bétaincourt, master of Marie de Guise's household. He too was travelling officially with news of peace; he too had another and secret errand.

The other negotiators remained at their posts along the Border. The Earl of Northumberland had grown worried about stories spread at Court of his misgovernment in the North. Aware that he had many enemies there, 'specially in this change', he instructed his brother to travel south and tell the Council how things really stood; the authors of the stories must be punished. He had always argued that without the Wardens' intelligence matters would be even worse. It soon became a question whether his intelligence service might not be literally his own, and whether he might not perhaps know a great deal more than the conspirators supposed; Sir James Croft later reported a suspicion that a clerk of the Privy Council advertised the Earl from time to time of all secret discussions among the Councillors that might concern him.

ii. The Peace Treaty: Spring 1559

The negotiations for peace in Europe moved from place to place during the winter of 1558–9 and ended up in early spring on neutral territory at Cateau-Cambrésis, with the Duchess of Lorraine as hostess, intermediary and chairman. The Duke of Alva, the Prince of Orange, Ruy Gomez, and the Bishop of Arras (Cardinal Granvelle) represented Philip II; the Constable Montmorency, ransomed, and both Cardinal of Lorraine and Duke de Guise represented France. It was the first great trial of Elizabeth's diplomacy, indeed its first international exposure, and to face these giant guns and practised poignards she sent Lord William Howard, Lord Great Chamberlain of England and her great-uncle, with the Bishop of Ely and Dean Wotton.

A succession of French manœuvres to divide Spain and England, and obtain with one a separate Treaty which would exclude the other, led the English an exacting dance. Calais became the sticking-point. Elizabeth was determined, if possible, to have it back as a fanfare for the opening of her reign. But peace took precedence, and in their last-resort instructions her Commissioners were ordered to take peace at almost any price. They skirmished in continual dread of a miscalculation, which would cause the French to break off in earnest and start the war afresh. The Spaniards assured the English that if Elizabeth decided to go on fighting she would find Philip at her side. All the same, the Duke of Alva hinted, her soldiers would be expected to do rather more than they had done so far. With grave but disconcerting courtesy he questioned their ability to do anything at all; and since England at that moment possessed neither ability nor inclination, Calais stayed French.

It proved an unhappy conference for Dean Wotton. He felt himself to be representing an England which Mary Tudor had turned into a poor relation. The French delegates had ears everywhere. He could not make out how they contrived to know so much, unless (this in Latin) 'there is nowhere money cannot penetrate'. Even the English ciphers were out of date and could easily be broken; it was high time they had a new set, with plenty of substitutes and 'a good number of nihils [blanks]'. The Treaty confirmed his fears of a Franco-Spanish alliance. Philip was to marry Henri II's daughter Elizabeth of Valois, and Emanuel Philibert of Savoy Henri's sister, and the French had consented to surrender most of their claims in

Italy, in order to keep Calais. 'It is not Calais,' Wotton lamented, 'but England and the Low Countries that may countervail Savoy and Piedmont.' Christopher Mount, the Queen's envoy to the German Lutheran princes, expected that the Kings of France and Spain would soon launch a massive crusade against all Protestants; indeed the Cardinal of Lorraine openly boasted that Henri II would have accepted peace at any price, in order to be free to exterminate the Calvinists.

On April 19, Mary and the Dauphin initialled the Treaty on behalf of Scotland. Maitland of Lethington was within call, but nobody thought it necessary to summon any Scottish delegates; he was merely given a copy and departed homewards with it on the 21st. Sir Nicholas Throckmorton received his letters-patent as Ambassador to Paris; and the Queen appointed him to join Wotton and Howard for the ratification.

*

The élite of half the western world now began to prepare for ceremonies and festivities; no treaty, least of all so great a treaty as Cateau-Cambrésis, being complete without oaths, benedictions, Te Deums, exchanges of carefully assessed gifts, balls, masques and tournaments. The climax would be the double wedding of the Valois princesses in Notre Dame. A brilliant embassy of Spaniards and Burgundians made ready in Brussels, headed by the Duke of Alva, who was to stand proxy for King Philip. In early May the humbler cavalcade of the three English Commissioners set out for Paris, and the French for London, headed by the Constable Montmorency's eldest son François. The highways to the Channel coast became crowded with magnificos.

Western Europe seems, as on other occasions after a great war has ended, to have entered a brief interim, as it were the vestibule of a new epoch, where the principal actors of both past and future are corralled together in the temporary role of peace-makers. Sooner or later they would separate again into opposing camps. A few men knew the direction into which they hoped to guide events; the rest were waiting. All eyed the leaders and one another. All understood, with varying degrees of lucidity, that things had changed dramatically; some wished to accelerate the change, some cautiously to steer it to their own and their country's advantage, some if possible to reverse it. Those concerned with Intelligence were on the look-out for possible agents and fifth-columnists; and it became important to recall what opinions people had evinced, and what their records had been during the periods of peace.

The embassy sent to Paris to sign the Treaty provides an illustration of strange new juxtapositions. Lord William Howard had found little difficulty in co-operating with Philip and Mary. This same choleric Lord High Admiral, who five years ago had prevented the rebel Wyatt crossing from Southwark into the city of London, who had closed Ludgate to Wyatt when he marched round by Kingston, and who had lost his temper with the more-than-conniving French Ambassador, now found himself yoked with Sir Nicholas Throckmorton, who had been among Wyatt's chief supporters and had asked that same Ambassador for arms; while Wotton, who had enlisted Sir Nicholas as a spy three years ago, was now to be succeeded by him in Paris. Lord William must be placed among the old nobility, who in France as in England desired as little change as possible. Wotton was timid, Cecil and Throckmorton not themselves radical. But all three belonged among the up-and-coming gentry, and the last two had formed connexions with radicals in Europe, which they were aware might now be useful. None of them could be certain so early in the reign to which arc of her genealogical circle and entourage, the upstart or the aristocratic, the Queen might decide to turn, nor how far she was prepared to take reform. 'It shall not be meete', Sir Nicholas had himself advised her, 'that either the old or the new shall wholly understand what you meane, but to use them as instruments to serve yourself . . .'[20] In France 'the old', by which he meant those dominant in the days when Philip had been King of England, was represented by the Spanish Ambassador, and 'the new' by the Huguenots, and he soon proceeded to make as good friends as possible of both.

On Sunday, May 7 Dean Wotton reached Canterbury, where he caught cold sitting in Chapter. Lord William found him on Thursday with an ague, taking pills and worried because the second fit fell due on the first day of his climacteric year; without waiting for him or for mere 'Mr. Frogmerton', and hearing no lodgings were ready at Calais, the great nobleman took his suite straight across to Boulogne and occupied every room available. Sir Nicholas had delayed long enough in London to extort a promise from the Queen that his embassy would not last long, 1,683 ounces of plate from the Jewel House, and a loan of 1,000 marks. At Sittingbourne he remembered that he had forgotten to ask how he should behave towards the Guises and wrote back urgently for instructions. If they showed friendship, Cecil replied, Throckmorton could meet them with friendship; if not, he should pretend, since 'if any harm be ment, it is to be lerned there'. Next day he and Wotton arrived at Dover, the Dean having escaped a fatal fit and being now troubled with nothing worse than a cough and anxieties about the Channel crossing, concerning which he sent Cecil a quotation from Plautus.

Sir Nicholas at once became busy with secret agents. A certain Richard Harrison had just got back from France. Throckmorton described him as a spy sent over during the war. He may have been the man of the same name who was a member of John Knox's congregation at Geneva in 1556. He had seen Knox very recently at Dieppe, a famous resort of Huguenots. Calvin had sent Knox there to preach, and the citizens had found him a '*singulier organe du Saint-Esprit*'. The Great Reformer was now chafing for a passport to travel home through England, and had asked Harrison to take letters over for Cecil, promising that they contained nothing 'unmete' for Cecil to receive, Knox to write, or Harrison to carry. But Harrison knew the ropes. Knox had lately issued his *First Blast of the Trumpet against the Monstrous Regiment of Women*. Though intended against the three Catholic Marys, it attacked women rulers in general, and Harrison either knew or could guess how Elizabeth had reacted. It had infuriated Calvin himself; 'thoughtless arrogance', he had called it. Harrison brought the letters to Sir Nicholas, desiring 'to be rydd of the Carryedge'. The passport was refused, and Knox had to find his way home by sea.

Harrison also brought Sir Nicholas glad tidings of the swelling of the Huguenot tide and went on as his courier to London; but a Burgundian gave the less welcome news that King Philip had not yet demobilized his soldiers in the Netherlands. One final question to Cecil about protocol (one that had not arisen the last five years)—when Sir Nicholas met the Spanish Ambassador, which of them should take precedence?—and at ten in the morning dean and knight were aboard and by four in the afternoon at Boulogne.

Here a spate of intelligence greeted Sir Nicholas. Lewis Dives of Bedfordshire, captured with Lord Grey after the fall of Calais, was now on his way home to scratch together a ransom, bringing two of those outrageous scutcheons which showed the Queen of Scots' arms quartered with the arms of England and implied that Elizabeth was a

usurper. He fancied the French meant peace for the time being, but
reported talk of some enterprise stirring against Scotland, of which
he would give details by word of mouth. The French Catholic clergy
thought the time had come to root out the Huguenots. The Huguenots were resolved to resist to the death and thought Elizabeth's
time come to help them. And Sir George Howard was at Boulogne,
waiting for shipping, with a suspect Frenchman in his train, ostensibly on a mission to buy English geldings but 'noted to be as great
and as fine a practiser as any in France'. One of Throckmorton's
retinue had warned Sir George about the man, and Cecil must have
him watched in London.

At every post towards Paris the two Commissioners encountered
someone whom Throckmorton thought worth recommending for a
few kind and interested words at Court. Old acquaintance began to
be resumed: old acquaintance from the war, from previous days of
peace, from King Edward's reforming days, from the wars of Henry
VIII. Everybody in this military-diplomatic world knew everybody
else, or at least knew about them, had fought with them or fought
against them or negotiated with them. Throckmorton possessed a
great deal of knowledge about the standing of such a person, the
extent to which so-and-so could be trusted, and, most important of
all, about those who favoured the Reformed religion. A few words
of advice Cecil had sent him while still at Dover give us a lead to one
particular French enclave, where he might hope for spies: 'the Scots',
he had written, 'ye may have most hope of the Scots'.

*

Many secret informers have been men of foreign origin who, for one
reason or another, do not like or have become dissatisfied with the
country in which they have made a home. For generations Scotsmen
had fought for France, taken up domicile in France, been educated
at French colleges, traded with France, intermarried with and been
influenced by the French. James V had married two French wives;
and Lady Fleming had made her special contribution to the 'auld
alliance' by briefly displacing Diane de Poitiers and bearing Henri
II a bastard.

Louis XII had exempted all Scotsmen from the need to apply for
letters of naturalization, and granted them the right to inherit
property and hold lands, goods and hostages, as if they had been
born Frenchmen. It had also become their privilege to guard the

person of the King. This was their reward for the lives their two renowned companies, the Men-at-Arms and the Archers of the Guard, had given for France during more than a century. They thus enjoyed access at Court with the greatest Frenchmen. They were always in attendance; always marched behind the King in their white silver-spangled jackets, embroidered with his blazon; always kept the doors of the innermost rooms; always held the keys of the palace, and always remained Scots. (When challenged on duty, they did not reply *Me voilà*, but in Gaelic.) What a chance for an enemy Intelligence service, if someone in so honoured and intimate a position should become disaffected![21]

During the preceding decade an entirely new group of Scotsmen had arrived in France, of whom several were to play, and one or two already had played, a part in English Intelligence. Most of them had come involuntarily, as prisoners. They include John and Robert Melville, two of the eight sons of Sir James Melville of Raith, who had been executed in 1548 on a charge of treasonable correspondence with the Protector Somerset, 'every quarter putt upoun ane poirt of the burght of Edinburght . . . and his heid upoun ane prik upoun the tolbuith'. They include Sir James Kirkcaldy, who had married their sister Janet, and his son William, and the jurist, devotional writer and friend of John Knox, Henry Balnaves. All these men had been on Cardinal Beaton's black list. All desired an alliance, even a political union, between England and Scotland, now that England was Protestant again. All were bitter enemies of the ex-Governor Arran and the Hamiltons remaining in Scotland; they had helped the Governor in his early Reforming days, and he had betrayed them, taking many of the confiscated Melville lands for one of his sons.

Henry Balnaves and William Kirkcaldy, younger than Balnaves by a generation, were English agents of long-standing. Their lives had been violently swung by the storms of the age, unlike Cecil's life, a wind-tunnel that managed to contain most of the storms with little damage to himself. Balnaves, trained in the canon and civil law, had become a convert to the Reformed Faith about 1542, when he was forty, 'not for the hope of gain'. As State Secretary under the Governor during 1542-3, he visited Henry VIII and negotiated a treaty of marriage between the infant Mary and the child Prince Edward, but the project came to nothing when the Governor changed faiths and went over to the Cardinal, and Balnaves had been imprisoned until the English freed him. Hopeful of him again at the time of the Cardinal's murder, they gave him large political subventions and a pension to deliver Mary and the Castle of St. Andrews into their hands. When the Castle fell and Marie de Guise smuggled her daughter away to France, he became a prisoner of the French, who treated him with great severity at the Governor's request. Immured in Rouen Castle, he wrote his 'Confession of Faith, containing how the troubled man should seek comfort at his God . . .'. Knox, who himself endured months of hard labour in the French galleys, expressed an earnest desire that this book should be saved 'as almost nothing else'; and so it was, and was found at Ormiston after both Knox and Balnaves had died.

Marie pardoned Balnaves in 1555, and he had written to her from Paris at the time to thank her 'for that most undeservid gentil clemency I and my wife have received and hope to receive at your graces hands', and sent her certain 'instructions' of which no one was to know. He returned home and worked with her for a time, but now that her policy of conciliation appeared to have ended he had become her enemy.

William Kirkcaldy, 'frend till all men in adversitie and fell oft in trouble to debait innocent men fra sic as wold oppress them . . . belovit of all honest men',[22] is one of the true romantic heroes of Scotland. In 1559 he was about thirty. Circumstance had driven him into devious courses. What was consistent about him was his passion for the liberty of Scotland, for the Reformed religion, and therefore at this stage for the English alliance. For the sake of the English alliance his father Sir James had lost a great career. For the sake of the English alliance his grandfather, Melville of Raith, had gone to the scaffold. In hope of help from England Kirkcaldy himself, then sixteen years old, had kept the postern-gate of St. Andrew's Castle, while Leslie of Rothes and the rest were murdering the Cardinal, and there, during the siege that followed, he had met and come under the spell of John Knox, a spell which lasted all his life.

After the fall of St. Andrews the French had imprisoned him in the fortress of Mont St. Michel. On Twelfth Night the boy put himself in command of the other Scots prisoners, gagged and bound the drunken guards, seized the keys and fled across the quicksands. After weeks of wandering he found a boat to take him home, and reached Scotland. Knox had by now been reprieved and was preaching in the north of England. Kirkcaldy found Scotland too dangerous and joined Knox at Berwick. The evangelical life was not enough for him and when peace was signed in 1550 he returned to France and took service in the French Army, where his chivalry and courage became a legend. The Constable would never allow him to stand bareheaded in his presence, and Henri II called him the most valiant man of the age and 'chose him commonly upon his side in all pastimes he went to'. But war was no more his sole occupation than law and the composition of religious treatises were those of Henry Balnaves. Scotland remained his first allegiance, and the high regard of the rulers of Catholic France does not seem to have made France, even temporarily, his second; in fact he refused a pension from the French. In January 1551 the Privy Council in London wrote to their Ambassador in France, Sir John Mason, that they were sending him a Scottish spy recommended by Balnaves. The man arrived in terror for his safety, and next evening brought Kirkcaldy as a substitute, who, Mason wrote, 'has promised to communicate all that he can learn', and was to go under the name of Coraxe.

When Mary Tudor came to the throne her religion did not deter Kirkcaldy, and he offered himself again through Dean Wotton. He would serve anywhere for the same pension and 'says he shall have good intelligence of the affairs of Scotland and of France by his intimacy with those of both nations'. His record deterred the Queen, however, and his pension was withdrawn; in such a matter Mary had purer rules than most Catholic sovereigns, and held that no Catholic power should employ the murderer of a Cardinal. In 1554 Marie de Guise allowed him to come home. Before leaving France, he again approached Wotton, who advised cautiously that his offer of secret service should be accepted, summing him up either as 'a very great and crafty dissembler', or else a man who bore no good-will at all to France and 'next to his own country has a good mind to England'. Kirkcaldy asked that no one should know of his offer but Lord Paget and Sir William Petre; if others on the Council learnt, they might inform Marie, and his life would be in danger.

He proved himself after his return home by arranging a meeting with Lord Wharton on the pretext of a Border truce, at which he imparted a mass of intelligence about the doings of the French in Scotland. He reported a letter he had seen in which Henri II promised d'Oysel all the men and money d'Oysel needed. He gave details of the French garrisons and their expected reinforcements. A ship had just docked at Leith with funds to enlist five bands of horse, one of which he was to command himself. Marie de Guise and d'Oysel had gone to Edinburgh to receive the money, which they would keep secret, 'because the Scots will be greedy thereof'. All this was valuable intelligence and would give occasion, Lord Wharton remarked, for the rulers of England to think twice about a truce.

After Elizabeth's accession Kirkcaldy gradually entered into regular communication with the English. He has already been glimpsed in Maitland's company on February 10, 1559, three weeks after the Duke of Châtellerault's secret interview with Sir Henry Percy. Maitland had charmed him. Again, as with Knox, he had fallen under the influence of a superior intellect. Maitland was the brain, Kirkcaldy the brawn; they were lone wolves, both in their way brilliant and quixotic, and years later died wretchedly together for a forlorn hope.

All these Scotsmen—Kirkcaldy, Balnaves, the Melvilles—had become friendly with Throckmorton during his own French exile. Kirkcaldy and Balnaves were home and well-placed for intelligence. Some of the Melvilles had remained in France, and Sir Nicholas, riding respectably back as the new Protestant Ambassador, was in touch at once.

There met him at Abbeville James Melville of Halhill, fourth son of Sir James of Raith, and author half a century later of constantly quoted memoirs. He had been too young to be present with his brothers in St. Andrews. Marie de Guise had received him into her favour and sent him to France as a page to Mary Stuart, hoping no doubt that he would there forget his Protestant associations and obligations to avenge his father's execution. The Constable had taken to him. He was shrewd and discreet, and the Constable's household was one of the highways to success. Influence at the French Court had thus enabled him, though young, to perform certain services for the English and Scottish Protestants in exile. He had lent money to Thomas Randolph. Of Henry Balnaves (also of Halhill) he wrote in his memoirs that Balnaves 'loves me as his own son, by some acquaintance I had with him in France, and pleasures I had done to him during his banishment'. Sir Nicholas Throckmorton was 'one of my oldest and dearest friends by long acquaintance during his banishment in France . . .' Henry Killigrew, also a former exile and now in Throckmorton's suite, was another friend. Killigrew had last seen James Melville having his wounds dressed after the battle of St. Quentin, and had held his horse for him. After the Constable's return to favour following the Treaty of Cateau-Cambrésis, Melville had every reason to hope for a successful career in France. At this very moment, he was riding northward on a mission of the highest trust for someone of his background and years. Henri II and the Constable were sending him to Edinburgh, where he was to ascertain in secret whether Lord James Stuart, Mary Stuart's Protestant half-brother, had designs upon her throne.

Perhaps James Melville confided this mission to the inquiring English envoys, as in garrulous and slightly forgetful old age he sat down and confided his long life to posterity. It is obvious that he left his mark. Two months later, while he was still in Scotland, Throckmorton suddenly saw fit to remind Cecil about him from Paris, and advised Cecil to 'make him the Queen's . . . for he will be able to do her great service'. That night in Abbeville he merely noted his importance and asked for some courteous words for him on his way through London. Killigrew also wrote to Cecil, going so far as to call Melville 'desirous to help forward by all his power that work which you seek so earnestly to establish and confirm to God's glory', and added, even more to the point, that the William Kirkcaldy on the Border was Melville's nephew.

At Amiens Wotton and Throckmorton came up with Lord William Howard. Mayors, lawyers, and men of learning had received Howard the whole way from the coast with the respect due to his high rank and kinship with the Queen. At Abbeville there had been addresses; at Amiens there was 'a greate present of fish . . . and also thurty greate pottes of wyne, whereof six were of ypocras'. The three Commissioners rode on together and approached the capital in state. Banquets awaited them at the Constable's great palaces of Ecouen and Chantilly, though the Lord Great Chamberlain had toothache 'and could not be at it'. As they entered the capital they learned that the King was so eager to receive them, they must needs ride straight to the Louvre, 'booted and spurred and well washed with the rayne' and even without their letters of credence. Every elegance of the French Renaissance, every grace and flattery this Court (still the gayest in Europe) could furnish, had been assembled to impress and give delight, but Sir Nicholas kept an eye open for darker, less seductive things. After the weddings, he reported ominously, the King would go off to Poitou and Gascony and Guienne to repress the Huguenots, and persecution could be expected to increase in Scotland.

On Tuesday, May 24 the three Englishmen were received by the Queen of Scotland and her consort the King-Dauphin. Jointly they concocted for Elizabeth, in respectfully appraising language, her first official impression of the girl who was for a while to be a prime mover and for long a principal piece in all their games, and her enemy for life. Later the same night Throckmorton wrote privately to Cecil: 'Assuredly, sir, in myne opinion the Scotish Quene loketh very ill on it, very pale and grene, and therewithall short breathed, and it is whispered here amongs them, that she cannot long live.' She still had twenty-seven years, and her death was not to be from illness.

iii. 'Most Hope of the Scots': James Hamilton

Sir Nicholas Throckmorton has been styled the ablest intelligence-man of his time, and the *grand provocateur de l'époque*. Some might say that in the later stages of his embassy in Paris he went too far and failed; on his arrival, however, he was circumspect and undeniably succeeded.

Seeing himself as an English Protestant encircled by a Catholic conspiracy, he looked first to the Huguenot leadership for news as later they turned to one another as military allies. His dispatches suggest that (like many others) he treated religion partly as a means to a political end, that end being the security of England. He was astute, militant and impetuous. His warnings, injected with anxiety that people in London would never understand what he, the man in the field, sensed all round him, became increasingly bellicose. He dreaded that, through blindness or timidity, they would allow France and Spain 'to make a Piedmont of us'. They *must* listen to him. In message after message he hectored the Privy Council 'to entertain the garboil' in Scotland. He was ready to use anyone, Knox included, whatever the Queen might think about that wretched book of Knox's; he even wrote to Elizabeth direct, suggesting she should show kindness to Mistress Knox. It is not surprising that he had enemies on the Council, or that the Queen and Cecil preferred to keep such a hornet out of London and let him annoy the King of France instead.

It has been estimated that, by the time Throckmorton arrived, France had 400,000 declared Protestants in a population of fourteen million. He could expect to find most sympathy in the highest reaches of the Court from the two Bourbon princes, Louis, Prince of Condé, and King Antoine of Navarre, and from the Constable's three nephews, the Cardinal de Châtillon, François d'Andelot, and Gaspard de Coligny. These were the potentates who, at the very least, could tell him what was going on; but towards all he had to behave with extreme caution, since none had yet irrevocably declared himself on the side of Reformation, and one or two were unreliable. Once the civil wars had started Throckmorton became deeply embroiled with these Huguenot leaders, but for the moment we hear more of his reconnaissance, on Cecil's advice, among the Scots. He wrote to the Privy Council that certain Scottish companies were owed 200,000 francs from the war, and had received only 12,000, 'wherewith theye be moch offended, and a great many of them are departed out of France mervailously ill satisfied'. Early in July he sent Cecil a certain laird, Alexander Whitelaw of Grange, the future bearer of many secret dispatches, with a testimonial to his honesty, sobriety, godliness, and devotion to the English cause. In fact he had been in the pay of Edward VI and had helped to put the fortress of Broughty Craig into English hands.[23] Throckmorton reported that he would be 'content with what he had before', but since he was so religious, Cecil 'must let him see as little sin in England as you can'.

Not all the Scots who came to Sir Nicholas for passports home by way of England were to be trusted. He issued one to David Beaton only because his daughter was in great favour with the Queen of Scots; she was one of the 'Queen's Maries'. He warned Cecil to beware of Beaton himself, 'a great papist', and a nephew of the murdered Cardinal; but qualified the warning a few days later on learning that Beaton was a friend and kinsman of the most important Scotsman in France, James Hamilton, now to become a key figure in William Cecil's plot.

*

James Hamilton was son and heir to the Governor Arran, Duke of Châtellerault, and therefore second in succession to the Scottish throne. This unfortunate youth was never celebrated for any great achievement or gifts of character, and we should hardly know of him at all, had it not been for his position; he comes to us almost entirely through the letters of those who used him. For a few weeks half the courts of Europe had him constantly in their minds, and the future of two kingdoms, even of western Christendom, seemed to hang upon his escape or arrest; then, for much of his remaining forty-five years, he was more or less mad. Like Mary Stuart, he had been a pawn from the cradle. But Mary had also been a Queen from the cradle. James Hamilton was never more than a hapless might-have-been.

The congenital fickleness of his father had made an almost permanent hostage of the son. He was six years old when his father reverted to Catholicism and submitted to the Cardinal. Beaton did not trust his father; so he carried the child off to St. Andrews as a safeguard and to keep him out of the clutches of Henry VIII. He was still there three years later when the Cardinal was murdered. His father began to profess wavering support for England and the marriage of Mary Stuart to Prince Edward, but the murderers trusted him as little as the murdered had, and kept Hamilton where he was; it was part of the bargain in return for which Henry VIII, and after his death Protector Somerset, agreed to send them troops.

When the troops arrived too late and the castle fell, Hamilton passed into the hands of France. His father again appeared to change sides and became available for fresh bargaining. Giving Henri II of France the same kind of promise he had given Henry VIII of England, he now undertook to deliver Mary to the French fleet in return for a signed contract of marriage between his son and Mademoiselle de Montpensier, a Bourbon princess with an alluring dowry; secretly he continued scheming towards the one aim from which he had never wavered, that Mary should remain in Scotland and the boy marry her himself. The French were giving the Scots no help without pledges, and knew the Governor's wiles. In the summer of 1548 Henri II carried both children away; whereupon the Governor 'fell into a sharp sickness' and nearly died of disappointment. French armies and French money for Scotland came back in return; but his son had gone. He soon accepted the situation, sent another son and a daughter after him, and made a will consigning all his children to the King of France.

Eleven-year-old James Hamilton had arrived in Paris with three new shirts, a Scots whinger, and a French whinger. The marriage to Mademoiselle de Montpensier did not come off. An impoverished Scot was not much of a match, even if in some vague future he might become a King, and she had received a better offer. Other princesses of the blood were put forward. Diane de Poitiers thought he might marry one of her god-daughters. But somehow all these ladies became contracted to someone else. At fifteen the rejected youth, who had nothing more than a pension of a thousand marks from the

Bishopric of Aberdeen, wrote to his father for money to maintain the right sort of retinue; if he could not have it, he might as well come home. Mary Stuart wrote to her mother: 'Please make him a duke.' His father was made one instead; and with the title came the promise of an establishment at the French Court for his son. Things looked better for James Hamilton, who after his father's dukedom becomes known as third Earl of Arran. A Spanish Ambassador described him on hearsay as a comely young fellow. He took to soldiering, received a company of Men-at-Arms, led some light cavalry against the Emperor, and fought at St. Quentin. He still hoped for Mary Stuart; when she married the Dauphin, he was reported as being 'in despair and rabid'.

From that time he had fallen among the worst company imaginable for any hope of advancement under Henri II. He took up with the Huguenots. His father's Châtellerault estates lay in Poitou, a province particularly dear to Calvin, who had preached there as a young man and sent a Minister there from Geneva. By 1559 the Poitevin Huguenots had become so strong that they had rioted and actually got the better of the Catholics and the royal troops sent to suppress them. (Richard Harrison gave Throckmorton an account of this rising when they met at Dover.) Perhaps Arran picked up his Protestantism among his neighbours. He was excitable and ambitious. The atmosphere of revolt found him sympathetic. It began to be whispered in Paris that he had changed his faith and turned Calvinist; it was even said that he had preached in person. All this happened, perhaps not accidentally, about the same time that his father had decided again to turn Protestant, and was having secret talks with Sir Henry Percy on the Border. New hopes had dawned for the Hamiltons. The son and heir suddenly emerged not merely as a possible successor to Mary, but as an eligible alternative.

Even Elizabeth began to show interest in him. She had by now made it clear that she would not marry Philip. She was rumoured to have a domestic lover in Lord Robert Dudley and to be spending most of the day and night with him at the same time as she was sending inquiries about the 'age, stature, height, fatness, strength, complexion, nature, condition, possessions, education, faculties, affection, temper, judgement in matters of religion, affection to the Protestants, etc.,' of two Austrian archdukes. There was no harm, and a good deal of advantage, in adding Arran to her list.

*

The Treaties were ratified at the end of May. Coligny conducted Sir Nicholas to Notre Dame to receive Henri's oath and, as they rode together through the streets, asked questions about the state of religion in England. Sir Nicholas noticed that he slipped away from Mass. After the ceremony he reappeared and on the way back praised Protestant Edward VI, Sir Nicholas's quondam patron, as 'the most virtuous and godliest Prince, and of the greatest hope to do good for Christendom that was for many years'—an odd comment from a subject of the Roman Church's eldest son.

The Treaties were exchanged. 'Our monsieurs', as Cecil called the French Commissioners, returned from London. Howard and Dean Wotton went back and Sir Nicholas was left in the lion's den alone. Outwardly Paris seemed abandoned to preparations for the double wedding. The Duke of Alva, with a train of 1,500, was on his way from Brussels. Philip was sending Elizabeth of Valois jewels to the value of 133,000 ducats and had already given one to the Cardinal of Lorraine worth 8,000 crowns, as well as plate worth 15,000. Unheralded, three Calvinist ministers slipped into the city from Geneva; and as the paving-stones in the rue des Tournelles were torn up to make a tilting-ground, the first General Synod of the Calvinist Churches of France assembled in secret, with Gustave Morel as President, and drew up their Confession of Faith on the Genevan model.

Near-by a great scandal was developing in the Parlement of Paris. One of its departments, the criminal court of La Tournelle, which had become more and more notorious for moderation, had just tried three heretics and dared to commute the death sentence to imprisonment for life. The Catholic extremists demanded a full session of the Parlement's Grand' Chambre to reassert its legal obligations. There was furious debate, while the King and his knights rehearsed their jousts almost underneath the windows. The moderates refused to yield. Led by Anne du Bourg, they made a passionate onslaught on the corruption of the Church. They demanded that a heretic should be given six months to abjure and, if he would not, suffer nothing worse than exile. The proceedings were supposed to be privileged and private; but Minard, leader of the extremists, told the Cardinal and the Constable, who told the King.

Throckmorton was secretly informed about the proceedings in both Parlement and Synod by people he does not name. He sent the Queen and Cecil warning after warning to forward to Sir James

Croft and the Protestants in Scotland. Everything possible must be done to keep the good-will of Spain and prevent a Franco-Spanish coalition. He did not care to live too near the Court, and moved a little way off to lodgings near the University. People offered themselves, of course. An unnamed Frenchman turned up, 'great with all the secretaries at Court', who wanted fifty crowns a month for supplying information. He had offered himself to Wotton while Wotton was Ambassador and could have saved Calais if only he had been paid enough. Or so he said. Sir Nicholas wished to know if the Queen could afford him. Henri was going on a week's progress through the Constable's and Diane's châteaux. No Ambassador had been invited, 'but I mind to have one to follow'. While the King was absent, the Guises approached some of the English exiles they had employed during Mary Tudor's reign, and offered to renew their pensions; the Cardinal particularly wanted to know about the movements of English ships. A Frenchman turned up at Throckmorton's lodgings when he had just sat down to supper, with no apparent purpose 'unless to see how I was accompanied and occupied'. Some Scotsmen appeared, representing themselves as friends of Arran's, to find out what Throckmorton thought about him. Throckmorton listened and said as little as he could. He was becoming alarmed, and asked to be recalled, a plea the Queen ignored.

All the time he had his routine work to do. There were wages to be found; long dispatches to be composed, ciphered, and copied; comings and goings to be reported; the usual diplomatic gossip, especially concerning the health of the Queen of Scots (whom the Spanish Ambassador in London, the Bishop of Aquila, believed to be suffering from an incurable disease). Influential visitors from home, come to study French or see the wedding pageants, had to be entertained. Sir Thomas Gresham's son was one, Cecil's heir Thomas another, whom his father wished the Ambassador to encourage in honesty, courtesy and cleanliness—'gayness I care not for'.

Within four or five days the Duke of Alva would be in Paris. The city must be at its most beautiful and most orderly. On June 10, Henri struck. Taking with him the Constable, the Duke de Guise, and the Cardinal of Lorraine, he entered the room where the Parlement was meeting and instructed its members to continue their arguments in his presence. The moderates refused to be overawed. They demanded that all action against heretics be suspended and a General Ecumenical Council called for reform of the Catholic

Church. Du Bourg protested fearlessly against the frightful punishments. 'It is not a light thing,' he cried in a loud clear voice, 'for us to condemn those who in the midst of the flames call on the name of Christ.' The King rose, and after a few words with the Cardinals ordered the arrest of du Bourg and three other moderates, who were at once taken to the Bastille.

Next day M. de Bétaincourt suddenly returned from Scotland with dreadful news for Catholics. The Court were keeping it extremely close, and Throckmorton could not at first find out exactly what it was. He surmised that it had something to do with the rising of the Calvinist Lords of the Congregation against Marie de Guise; Cecil had informed him a fortnight ago that Scotland was on the verge of civil war. Sir Nicholas reported the French Court 'greatly perplexed'. The Guises had been so jubilant about the King's arrests; and now, in that half-savage northern land, their own sister, the mother of the Queen of Scots, the Dauphin's mother-in-law, had been defied by her own subjects. And the Duke of Alva had arrived, with the Prince of Orange, and Count Egmont, and the rest; what an overture for the wedding marches!

There followed another rebuff to the French. The Earl of Arran was expected in Paris for the celebrations. He had promised the Queen of Scots and the Dauphin, his sovereigns, that he would come if he could afford it, and gone off to his estates in Poitou to fell timber and make some money. Since Throckmorton had arrived, according to Mary and François, he had changed his mind and 'conveyed himself out of the way'. It was the beginning of an intricate and dangerous operation to smuggle Arran back to Scotland, where the Lords of the Congregation were demanding that he should come to lead them. Cecil probably initiated it, with Throckmorton and Thomas Randolph as the agents in the field. On June 13 Throckmorton sent Randolph to Cecil about some purpose evidently agreed beforehand, and about the same time Mary and François summoned Arran to Paris from his timber-felling. Throckmorton informed London, from 'one that taketh upon him to know something of his mind', that Arran would not come. A Court messenger was sent post-haste with offers of money and preferment. Still he did not come. He had never behaved like this before; money and preferment had always been his needs. The Court gave up coaxing and tried coercion. This time Henri himself sent three noblemen to bring Arran to Paris alive or dead. Andrew Cunningham,

a brother of the Reformer Earl of Glencairn, informed Throckmorton that they had scoured Poitou and failed to find him. French
distrust of the Scots increased, while the Scots became incensed at
the threats to their young captain.

Henri had a sufficiently clear idea of Arran's destination and wrote
to Gilles de Noailles, his Ambassador in London, that the Earl had
behaved scandalously on his estates, and made Huguenots of many
of his neighbours; if he arrived in England, Elizabeth must be
required under the Treaty to arrest him and extradite him as a
fugitive from France, guilty of lèse-majesté. Throckmorton advised
Cecil that if Randolph had not already left London he should come
disguised as a merchant and travel with all secrecy. He arrived on
some date between June 24 and 28, bringing letters from the Queen
and Cecil. Throckmorton sent him to Arran's estates, accompanied
by Arran's Master of Horse, and made arrangements for the Earl to
be received by the Protestants in Zürich. An anxious period ensued
during which he knew nothing of Arran's movements apart from a
rumour from a neighbour in Paris that he had travelled eastward on
his way to Geneva, 'enduring great penury and hiding himself for
15 days in a wood and subsisting on fruits'. The Bishop of Aquila,
Spanish Ambassador in London, found out that Randolph had seen
the Queen and joined in the detective work, deducing that Arran
was already in England and very near London. 'We shall soon hear
of the marriage.' He felt sure of it. Cecil continued to make mysterious journeys; he had just left suddenly for Greenwich, and it
must be to call on Arran. Ten days later the Bishop hazarded a new
guess; Arran was probably hidden in Dover Castle.

The Bishop was new to the coil in England. He had few informants of importance, his intelligence was often incorrect, as here,
both in general deductions and in detail, and he was playing into the
Queen's hands by allowing himself to glimpse a husband for her
behind every arras she chose to rustle. But one must notice, in this
letter, his description of Thomas Randolph, as 'a brother of one of
Your Majesty's servants'. It is an assertion reiterated by Spanish
Ambassadors. The 'servant' of the King of Spain must therefore
have been the same Captain Edward Randolph whom we have seen,
first, among the Wyatt conspirators; then in exile in Paris; then
acting as a double agent between the English and the French,
pardoned by Philip and given a captaincy of artillery, but living
next-door to the French Ambassador and ready to assist Henri II in

an invasion. The Randolph brothers rouse even more curiosity when we learn that Edward had married Sybil Croft, a sister of Sir James.[24]

The Earl of Arran had vanished, by whatever route, and had been intended to vanish by the English, and the hue and cry after him from Paris began too late. There was a fight at Court between some of his company of Men-at-Arms and the French, during which several lost their lives. Throckmorton reported that all the Scottish bands were to be put under the control of Frenchmen. The three nobles were again sent to Poitou to find Arran and again returned without him. When one of them went, in polite but foolish innocence, to apologize to Mary Stuart for seeking the arrest of her kinsman, she riposted that nothing would give her greater pleasure, since her kinsman had turned traitor. Arran's brother was seized in reprisal and imprisoned in Vincennes, and more fights broke out between French and Scots. Throckmorton gleefully reported it all to Cecil for communication to Sir James Croft and the Scottish lords; the Duke of Châtellerault and the Hamiltons in particular might like to know how their flesh and blood were being treated.

Amidst his many preoccupations one item of gossip must have brought Sir Nicholas up with something of a shock. It reached him from Dorothy, widow of Sir William Stafford, whose first wife had been Anne Boleyn's sister Mary. Lady Stafford was someone to be reckoned with. Both she and her late husband were of royal descent. Strong Protestants, they and a large household had gone into exile at Geneva early in Mary Tudor's reign without leave. She was now in Paris trying to make her way home, and bombarding the Ambassador with petitions.

She had told him the gossip twice, and he had refused to take it seriously. The third time he felt he should report it privately to Cecil. According to Lady Stafford, the Queen of Scots had informed her that Sir James Croft's secretary at Berwick was in French pay, and passed on everything he could find out to Marie de Guise. The story seemed absurd. Why should the Queen of Scots give away one of her mother's secret agents, unless deliberately to discredit Croft? Sir Nicholas must have recalled the grim trial at Guildhall five years ago, and the so-called 'confession' by Sir James, which might have proved his own death-warrant, had not Sir James refused to support it. 'I am loath to hurt any person. . .', he wrote to Cecil, '. . . I believe most assuredly, that Mr. Croft himself is utterly void of all suspicion; and what his secretary may be God knoweth . . .'

Sir James's secretary was a man called Louvel. He did maintain contact with Marie de Guise's household in Edinburgh, that was true, but only apparently with her doctor, M. du Faubusson. Faubusson had sent him some pills, inquired after his deafness, and asked him to convey respects to Sir James and Lady Croft.[25] On the surface there was nothing wrong there. Good doctors were scarce, and England and Scotland officially at peace; all the same M. Louvel might sound to some an odd kind of person to employ, at this moment, in a confidential post at Berwick.

iv. Between Paris and the Border: Summer 1559

Sir James Croft did not care for Berwick. It was the worst station in the kingdom. As a former Governor of Haddington he knew the Borders, but he had been younger then. During all this last spell in the 'sourness of this Northern air' he had been in bad health. He had a Herefordshire wife and children in the castle with him and Cecil, he wrote, must do something to help them all if they were not to starve, or else appoint somebody to Berwick who could afford it. To the soldiers under his command, and the labourers sent from the south to work on the dilapidated fortifications, leave to go home was almost as good as wages, and lately about all the wages they had got. The labourers Sir James reported as being without shirts or shoes and, when they were ill, unable to afford fresh meat. The soldiers, refused further credit in the town, had to promise the Surveyor of the Victuals sixpence for what they could have got in the market for a groat down. The Surveyor furnished them with food that had gone bad; it gave them scurvy and made them 'sore in the mouth and swollen in the legs and other parts', some becoming lame for life or dying. The Queen insisted on economy. So Sir James increased the fish days. But the fish arrived late and there were so many complaints of its 'naughtiness' that he had to make mess inspections; on one round he found 396 barrels of stinking herring, apart from an abundance of rancid butter and bad cheese.

Unpaid, ill-fed like everybody else, the captains continued to take it out of the Treasury. They sold their armour and even when the Council did send their money neglected to pay their bills. The Queen wanted more men demobilized, but the place still had to be defended, like all the other crumbling outposts strung out from Holy Island to Carlisle. Sir James reminded the Privy Council that the town walls had a circuit of 10,000 feet. A reduced garrison would have to be on duty eighteen hours at a stretch, and their Lordships in London might like to consider what that would mean in winter, in the long northern night, with an east wind blowing from the sea. And this was the citadel expected to defend half of England, the Queen's title to the throne, and the Reformed religion, to say nothing of those great houses Cecil and the rest were busy building in the south, against a French invasion.

Berwick remained safe so far only because Scotland had other things to think about. A hundred miles to the north Catholics and Reformers were moving headlong to a clash. The secret letters with which M. de Bétaincourt had passed through Berwick had included instructions from Paris for Marie de Guise to proceed more vigorously against the preachers and the Lords who protected them, and she had summoned the preachers to appear before a civil court at Stirling on May 10. Huge crowds assembled to hear John Knox and fired by a clarion sermon resolved to follow him to the trial 'to make confession of their faith'. The Regent undertook to defer the trial, on condition they dispersed; they agreed, but as soon as they had started to go home, she put the preachers to the horn. Knox preached again in Perth. Scarcely had he finished when a priest came forward to celebrate Mass. A boy in the crowd threw a stone at the Host, and two days of rioting ensued that left the Franciscan, Dominican and Carthusian monasteries in ruins. Marie marched on the city with an army led by d'Oysel and Châtellerault, still outwardly a Catholic and loyal to her. The Lords of the Congregation marched to confront her and for a few hours battle seemed unavoidable. Again she yielded, on the understanding that she would permit no reprisals, no more French garrisons, no restitution of the Mass. She entered Perth, had Mass said, changed the Provost, and left a garrison of four hundred 'Scottishmen', Knox wrote, 'but paid by France'.

The Earl of Argyll and Lord James Stuart now openly joined the Congregation, and with Knox and the preachers moved on to St. Andrews. Altars were broken, images and missals burnt, priests and monks expelled. The Regent marched once more, and the Lords awaited her on Cupar Moor. Two agents of whom we have already heard arrived in the opposing camps. The Laird of Ormiston brought reinforcements to the Lords, and Knox found him 'very comfortable that day by his good counsel', and James Melville reached the Regent on his secret mission from the King of France

and had a meeting with her in the old tower of Falkland. Henry
Balnaves, his friend from the old days in France, took him across to
the other side to see Lord James Stuart; and Melville came with
startling and questionable promptness to the conclusion that the
Reformer Lord did not want his sister's crown. Once more, when the
armies were within cannon-shot, Marie sent messengers of peace,
and an eight-day truce was signed on Howlet Hill. This insurrection
was the news with which M. de Bétaincourt had rushed back to
Paris and which, as Throckmorton reported, had so 'greatly perplexed' the Court.

On May 24 William Kirkcaldy wrote to Sir Henry Percy. He
accused Marie of deceit and asked outright what Elizabeth would do
to help the Lords of the Congregation to expel the French. Marie
was beginning to suspect him. He was still in her service and events
in Scotland were moving so fast that he found it dangerous to get
away or write. Percy set up a link between his confidential servant,
Ralph Lawrence, 'one of my practisers in Scotland', and Kirkcaldy's
cousin Robert, who was to have a guide so that he might pass and
repass the frontier. A week later Maitland returned, having handed
the ratification of the Treaty to Elizabeth, and continued north to
resume his official duties with the Regent. Of him at least she seems
to have had no suspicion. George Buchanan wrote in his savage
depiction of Maitland that 'she could not espy the gilded Vices hid
in that Monster under the Colour of Virtue'. Some people believed
he was her lover.[26]

Sooner or later, Croft knew, the Lords would have to be given
precise answers about aid, about the whereabouts of Arran and the
chances of his marriage 'you know where'. This was highly explo-
sive, as any suggestion of a husband for the Queen continued to be
till well into the eighties. Sir James did not want to touch it and
asked that someone trained in such affairs should be sent to Berwick
under cover of inspecting the fortifications. Kirkcaldy raised the
marriage in a letter to Cecil written on June 23, but with such
circumspection as to be almost unintelligible. About aid to the
insurrection, he could speak his mind. Left to her dwindling Scottish
supporters, Marie de Guise could (in his view) be compelled to
yield. He thought she knew it herself and was preparing a
retreat on Edinburgh, there to hold out while her brothers in
France shipped reinforcements. What, for the second time, would
England do? He asked Cecil, as he had once asked Wotton, to

keep what he had written out of sight of anyone who might harm him.

About Kirkcaldy Cecil wrote to Percy with reserve as 'a private man, and not before known otherwise to them but as one in good grace with the Dowager [Marie de Guise]'. This is surprising, and leads one to wonder if Cecil knew about Kirkcaldy's former approaches in Paris to Mason and Wotton. Or perhaps he did know, and may have discussed him with Wotton, now in London and a member of the Council, and heard Wotton's doubts whether Kirkcaldy was really a friend to England or 'a very great and crafty dissembler'. Maitland was the one they were waiting for in London. His charm and adroitness had made a great impression there, and Elizabeth herself had called him 'the flower of the wits of Scotland'.

*

On July 4 a fatal accident occurred in Paris within a few yards of Sir Nicholas Throckmorton. A young Scotsman, James Montgomery, Seigneur de Lorges, a lieutenant in the French Life Guards, whose father had been for years their captain, was tilting against the King. At the last assault his lance broke against Henri's visor and the splinters penetrated through the eye. Henri lingered for several days in agony, attended by those two great pioneers of surgery, Vesalius, sent by Philip of Spain, and his pupil Ambroise Paré. Four criminals in the Conciergerie and Châtelet were beheaded, so that experiments could be made on their skulls. The King died on the 10th, and Henry Killigrew was happy to take the news to London 'with a speed I think be not forgotten'; five days after his arrival, the English Court still doubted it. The Huguenots called it Heaven's retribution on their oppressor; over the deathbed, until some faithful Catholic removed it, had been strewn a tapestry embroidered with the story of the conversion of St. Paul and the words, 'Saul, Saul, why persecutest thou Me?' Henri's death was the kind of crucial accident no Intelligence service could have foreseen, though many people chose to think that Nostradamus had foreseen it. Some time ago the Jewish astrologer had prophesied that the young lion would vanquish the old in single combat, and gouge out his eyes in their golden cage, and it was now recalled that the King had been wearing a golden helmet.

The death of Henri II removed one arch-enemy of the Reformers and gave place to two, if possible, even worse: the Duke de Guise and the Cardinal of Lorraine. A sixteen-year-old weakling, dominated by them and by his wife, became King as François II. Mary Stuart became Queen of France, Scotland, and, in the eyes of the Pope and perhaps half of Christendom, of England too; she in turn was dominated by her uncles. They seized power at once. Henri's old hero, the Constable, fell overnight and after the funeral the new King turned his back on him. The Huguenot princes of the blood, Navarre and Condé, rode hurriedly and nervously to Paris to find themselves forestalled by a palace revolution. Catholicism in its most militant form seemed triumphant, and the gates swung yet wider for the Franco-Spanish anti-Protestant crusade. Throckmorton began to fear for his life. In Scotland Marie was jubilant. The Lords of the Congregation renewed their appeals across the Border on an even more urgent note. What would Elizabeth do now? And where was the Earl of Arran?

For some days not even Cecil or Throckmorton knew; when they did know, it was not immediately in their interest to tell. The Lords of the Congregation thought he had reached Geneva. Marie de Guise thought he was still in France. The wish was in each instance father to the thought. Early in July the Constable said he was in Geneva. On the 8th Cecil allowed Sir James Croft to tell the Congregation that he had left France. Sir James wanted to know exactly where he was, since everything in Scotland depended on his arrival. Geneva it turned out to be; he had entered Switzerland by one of those routes the refugees were taking and by which Calvinist propaganda was pouring into France.

The English must now get him home to Scotland, either direct or, preferably, by way of London, where the Queen and Cecil could inspect him. The operation had to be entirely secret, and communication could only be through the most trusted bearers either in cipher or by word of mouth. On July 10 Throckmorton sent Henry Killigrew over to Elizabeth. The instructions with which she sent him back included one letter composed with a deliberate eye to interception. She and Cecil pretended to believe that Arran was still in France (at least a fortnight after he had left). They hoped, they wrote, that he would know how to keep out of the clutches of the Guises and the King; but in the last resort he must don a disguise and travel to Geneva (several days at least after they knew him to be there), or else to Jersey (in the opposite direction). Elizabeth gave her true motives a virtuous cloak. In the first draft for Throckmorton

which Cecil prepared for her, she declared that she wished to help
Arran because he had been persecuted for the Protestant religion;
in the messages Throckmorton finally received, it was compassion,
her own princely nature, common charity, the Earl's rank, and her
own experience of similar troubles, which had impelled her. Arran
must not presume too far. The poor youth had written to her and
been imprudent enough to mention hopes held out to him by her.
Marriage was the implication. He had missed Mary Stuart and
Mademoiselle de Montpensier, but here, in the greatest catch of all,
might be his revenge and the fulfilment of his bounding hopes.

The Queen thought such presumptions strange. She did not know
what to think. She was not at all pleased that he had received
encouragement of this kind. But while denying it in private she did
not mind if people at her Court, particularly the Spanish and
Imperial Ambassadors, believed it. Both of them had been urging
the charms of Philip's nephew, the Habsburg Archduke Charles, of
whom it had now been established that he was preferable to his elder
brother, and had everything to recommend him except for his
religion and a head even bigger than the Earl of Bedford's. On June
27 the Imperial Ambassador, Count von Helfenstein, saw Elizabeth
and tried to draw her out—or else was made use of as an audience—
about this Scottish suitor. Her father, she remarked, had once
betrothed her to Arran; but she had never liked him. It was true that,
though Henri II had sent his portrait to all the ports, he had escaped
from France. Henri thought he was now in England. She herself
thought Henri was mistaken; or if Arran was in England, nobody
had told her. She did however know that he had been lately 'in a
certain kingdom . . . and thereupon smiled and looked archly'.
Afterwards she repented, or seemed to repent, of having said so much.
Henri was 'bursting with rage, and she did not want him to burst
more'. She begged Helfenstein not to repeat what she had told him.
The Bishop of Aquila, to whom he repeated it the same evening, had
made up his mind that Elizabeth was sure to marry Arran and would
use him to control Scotland and spread heresy; if she had been
joking, he thought the joke a poor one.

Mr. Charles Howard (Lord William's son) was crossing to Paris
on a mission of condolence for the King's death. Elizabeth gave
him a thousand crowns for Throckmorton to pass on to Arran as
travelling expenses, with instructions to make for the coast disguised
as a scholar or a merchant. He must avoid the Low Countries and all

dominions of the King of Spain, the Emperor, or the Three Bishop-rics, since, if found there, he would be returned to France; Lübeck or Hamburg seemed the likeliest ports of embarkation, or East Friesland, if the Countess of Emden could be trusted. Throckmorton was to appoint one man to escort him. The Queen and Cecil sugges-ted Richard Tremayne of Collacombe, a member of another West-Country Protestant family and a cousin of Francis Drake. He and his twin brothers had conspired against Mary Tudor, taken refuge in France, and received French pensions for a time. Throckmorton knew him and agreed that he should be used; Tremayne knew German well, and no one would be a better guide. 'A great heretic', the Bishop of Aquila called him, 'who goes to and fro with messages to the heretics' in France. Most of this work took him to Brittany, but special permission was now given him to 'continue his studies' at Geneva.

The friendships which Throckmorton, Randolph and Killigrew had established with the German and Swiss Reformers now proved their use. Arran wrote to Throckmorton that he had left Lausanne on July 6. Cecil put in his almanac that he 'escaped out of France to Geneva' on July 11, 'accompanied by Mr. Randolph'. The Cardinal of Lorraine asked Philip of Spain to order Margaret of Parma, his Regent in the Low Countries, to arrest him. They were all too late. News reached Brussels that he had passed through the Low Coun-tries, accompanied by one Englishman. He reached London at the beginning of August, and Cecil hid him in his house. The Bishop of Aquila wrote to Philip that Arran had been secretly received by Elizabeth.[27] He had escaped the spies and soldiers of the Catholic powers, passed mountains, and crossed the sea; only the Border and the agents of Marie de Guise remained.

Chapter Four

INTERVENTION AND ESCALATION

i. 'Promises . . . Money . . . Arms':
From Promises to Money

THE active head of a country's Intelligence services is seldom the master of its political decisions. An ambitious man may seek to become so, and now and then succeed. Usually there will be some Government, or group, or person, monarch or dictator, whom he will have a duty to obey as well as inform, but perhaps also endeavour to persuade. Many chiefs of Intelligence have found the work of obtaining it enough and not sought political power at all.

William Cecil was as loyal a servant of Elizabeth as ever sovereign had anywhere. His control over Intelligence was a part of his work as Privy Councillor and State Secretary, concerned with policy. He did endeavour to persuade, and his Intelligence supplied him with evidence for his persuasions. Elizabeth's mind was not easily made up. She preferred, if possible, not to come to any decision at all and, if she could not avoid it, to come to two, each contradictory of the other.

Scotland had furnished her with the first crisis of her reign. She wanted French influence and soldiery sufficiently removed to cease to be a threat, but her religion was not militant and she had never had a taste for martyrdom or crusades. She believed entirely in the sanctity of crowned heads and did not intend to push a Protestant, even less a Knoxian, rebellion in Scotland one inch further than was necessary for her own security, which she identified with the security of England. Cecil himself favoured action, as much of it as possible to be taken by the Scots, but to be reinforced if necessary from England. So Sir James Croft was instructed to 'kindle the fire' of Protestant insurrection; Sir Nicholas Throckmorton needed no telling, but had less scope. The rest was for the Secretary in London; patient argument supported by Intelligence on the one side, against the less complete information and also lesser intellects of the Council, and the emotions of the Queen, upon the other. At the end lay either success or resignation.

Two days after Arran had ridden out of Lausanne, Cecil wrote to Croft that the Lords of the Congregation were to be 'essayed with all fair promises first, next with money, and last with arms'. It is a classic formula of escalation. Fair promises were easy. The Queen would need intensive wooing to send money and much more to send arms; the country had little to spare of either. The initiative at each stage rested mainly with Cecil, and to make up, or satisfy, his own mind he needed to be informed first, how much the Lords would and could accomplish on their own; second, how far the French were able and prepared to go to stop them; third, what the King of Spain would do.

By July it had become clear that Marie de Guise's attempt to silence the preachers had so far failed. She retreated to Dunbar. Her latest instructions from Paris, combined with necessity and her own judgment, told her to temporize again and hang on to the vital ports until reinforcements could be landed there. If during this period the Lords could persuade her to send the holding forces home or, alternatively, drive them out, France and the Catholic cause were lost. In all three countries it became a race with time. We assume now, as we assume of most past events in whose wake we have lived for centuries, that they could not have happened otherwise. It seems 'obvious' now that Protestantism would be victorious in Scotland and union with England sooner or later follow. In the summer of 1559 it seemed just as likely to everyone, John Knox included, that Marie de Guise would win, Scotland thereby becoming a French protectorate and a springboard into England.

Throckmorton wanted to come home. Living was dear, his half-yearly allowance only enough for a quarter, he himself 'bare and ruined'. Three hundred crowns spent on goldsmith's work for the Queen were still owing him. The French Ambassador in London had had a credit for 10,000 crowns opened; why should Throckmorton not have a thousand or two? The Guises hated him. Until he had arrived, they were all now saying, Arran had always been amenable. It was the Ambassador's doing that he had defied his sovereigns and absconded. A player on the virginals he had brought over from England was kidnapped and sent to the galleys; despite the most courteous assurances from the Duke de Guise, the Ambassador had great difficulty in recovering him. Watch was set on his lodgings, and his letters were laid in wait for.

He had been instructed to send duplicates of all letters of importance either with the merchants of Rouen or Dieppe, or via the Protestant fortresses of Geneva and Strasbourg. Sometimes he used the professional couriers, and on one occasion Sir Peter Carew, whom the new reign had freed from further acts of penitence, and on another Cecil's son Thomas, who had 'cared for gayness' and was being sent back to father in disgrace. For exceptional encounters he dispatched a senior member of his suite. After the death of Henri II and the Guises' triumph the King of Navarre became the obvious man to cultivate; and as Antoine de Bourbon rode up to Paris and the Guises rode out to meet him, Throckmorton sent out Henry Killigrew, who intercepted him at Vendôme and was granted a confidential talk.

The supple King, now heir but three to the throne of France, declared that God must have preserved Elizabeth and himself to preach His word, suggested an alliance, and asked where the Earl of Arran was. He invited the Ambassador to meet him at St. Denis 'in cape', and the encounter took place at midnight in Antoine's *garderobe*. The King told the Ambassador that France and Spain were extracting more secrets from England than he would believe possible. He expressed special interest in Elizabeth's marriage and asked for a secret courier between them whom both could trust. He offered Throckmorton a bed for the night, or alternatively an escort to the Embassy, but Sir Nicholas declined for fear of spies and towards dawn rode back with his own lackey and page. He was right to have been cautious. The interview became known; and the Guises, to occupy Antoine with less harmful matters, gave him the doubtful honour of escorting the new Queen of Spain from Paris to her consort.

By now many of the Marian exiles had returned home. To those who remained in France Sir Nicholas became much as Dean Wotton a couple of years ago had been to him. There were able and vigorous men among them. Elizabeth would be glad to have them back, 'but circumspection must be used' in case they returned (like Edward Randolph) as double agents. It was left to the Ambassador, as a man experienced in such affairs and well acquainted with them all, to prove them. A good deal of intelligence reached him about Scotland, probably from the Archers of the Guard and the Men-at-Arms. 'And

VIVE PIE·VT·SOLITVS·VIVB·DIV·VT·MERITVS

WILLIAM CECIL

MARIE DE GUISE-LORRAINE

there is in this Court one Master John Melvin [Melville],[28] a gentleman of Scotland, from whom I have learnt divers things for the advancement of the Queen's service . . .' This John Melville was a brother of the more famous James, who had talked with Throckmorton at Abbeville. He wished to serve the English cause in Scotland 'especially with those who dislike the French and are desirous to advance religion'. He was a zealous Protestant, who expected no pay until he had deserved it. Throckmorton advised that he should be given a chance; 'he may enter upon the Border to learn intelligence, and to practise, with less suspicion than an Englishman may.'

All the time Sir Nicholas watched Mary, chronicling her every swoon; one occurred at a banquet, and another in church, when she had to be revived with the Communion wine. She might be pregnant . . . a male heir to the thrones of France and Scotland, union in a Catholic Guise Empire? Pages of Franco-Scottish intelligence crossed the seas to London, to be galloped up to Croft or Percy at Norham or Berwick, and so sneaked north in the saddlebags of Ralph Lawrence or men unnamed, past Marie's spies and into the hands of the Congregation.

A vital branch of English espionage in France was concerned with preparations in the Channel ports; of this the Privy Council in London received reports by almost every post. Francis Edwards, a merchant and a man who knew ships, was riding to and fro along the Normandy and Picardy coasts during July and August and reporting direct to Cecil the movements of horsemen, and what they said to him, the numbers and tonnage of the ships in Rouen, Fécamp, Dieppe, Calais, and Boulogne, the bustle in the yards. One ship was being 'new made from her chainholes upwards', she could not be ready for at least three weeks. Brass cannon had been mounted all round Dieppe, facing seaward; some said they were to salute Philip on his journey from the Netherlands to Spain, but Edwards attributed them to fears of an English raid. He was an excellent spy, who separated what he or one of his men had actually observed from what they had been told. All that he collected tended to confirm the Ambassador's intelligence in Paris.

Two fleets were being prepared to transport enough men and munitions to reinforce Marie's garrisons at Eyemouth, Dunbar and Leith. Captain John Ross would command the seamen, M. de la Brosse the soldiers; Francis Edwards had himself watched de la Brosse arrive at Rouen and leave next day for Le Havre. As soon as

possible after the French exchequer had recovered from the weddings—Henri II had had to borrow over a million crowns to pay for
them—the Marquis d'Elbeuf and probably the Grand Prior of
France would follow with an army. They were both Guises, a family
as Bonaparte-like in its arsenal of brothers and sisters as in its
ambition. Having crushed the Lords of the Congregation, they would
join with the Scots loyal to Marie and invade England.

This was the Ambassador's assessment. He also reported that the
French were afraid England might attack them first, and just as
anxious as the English to know why Philip and his troops still
loitered in the Netherlands. Privileged by old acquaintance, and
never the most tactful of men, he almost hectored the Queen. She
must have a good eye to her navy. She ought to get more spying done
by the cross-Channel merchantmen. She would do well to warn Sir
James Croft of a plot to surprise Berwick 'by way of the cliff there,
at low-water mark'. Spain must be courted, but if no alliance could
be signed, and at once, England must turn to some other Prince.
His urgent imagination envisaged his dispatches vainly shredded
among a divided Privy Council and disappearing into the same
limbo as Dean Wotton's about Calais. 'Let us not tempt God too
far as Queen Mary did . . . it may be too late when our enemy is at
the door.' He grew so desperate that he asked leave to come over to
speak to the Queen himself.

In July Marie de Guise's spies got the scent of the secret conversations. They began by tracing it to the wrong man; most surprisingly, to the Earl of Northumberland. William Kirkcaldy became
alarmed. If spies suspected the Earl, sooner or later they would
certainly suspect the Earl's brother or Sir James Croft and the trail
would lead to him. He pretended to be ill, daring neither to present
himself at Marie's Court nor yet to declare himself openly her
enemy. Croft, in a letter to Cecil, explained why he could not do the
latter. 'The man is poor . . .' Wages from the war were due to him.
'They be all poor, and you know,' Sir James added feelingly, 'in all
practices money must be one part.'

Neither side was yet prepared to commit itself wholly to the other.
Each feared France and suspected the other might come to an
arrangement with France. Cecil would not allow William Kirkcaldy
possession of his letters; in Norham Castle, by a ford, in a forest,
wherever it was Kirkcaldy met Sir Henry Percy, he had to read them,
digest them, and then hand them back to Sir Henry, who returned

them post-haste to the Secretary's office in Cannon Row. On July 4
Cecil asked for messages from people less 'private' than Kirkcaldy.
On Sunday the 15th Kirkcaldy repeated this letter to the inner
Council of the Lords at Edinburgh, who replied four days later.
Pledging their own names, they vowed they would never return to
the French allegiance, and required the 'counsel and furtherance' of
England. But England must hasten. Some of them were already
beginning to slip away home, taking their clans and followers with
them. Marie de Guise heard of it and advanced on Edinburgh.
Between the capital and Leith the two armies again came within
striking distance and on July 24 again compromised. The Reformers
handed back the printing-irons they had removed from the Mint
and Marie re-entered Edinburgh. Both sides took hostages and kept
men in arms against non-observance of the truce. About the same
time Marie's spies got wind of Kirkcaldy's talks with Sir Henry
Percy. He now had no alternative but to declare himself publicly with
the Congregation and leave her, having received no wages from her
and nothing so far but fine words from the English.

To Knox the Edinburgh truce had been surrender. In London the
Privy Council waited for the Lords of the Congregation to expel the
French garrisons; while the Lords, withdrawn now to Stirling,
waited for the Privy Council to send them money. Something had to
be decided quickly, and on August 1 the Great Reformer himself
descended upon Berwick with twelve articles of alliance for submission from the Congregation to the Queen.

John Knox was a great man. He roused multitudes and feared
nothing human. He played St. Paul to many timorous and back-
sliding congregations. He was consumed by almost daemonic energy
and sense of mission. Like Julius Caesar, Lenin, and Churchill, he
wrote history which he himself made. What he could not do, apart
from believing that he might ever be in the wrong, was to pass
anywhere unnoticed. He arrived in a fishing-boat from Holy Isle 'in
such unsecret sort', wrote Sir Henry Percy, 'that it is openly known
both in England and Scotland'. Marie de Guise found out at once
and two days later accused Percy of conspiracy with her enemies.
Sir James Croft hauled down a curtain of security and had Knox
brought into Berwick Castle, 'so secretly,' he hoped, 'that my speaking to him can be suspected but not known'.

Knox gave him the twelve articles. Those 'to be specially remembered and diligently answered' were marked with a dagger. The

Queen was asked to make 'comfortable support' available on the Borders at once; to influence the Borderers, especially the wavering Homes and Kers, in favour of the Congregation; to seize the fort at Eyemouth as soon as the French fleet came in sight; and to provide money for garrisoning Stirling, the hinge of Scotland. In return the Scots would bind themselves in friendly union with England for ever. Knox went on to expound the articles, which sorely tried Sir James's patience and simple soldier's mind. 'To declare the circumstances of their meaning as Knox declared them,' he told Cecil, 'would make a large paragraph and not easy to understand, nor the objections thereto answered, unless someone were there to answer them . . .' All Sir James could do was to repeat that the Queen could not ally herself with a mob. Knox thereupon asked to have the Earl of Arran brought from wherever he was to England, so that he could be secretly detained 'until wise men may consider what is in him'; if they did not like what they found, they would put Lord James Stuart in his place.

Sandy Whitelaw arrived from London next day, and the two Reformers rode out the same night for Scotland. Knox's neglect of security had put Marie's spies on to them, and they only just escaped, Sandy Whitelaw being chased three miles. From Stirling Knox wrote in disgust that if the English would not send help, 'they will utterly discourage the hearts of all here'. What the Scots wanted, and he wrote it twice, was enough money to pay the soldiers they still had, now reduced to a mere five hundred, and to enlist a thousand foot and three hundred horsemen more. Otherwise, anything might happen. Argyll and Lord James Stuart wrote more briefly and less bluntly, but in the same sense. By the middle of August Croft reported that an urgent messenger from Knox was with him, and that the Reformers were in despair.

But something had been started from London, which caused the messenger to be detained. On the very day that Knox and Whitelaw left Berwick, the Queen had authorized a warrant to pay three thousand crowns to Sir Ralph Sadler, travelling to the North on her behalf, 'to be employed according to such instructions as she shall give him'. His official orders charged him to inspect Berwick and settle various disputes along the Border. His real job, conveyed secretly by the Queen a day or two later, would be to take over the secret negotiations and use the money to keep the Congregation in the field. It must not be suspected to have come from the Queen;

Sadler must have a cover for everything, and on no account jeopardize the peace treaty.

Sir Ralph Sadler was over fifty, in those days an overripe age to ride off on secret missions, especially to the uncouth and rainswept Border. But it took more than that to defeat Sir Ralph and he had a generation still to go. He was one of those who had risen under Thomas Cromwell into the favour of Henry VIII, and survived his master's fall. His familiarity with influential background figures and his own financial quickness and colossal industry had given him a name as 'the richest Commoner in England'. It was said of him that he regretted losing any hour of the morning between four and ten. He tells us himself that at one time of his life he rarely slept past four and scarcely went to bed one day in seven before midnight.

No Englishman knew Scotland better. Scotland was his department. He had worked and fought there during the blood-soaked forties, negotiating and plotting (mostly in vain) for Henry VIII, and marching in with Protector Somerset to lay waste the Lowlands. It was he, fifteen years previously, who had first used the Laird of Brunstane as a spy. On one of his missions the Scots had tried to kill him, and he had had to take refuge in Tantallon Castle. Knox, Balnaves, Kirkcaldy, Lord James Stuart, Glencairn, treacheries, deadly feuds, Anglophils, Francophils . . . his memory was a dossier of them all. He understood soldiering, administration, and money, and ciphering and conspiracy were second nature to him.

His mere name gave the Reformers heart; he represented Henry VIII's policies without Henry's savagery. The state in which he found the Border made him indignant and he did not mince his words. Berwick was no stronger than it had been before the fortification started; if Marie de Guise had had better intelligence, she could easily have surprised it. Lord Dacre, the Earl of Northumberland, and Sir Henry Percy must all go; Sadler was one of the 'new men' and great names did not awe him. Lord Dacre and Northumberland were 'rank Papists'. The Graemes, in Dacre's wardenry, were regularly raiding the Maxwells in Annandale and preventing the Maxwells from joining the Congregation, while Dacre sat in Carlisle and did nothing. Sadler suspected the whole semi-royal Percy entourage, especially Thomas Clavering, who farmed the border demesne of Norham from Sir Henry Percy and was deputy-Warden to Northumberland. As for Sir Henry, other duties had kept him away from the frontier far too long, 'and I do not judge him

a man of such integrity as in anywise to be comparable to Croft'.
Elizabeth had now had it suggested to her that of the four men
charged with the defence of her most vulnerable frontier, three, and
the secretary of the fourth, were conniving with, spying for, or
actively co-operating with her enemies. So far, but so far only, Sir
James Croft alone seemed blameless.

On August 23 the Spanish Ambassador in Paris was having supper
with the Queen of Scots, François II, and the Cardinal of Lorraine.
Mary 'looked very evil', he told Throckmorton, and had swooned
again. After she had been revived with eau-de-vie, he tried to improve the hour by telling the Cardinal that Arran would never risk
crossing the Netherlands and, if he did, Philip would arrest him. At
that very moment Arran was snug in Cecil's house in London. In
another letter to Throckmorton intended for interception, Cecil
wrote that anyone was mistaken who thought Arran had reached
England; on the contrary, he was at Cologne, and would travel home
by way of Denmark. Meanwhile Arran had an audience with
Elizabeth; and on the morrow, borrowing two hundred crowns from
Cecil and passing as M. de Beaufort, a gentleman of the French King,
he set out along the Great North Road. Elizabeth saw fit to have him
accompanied by the assiduous Thomas Randolph, who took the
name of Barnaby. She signed one passport herself, commanding a
journey for the pair without search or stay, and Cecil signed another.
Perhaps the Secretary feared an accident. Highwaymen beset the
Great North Road, and innkeepers sometimes made pacts with
highwaymen. The further north a traveller went, the more dangerous
it became; the soldiers' pay had lately been waylaid south of Aln-
wick, and Sadler suspected that his letters were being rifled. Or
perhaps Cecil had his doubts of the young hopeful, since he sent
separate instructions north that, if Lord James Stuart also thought of
pressing that claim to the Scottish throne of which James Melville
had acquitted him so glibly, he should not be discouraged.

A small vanguard of the French fleet anchored in the Firth of
Forth. Cecil heard from his spies in the Channel that de la Brosse
had embarked at Le Havre with eighty horse, heading for Scotland
by the western approaches, and instructed Sir Thomas Gresham to
hurry with the munitions he was buying for the Queen in Antwerp.
From Edinburgh Marie de Guise issued a proclamation denying that
she had sent for an army from France or had ever pledged herself not
to send. The Congregation retorted with a passionate indictment of

the bitter wrongs the French garrisons had done to Scotland, which reads like a catalogue of every evil every occupying army has ever been accused of, raping, murdering, dispossessing, 'their idle bellies fed upon the poor substance of the community'. Official courtesies and official negotiations continued meanwhile between Councillors and Heads of State, as if nothing else was happening. The Commissioners of peace between England and Scotland met at St. Mary's Church, Norham, and signed the articles left undecided at Cateau-Cambrésis. Northumberland and Sadler gloved their mutual mistrust and dislike in the language of courtly disagreement. François II wrote to Elizabeth of his pleasure that she would re-accredit Sir Nicholas Throckmorton as her Ambassador. The Duke de Guise sent assurances that the death of Henri II had not altered his goodwill towards her. Sir William Cecil went off to Burghley House for a fortnight, feeling 'like a bird out of a cage'. And at midnight on Wednesday, September 6, Henry Balnaves arrived at Berwick from the Congregation, to confer secretly with Sadler and Sir James Croft.

It was a momentous meeting. At last men with full authority to speak for both sides had come together. Balnaves and Sadler were both used to affairs of State. They had worked openly or covertly for a Protestant alliance between England and Scotland most of their lives; indeed Balnaves's autograph register of two hundred Scots pledged secretly to serve England had been found after his capture in St. Andrews. They talked in the great keep of Berwick all Thursday morning. Balnaves alleged that Marie had committed fresh breaches of the Edinburgh agreement. She had celebrated Mass again at Holyrood, and was bringing in more and more French soldiers. The harvest was late this year and the clansmen still in the fields. Once it was in, they would assemble. Within the next few days the Lords themselves would meet at Stirling, hoping—this was why Balnaves had come—for some 'good comfort' from Elizabeth. The Duke of Châtellerault stayed neutral, awaiting the arrival of his son. On all sides the preachers were bringing in recruits. The older generation hesitated, or clung to the old allegiances, but let their sons, 'young and lusty gentlemen', go forward with the new.

Sadler and Croft warned Balnaves that the Queen of England could not risk breaking the peace with France and the Queen of Scots. Balnaves did not demur. The façade must indeed be maintained, since, if war broke out again, no one could object to French reinforcements. The English knew, Sadler went on, that the Lords were in arms for true religion and the liberty of Scotland, but in the world's eyes their actions would be taken as a rising against authority. Discarding all pretence, Balnaves replied in the strictest secrecy that, whatever they might feign, what they in fact intended was 'an alteration in the State'; they would depose Marie and put the Duke or, better, the Earl of Arran in her place. The two Englishmen closed the talks by promising them £2,000 from the secret service money; if they used it well the Queen would send them more. It was agreed that the money should be collected from Holy Isle within the week. Only the most trustworthy of the Lords must know its source; the rest would be told that it had been raised by levy. Sadler could not help hoping aloud that it would be better used than all the subventions King Henry had sent to Scotland in the old days.

If any whispered message interrupted these conversations, if the night before the sound of hooves had disturbed Balnaves's sleep, the elderly conspirator was not told the cause till morning. But the Earl of Arran had arrived. Dawn must have been breaking when he and Thomas Randolph rode through the gates of Berwick, and later in the day Balnaves met the young man he had known thirteen years earlier as a boy-hostage in the Castle of St. Andrews and was now proposing to make King; and Croft met his sister's brother-in-law, disguised as Barnaby. At nightfall Arran was rowed across the Tweed. A guide arranged by Sadler and Croft met him. They galloped 'over the waste grounds and under the hills of Cheviot' into Teviotdale, where a Scottish friend of Arran's took over soon after midnight. Croft and Sadler felt sure they had managed it all so well that Marie's spies could never have evidence by what route Arran had entered Scotland. At night too Balnaves was rowed across to Holy Isle. Gales delayed him there six days, and finally he took the money with him.

For a week Cecil did not know what had become of de la Brosse and his reinforcements; then Throckmorton reported that he had put back to France and set out again by the eastern approaches. Within days Cecil heard that Arran had been brought safe to his father's arms in Hamilton Palace, whence, to the Secretary's amazement, he sent back the borrowed two hundred crowns. There was joy in Scotland, but his escape produced awkward moments for his former neighbours in Poitou. The town of Châtellerault happened to be the stage François and Mary had chosen for their farewell to Elizabeth of Valois on her way to Spain. Mary stayed in the house Arran had lately vacated, and took what revenge she could by placarding the arms of England on her canopy. 'Divers justices and officers' hurried to dissociate themselves from Arran and 'divers gentlemen' found it convenient to disappear. From Scotland the Duke of Châtellerault composed a disingenuous letter to Henri II, asking what the King knew about his son's departure and what could have induced him to depart, 'whereunto', Throckmorton commented, 'what answer has been made, as yet I cannot learne.'

Thomas Randolph soon followed Arran across the Border. Unsuspecting, Marie de Guise requested a passport for James Melville, his French mission completed after his own fashion, to return to his service with the Constable. Melville reached Berwick and gave Sir James Croft a message. Sir James passed it on to London, mostly in cipher, including Melville's name.

It was from young Maitland of Lethington. Maitland now formally offered his services to Elizabeth. He remained with Marie de Guise, he said, 'no longer than he might have a good occasion to revolt into the Protestants'. On September 27 Sadler and Croft watched a great ship sail past Berwick northward; they took de la Brosse to be aboard. Any day d'Elbeuf might follow with the great army. Marie and her Frenchmen withdrew from Edinburgh into Leith and began to fortify it. Any day, Sadler and Croft wrote, Maitland (his name of course in cipher) might be expected to leave her, declare himself with the Congregation, and arrive at Berwick as their official emissary. He delayed, and their letters betrayed nervousness. If he was to come, it must be in the greatest secrecy. Marie had many spies around and probably inside Berwick; two French soldiers and a Scot had lately been captured in the neighbourhood without passports, and on one of the soldiers were found letters belonging to the French Ambassador. On October 2 Randolph, now installed with the Congregation, sent his masters a long letter all in cipher. Maitland, he wrote, still intended to make his way to London. At the moment, however, he had accompanied Marie right into Leith itself, 'advised thereunto for summe good purpose'.

James Melville had continued on to London on his way back to France, intending there to inform the Constable that Lord James Stuart had no designs upon the Scottish throne. 'The way', it has been observed, 'in which he executed this commission argues either extreme simplicity, or a predetermination not to seek the truth.'[29] He reached Paris to find the Constable out of power, and all Scotsmen distrusted and disliked. He then, he tells us in his memoirs, 'required licence at the Queen my sovereign to visit other countries, whereby I might be more able afterwards to do Her Majesty agreeable service.' The Constable sent him into Germany 'to learn the language' at the Court of the Elector Palatine, a Protestant Prince much sought after by Elizabeth and Cecil as an ally on the eastern frontiers of France.

But in the English State Papers we find this put a little differently. A letter from Elizabeth, dated January 9, 1560, instructed Sir Nicholas Throckmorton that 'for the furtherance of her service he shall procure James Melville to be placed by the Constable with the Elector Palatine, and give him in reward a hundred crowns, and promise a pension of two hundred crowns per annum'. Sir Nicholas was to use his discretion whether or not to obey, 'as shall seem most profitable for her service.' Sir Nicholas obeyed, and Melville in his memoirs thanked him . . . 'my dear friend, who had procured a pension for me from his mistress, to help to entertain me when I was willingly banished from the court of France, so long as there was civil wars between France and Scotland . . .' Did Mary Stuart know of this subvention from Elizabeth? Perhaps she did. Perhaps it does not matter. Melville had to live. It was not thought amiss for a diplomat of one country to receive money from the sovereign of another. What is remarkable is that the message about William Maitland's defection from Marie and France, which Melville delivered to the English at Berwick while he was still in the King of France's service, somehow finds no mention in his memoirs; one can hardly believe he had forgotten it.

ii. From Money to Arms

Wars and conspiracies have often brought international struggles to so concentrated a point that all the Fates seem to be hovering above one place. Such a place, from autumn 1559 until early summer 1560, was the fortress-port of Leith. Marie de Guise had to hold it until, or the Lords of the Congregation seize it before, her reinforcements came; whoever succeeded had won Scotland, and much else besides.

Mary Stuart achieved little but disaster in her life, but something admirable, certainly memorable, by her death. Marie de Guise achieved much while she lived; her last months seem to have swept away even her memory. Mary Stuart's son survived to inherit England and Scotland; both Marie de Guise's sons by James V had died in infancy. James took mistress after mistress. Marie had a share of her daughter's unhappiness with the men she chose, or was compelled, to trust; and she missed France as deeply as Mary Stuart. She returned home once only during her reign. Her son by her first marriage to the Duke de Longueville died there in youth and Mary was taken from her at the age of six. 'You have had so little joy in this world,' her mother Antoinette de Bourbon once wrote, 'and are so inured to cares and hardship, that I think you must have ceased to know what pleasure is.' Inevitably rumours were spread about her. At one time she was reputed 'Cardinal Beaton's whore' and it was ancient gossip that Mary Stuart's evil genius, the fourth Earl of Bothwell, was her mother's son by the third Earl.[30] If Maitland had indeed ruled Marie de Guise, as a Spanish envoy wrote, 'body and soul', it is not surprising; he had brought her wit, *savoir-faire*, and a breath of the Renaissance.

Scotland was supposed to be paid for from its revenue, on top of which she had to provide for her own household and, after 1554, supply a suitable establishment in France for Mary. Though she was rich by Scottish standards; though after she became Regent she controlled the administration; though she had available the pension granted her by François I, and revenue from French and Scottish estates acquired by her two marriages, Henri II paid the pension irregularly and her Longueville in-laws involved her in a long and costly lawsuit. She inherited a deficit of £30,000 from the Hamilton administration. At one moment she owed for two years' supply of wine; at another her daughter's servants had received nothing for fifteen months and the comptroller nothing at all. In 1556 Lord Home's pension from France, theoretically 2,000 livres a year, was well in arrears. War stretched her resources past their limit. When the French fleet arrived with reinforcements in 1548, she melted down her plate to pay the cavalry, and the Constable sent her 100,000 crowns of his own.

Perhaps she was extravagant. We hear of her buying jewels on her one visit to France, and losing 6,000 crowns at cards to the Marshal d'Essé, pledging another 6,000 and getting it all back. She borrowed wherever and whenever she could, from d'Oysel, from the Scottish merchants she encouraged, £4,400 from the Bishop of Dunblane, even two hundred crowns from Lady Moray, who had difficulty in recovering them. After the 'tumult of Perth' she sent three messengers and several urgent letters to France, imploring money. Soldiers were coming to d'Oysel two or three hundred at a time for food, pay, and leave to return to France; they were even—crowning ignominy —accepting shelter and the odd shilling or two from their impecunious Scottish enemies.

In the past she had managed to entertain some kind of intelligence service of her own. During her struggle with the Hamiltons after the death of James V she maintained a spy in their household. When Protector Somerset invaded Scotland, she sent a certain George Paris to agitate the Irish against England, but he soon betrayed her. Ker of Premsideloch and Macdowall of Mackerston in Roxburghshire kept her informed of the English army's advance north in 1549, but hinted that if she could not offer them a living they would have to beg their meat elsewhere. By 1559 she depended to a great extent on the organization of two Frenchmen, Gilles de Noailles and Henri Cleutin de Villeparisis d'Oysel. De Noailles was the youngest of those three gifted brothers who succeeded one another as Ambassador in London during the 1550s. D'Oysel, a Guisian, first went to Scotland as Ambassador; he now commanded Marie's armies and was trusted by her as thoroughly as he was hated by the Congregation. In 1557 he had argued that the capture of Berwick would throw open the whole of England, since there was no other fortress to stop an army before London; in 1559 nothing had occurred to contradict him.

So far the game was still a game of chess. William Drury, sent in by Sadler to spy on the fortifying of Leith, noted that Arran and Lord James Stuart now bore all the responsibilities and costs of leadership. Thomas Randolph reached them after a dangerous journey from Berwick and attached himself half as secret ambassador, half as spy. Cecil had instructed him to find out as much as he could about Marie and the French, while keeping his presence in Scotland hidden from her. He crept close to Leith, obtained a plan of the fortifications, and reported it strongly sited and apparently well supplied with food, but undermanned. He had his cover story; if detected he was to pretend that he had incurred Elizabeth's anger for keeping company with Arran and dared not show his face in London.

It had become imperative for Cecil in his skirmishes with Elizabeth to have Maitland in position soon. The Lords wished to send Henry Balnaves to London, but Balnaves was too much of a Calvinist for the Queen. Only Maitland would know how to reassure her that, in trying to quench the French-Catholic fuse smouldering towards her throne, she was not hastening the Scottish-Calvinist one. Some time during November Maitland at last did what England expected of him; he rode out of Leith, went through the masquerade of 'surrendering' to Kirkcaldy, and joined the Congregation. Marie sent spies deep into England after him for months, but only once again set eyes on him.

A river of clandestine mail began to flow across hills and moors from the Lords to Thomas Randolph, from Randolph to Sadler and Croft, and from Sadler and Croft to Cecil and back again. The Scots demanded money to pay their soldiers, powder, and munitions. The Queen agreed to stump up another £3,000. Mr. Overton, clerk of the musters, 'perceiving himself to be dogged by false varlets', hired a bodyguard and brought the money safe to the Lords on November 15. Sadler was authorized to send any powder and munitions that could be spared from Berwick, and Cecil gave permission for five or six experienced English captains to 'volunteer' for service north of the Border. They were to be chosen from among the Marian exiles who had lately returned from France and not yet been restored to royal favour, but must go disguised and under assumed names. Edward Randolph was to be one. They too would have their cover; if captured, they must say that the Queen had refused them a living and that, disillusioned with their native land, they had turned to Scotland. All the time John Knox continued to clamour for men, munitions, money, regardless of the means of sending them. Englishmen, he wrote to Croft, were free to serve anywhere as mercenaries; if the Queen feared that their soldiering in Scotland would lead to war with France, let her wait till they had arrived there and then declare them rebels. Croft riposted with a tartness Cecil approved, 'Ye are so open in your doings as you make men half-affrayed to deal with you'.

On October 21 the Lords 'deposed' Marie from the Regency 'in the name of the King and Queen', her son-in-law and daughter, who had not been consulted. She responded with defiance and disdain. Thomas Randolph, to whom she was the arch-enemy, jibed at her bulk: 'men think, the more sorrow she hath the fatter she waxeth; which makes me believe that shortly, if she wept not oft, she would die for fat, seeing as no other disease is able to take her out of this world.' For a time, she remained well informed, though the sands were running out and d'Oysel had to ask de Noailles to find out the relationship between the rebels and 'the people your side' in London.

In Scotland it was becoming more and more difficult; 'a man with us in the morning might be with them after dinner.' Intelligence might come a little late, but still it came, and still it could prove correct. A month passed before d'Oysel understood, or put into writing, the real reason for Sir Ralph Sadler's arrival on the Border. But he knew within days of Henry Balnaves's embarkation for the top-secret meeting in Berwick Castle; 'the most ungrateful rascal in the world,' he wrote, '. . . an English agent from the time of the Castle of St. Andrew's onwards . . . the greatest sedition-monger in the whole of the British Isles.' He reopened the packet containing this intelligence to add that a Scotsman called Forbes, a gentleman of Arran's, already under observation by French couriers, had been allowed the unusual privilege of buying two horses at Berwick and had galloped off to Arran's father at Hamilton, where 'as I know for a fact' he had been very well received. And he reopened the packet once again to put in the news that Marie had just heard of Arran's arrival somewhere in Scotland from three different sources. Croft and Sadler had not managed things at Berwick so secretly as they had supposed.

*

De Noailles had two principal informers at the English Court. He does not say who they were, and during September and October one was absent and the other ill. This proved a big handicap. Security in London had tightened. Elizabeth now settled her Scottish policy with not more than two or three Privy Councillors, of whom Cecil and Sir Thomas Parry were certainly two. The rest, Noailles reported, had never known anything like it. They resented this little upstart group . . . '*petits compagnons*', he called them. Cecil wrote, ciphered and deciphered the secret dispatches entirely on his own and when the Privy Council assembled in full session, no clerks attended; this extreme caution was perhaps a reaction to Croft's warning that one of them was a spy of the Earl of Northumberland.

De Noailles faced one permanent impediment, exceptional even in a Renaissance Court. This was Elizabeth herself. She was sly beyond belief, and he in person, and Marie de Guise by correspondence, vainly manœuvred to outflank that elastic wall of artifice and charm. She lied as eagerly about her help to the Scottish Reformers, as Henri II had lied to Wotton about his help to Sir Peter Carew and the other Marian exiles. In the summer Marie complained that the

English on the Border were secretly aiding the Congregation. Elizabeth found it most strange, she replied to the 'most high and mighty Princess, our dear sister and cousin', that any servants of hers could possibly embroil themselves with 'people of that sort'; if she could be allowed a glance at some precise evidence, she would see to it they were punished. This she wrote after the conspiracy had been afoot six months. In September de Noailles went to Hampton Court to protest that Scotsmen were being allowed across the Border without passports. Elizabeth replied that she had plenty of fools on her Council, and one of them might conceivably have encouraged some Scotsman to behave so stupidly; she would make inquiries and see that it did not happen again—this about the time that Henry Balnaves, passportless, went to his rendezvous at Berwick. Taking the Ambassador along her picture gallery, she showed him her portrait of Marie de Guise and expatiated on her 'good sister's' honesty and courage. She herself, she assured him, had written nothing to the rebels, promised nothing. Her seal was well known enough; now if that were to be found, that would be evidence indeed. Of course it was found on nothing; she and Cecil had taken care of that.

Again during September de Noailles conveyed Henri II's request that when Arran reached England, if he were not already there, Elizabeth should arrest and send him back. Elizabeth replied that she had no news of him (he had already reached Berwick), but that once he was in her power, for the Treaty's and friendship's sake, she would do what Henri asked. About three weeks later de Noailles saw her again. This time he could confront her with a list of agents' names. Her reply was again all innocence. Ralph Lawrence? a servant of the Percys? She had never heard of such a man, but of course she would tell Sir Ralph Sadler to inquire. Forbes? buying horses at Berwick . . . Sir James Croft would never, on his life, have dared to allow such a thing. She, Elizabeth, held her honour far too dear to let herself be thought the kind of person who said one thing and did the opposite. Almost the whole time she was running through this liturgy of falsehoods, she was 'laughing . . . and with the most cheerful expression'; the audience occurred soon after she knew for certain that Arran had reached Scotland.

It was not until mid-October that de Noailles, informed much later than the Spanish Ambassador, reported that Arran had seen Elizabeth. Marie knew that Randolph had entered Scotland without a passport under the pseudonym of Barnaby; and that some of the Berwick captains had slipped across to advise the Congregation; and that Drury had spied on Leith. But she and her supporters were becoming increasingly isolated. Perhaps her trouble was lack of money; perhaps, that the south had been longer habituated to secret service . . . it was an old saying that whatever the Scottish Council decided became known at Berwick within twenty-four hours; perhaps, simply that she was worn out.

For by the winter of 1559–60 she was dying on her feet. Nearly twenty years ago she had complained of sleeping badly and written about her symptoms to the doctor of François I. He had diagnosed palpitations of the heart and melancholia, which made her blotchy in the face and heavy and sluggish in her movements. He advised her never to let a day pass without some gentle exercise before meals. She should always inhabit a pure clear air as far as possible from marshes and the sea, and never remain for long where there was much cold, mist, wind or rain. This can hardly have been helpful to a woman called upon to rule from Edinburgh. The Guise vitality had kept her going. Even now she battled on, waiting for her brother d'Elbeuf to arrive and take over the Regency, so that she could end her days in France. The tenacity with which she clung to life and power drew from Randolph an exasperated 'Summe saye the devil cannot kill her'.

At the beginning of November her intelligence brought her two successes. She was alone now in Leith with some three thousand French and Scottish troops, Lord Seton and Lord Borthwick. Bothwell held Crichton Castle, but was it for her, or for himself? On the Border the Kers and Homes had still not made up their minds. Unable to keep their soldiers together, the Congregation had sent the Laird of Ormiston to Berwick on an urgent mission for more money. Returning through Lothian with £1,000 (or perhaps more) which Sadler and Croft had managed to scrape up, and 200 crowns for himself, he was waylaid by Bothwell, wounded in the face, and robbed of the whole sum. Arran and Lord James Stuart rushed from Edinburgh in pursuit of Bothwell, but missed him at Crichton by a quarter of an hour. Apprised of their absence, a party of French made a sortie from Leith, engaged a forage party of the Reformers outside the capital and routed them, killing one of their captains. The insurgent troops began to melt away. Arran and Lord James offered to remain in Edinburgh if they could have a thousand men, but at midnight on November 5 the demoralized Congregation decided to withdraw their forces to Linlithgow and then to Stirling, where John Knox resumed the trumpet-call of a sermon he had been compelled to interrupt at Edinburgh and put some heart back into them. Dividing into two groups, of which one took up its headquarters at Glasgow and the other at St. Andrews, they resolved to make up for the lost funds by melting down their plate; but Thomas Randolph reported their spirits sunk so low that 'I know not whom to commende'.

Ormiston had been spied on; it was inconceivable that a Reformer of such sincerity, and such long-standing as an agent of the English, could have betrayed them. Appalled at the collapse of security, Sadler and Croft instructed Randolph that the Lords must pretend the money had been Ormiston's own, or their own, or fabricate any story to conceal its true origin, and passed the double calamity to London 'in as good sorte as we can'. Cecil waited until November 13 before he dared to tell the Queen. Watch her countenance narrowly when you speak to her about it, d'Oysel told de Noailles, and notice whether she blushes. De Noailles's chief spy at Court, now returned, thought that the sum stolen was as much as 14,000 crowns. In Brussels Elizabeth's Ambassador Sir Thomas Challoner had an embarrassing interview with Philip's Minister, Cardinal Granvelle. The Queen, said the Cardinal, had decided to pretend that the money had been Cecil's. The French would never swallow that; 'for can they thincke a Cicile hath so much spare?' For the moment the loss kindled in Elizabeth a mood approaching resolution. She dispatched Edward Randolph to Berwick with £3,000. He arrived with the money on the 21st, and went on to the Lords with the even more important news that the Queen was levying reinforcements for the frontier.

Relentlessly, a decision to act effectively on the Lords' behalf was being forced upon her and upon her Privy Council. The 'doves' among them believed England far too weak to risk war with France, and argued that everything in Scotland immediately necessary to England's safety could be obtained by negotiation; later, when the country had arms, money, and political stability, something more vigorous might be done. The Catholic party opposed any action at all. But William Cecil, for the moment a 'hawk', his mind made up that it was now or never, mustered all his resources to convince Elizabeth. Sir Nicholas Throckmorton arrived on November 7, excusing his absence to the King of France on the ground that his wife was ill; in his eagerness he had forgotten to notify his wife of her illness, and she had unfortunately given de Noailles a letter addressed to Paris for him the same morning.

Maitland, fresh from Leith, joined him with Robert, a third Melville brother, at the end of the month, and gave a full report on Scotland: the numbers, arms, and provisions of both sides, the state of Marie's navy, the best land-routes, and a complete list of lords, lairds, and clerics, with her, against her, and undecided. He and Melville were hidden in the Palace of Westminster. De Noailles learnt of their presence, had the Palace watched, and reported that the two Scotsmen had been taken out by the water-gate and rowed in a small boat to Sir Nicholas's lodgings on the Thames. His informant at Court told him that the Congregation were thinking of offering Elizabeth the joint crown of England and Scotland, the kingdom to be united 'under the old name' of Great Britain; and he had accurate figures of the military and naval forces to be sent to the Border.

The combined impact of Cecil, Throckmorton, and Maitland, these three brilliant counsel for a policy of action, made up for the lack of dependable intelligence from France. Killigrew and Jones, Throckmorton's deputies, were now, like de Noailles, experiencing trouble in obtaining it. The French Court had taken up residence on the Loire, where the English could more easily be kept under watch. Accustomed informers, frightened of the Guises, avoided contact; the Queen was advised that if she wanted information she must be prepared to spend more money. One or two things seemed certain: the 'great fleet' was equipping, and would sail for Scotland in the spring under the command of yet another Guise, the Duke d'Aumale; convoys were to pass throughout the winter with arms and provisions for the garrisons; and any day the Marquis d'Elbeuf, with plenipotentiary powers to pardon Reformers who submitted and punish the remainder, would take over from his sister.

On December 15 Elizabeth informed Sadler and Croft that she was levying 4,000 foot to reinforce the Border, sending the Duke of Norfolk as Lieutenant-General north of the Trent, and fourteen men-of-war under Admiral Winter to block the Firth of Forth and use any opportunity to attack and defeat the French 'as of himself'. They were due to sail on the 20th. A week before, Cecil heard that forty sail had set out from France; 'so the English are likely to come too late.' At last, at midnight on December 23, he could tell Sadler and Croft: 'our shippes be on the sea, God spede them . . . the whole costs of France prepare to war . . . God gyve you both good night, for I am almost a slepe.'

The Privy Council had spent two whole weeks arguing, but the famous debate had ended in triumph for Cecil. Open war with France was unanimously rejected. But the Queen was asked to confirm Norfolk's appointment and send an army with him under Lord Grey. If the Scots could not expel the French with their own power, the English must move in to help. Since war would probably follow, the Queen must put the country in a state of mobilization; sell £100,000 of Crown lands; raise £200,000 through Sir Thomas Gresham in Antwerp; send Philip of Spain an embassy to obtain his support if possible, and, if not, to discover his intentions; raise mercenaries from the German Protestant Princes; and spend enough money in France to gain adequate intelligence. Cecil prepared a draft of the Council's resolution on Christmas Eve. On December 26 Knox was writing that a French fleet under d'Elbeuf, expected daily to attack Stirling or St. Andrews, had been driven north; if the English could reach the Firth in time, it could not escape. The English diplomats at Blois and Brussels, however, reported that d'Elbeuf was still at Calais. On the 28th Cecil marked his draft, 'disallowed by the Queen'. Perhaps then, perhaps earlier in advance, he asked permission to resign. This Elizabeth could not face. Before the end of the year she yielded. With or without her favour, Winter had already sailed.[31]

As soon as de Noailles had learnt full details of the Council's decision, his messenger to the French Court galloped away with them only to find the ports closed and all the rigging of the Calais mail dismantled. The Ambassador went to protest to the Queen. Hearing of his arrival, she left the Privy Chamber and began a game of primero with some of her courtiers in the Presence Chamber. Laughing as before, she told him that she knew nothing about the closing of the ports and thought it most peculiar. He accompanied her as far as her oratory, where she took a gay farewell and her attendant lords made him deeper bows than usual, leaving him to send his news as best he could.

Scotland's fate became a race between the fleets. The storms had been terrible all winter. Cecil learnt of sixteen French ensigns perished off the Dutch coast, but could get no confirmation till some

courier could clear Flanders. At last he heard from Sir Thomas
Challoner in Brussels. A thousand French on their way to Scotland
had been wrecked somewhere off Zeeland; the King of Spain's
Council in the Netherlands had broken with custom, so grave was
the news, and sat 'till dark night'. It was the first of Elizabeth's
'Protestant winds'. Storms in Scotland held up communication
between Sadler and the Lords. Marie's 'two little pinnaces' were
driven out of the Firth. A messenger from St. Andrews took seven
days by sea to reach Holy Isle and thought himself lucky to get
ashore. At Berwick the Duke of Norfolk anxiously scanned the seas
for Winter, and Marie sent her soldiers out on a bold venture.
Sarlabos, master of the camp, was ordered to drive the Congregation
out of Stirling and seize St. Andrews, which could be used as an
alternative beach-head for reinforcements if things went wrong at
Leith. The Lords withdrew and Sarlabos pressed forward into Fife.
D'Oysel sent three or four thousand men across the Firth of Forth to
join him. They took several hundred Scots prisoners and proceeded
to lay waste the northern coast of the Firth. Lord James Stuart and
Arran, fighting a harassing campaign in a grim winter, did not
change their clothes or even, according to Knox, remove their boots
for three weeks.

On January 12 there reached Brussels 'a gentleman out of Holland
to the Prince of Orange, governor of that country, with advertisement . . .' D'Elbeuf had been shipwrecked. Four ships and the
corpses of eight hundred men and eighty horses lay scattered along
the Dutch coast four leagues south of Amsterdam. People spoke of
two thousand dead; d'Elbeuf himself was said to be among them.
Challoner thought it too good to be true and sent to Sir Thomas
Gresham at Antwerp for corroboration. Nine days later Jean du
Faultrey, stationed with Marie at Edinburgh, wrote to his brother
with the troops in Fife that eight vessels had been sighted approaching the Firth of Forth. 'May God grant they are the ships of the
Marquis.'

They were the English. By clinging to a friendly coast and riding
the same storm that had wrecked d'Elbeuf, shelterless on the open
seas, Admiral Winter had arrived and won the race. It was the
second 'Protestant wind'. If the French could not get reinforcements
into Leith and were in no state to invade England, they had only two
hopes left: either treachery among the English or intervention by
the King of Spain.

Chapter Five

VICTORY

i. The Financier as Spy

WHAT would King Philip do? Whose side in Scotland, if either, would the Spanish take? All through the spring and summer of 1559 the King of Spain lingered anxiously and unwillingly on his inheritance in the Netherlands. Their commercial links with England, and the common enmity of France in the old Burgundian days, had made them a listening-post and observation-point for centuries. Elizabeth depended on two principal informants there: Sir Thomas Challoner, and even more the great financier and merchant-prince, Sir Thomas Gresham, who resided at Antwerp and succeeded Challoner as Ambassador about Christmas.

Where there is trade, there is usually Intelligence, and where a great deal of trade, intelligence that concerns the State. To the desk of the great merchant there pours in news not only about the special commodities in which he deals, but also about political conditions in the countries which produce them. For the great financier the commodity is money, which encompasses all the rest. His parish is a large part of the world. Political information is bound to reach him day by day, and a Government will be unwise that does not seek to draw on his supply.

In Sir Thomas Elizabeth had inherited a pearl among intelligencers, placed long since in a golden whispering-gallery. Magnificent Antwerp, despite the financial crash in 1551, was still the greatest entrepôt and money-market in Europe, the successor of Bruges, the superseder of Venice, the Rome of merchandise and finance, and the heart of news. Staffs included, nearly a thousand merchants had made their homes there. Every morning and evening the representatives of at least six nations sauntered to the English house to bargain in commodities from every corner of the trading globe, which had arrived, or were awaited or still at risk; then they moved on the splendid quadrangle and Gothic arches of the Bourse to negotiate bills and loans for Princes, Kings and Emperor. 'In Antwerp one always knows what is going on in the rest of the world.'

Sir Thomas Gresham had first come to the Low Countries in 1543, when he was twenty-three years old. He was one of a wealthy Norfolk family for some years engaged in the Flanders cloth trade. Both his father and an uncle had been Lord Mayors of London and knighted by Henry VIII. His father received plentiful Church lands from the King and supplied Cardinal Wolsey with intelligence from Antwerp. At Antwerp too he had become acquainted with Thomas Cromwell, while Cromwell was still a clerk filling in Merchant Adventurer account-books. Wolsey died owing Sir John Gresham £200. John Dudley Duke of Northumberland became Thomas's first patron and in 1551 appointed him Royal Agent in Flanders. In this role, over some twenty years, he was to borrow and repay hundreds of thousands of pounds for the English Crown. On the death of Edward VI, and subsequent execution of Northumberland, things looked black for him. The Duke went to the scaffold owing him twice as much as the Cardinal had owed his father, and about the same time all his plate and household stuff and his and his wife's clothing foundered in the North Sea. 'Now God helpe poor Gresham!' he exclaimed. God, operating mainly through Queen Elizabeth, did help, and generously. Poverty never became one of Gresham's problems. Great Ministers might fall; the Great Financier lasted.

As a Protestant, he incurred some danger at Mary's accession, but had a highly placed protector and escaped. As a businessman, he welcomed the defeat of Wyatt's rebellion, which had been bad for credit. He turned up to pay his homage to Elizabeth at Hatfield only a day or two after William Cecil. Perhaps he had been well-warned; he knew Cecil of old and his wife's sister married Cecil's brother-in-law, Sir Nicholas Bacon. Queen and Secretary were kindred spirits to Gresham; they understood the value of money and needed his trained hand. Elizabeth promised him that she would 'keep one ear shut to hear him against his enemies and, if he did no more for her than he had done for her late sister and brother, to give him more land than both of them together'. The good old times were back. It 'made me a young man agayen'.

Sir Thomas was foremost among those who put London in the place of Antwerp, and became a progenitor, almost indeed the Abraham, of that worldly priesthood, so feared, so trusted, so envied, so attacked, the City. He created the Royal Exchange on the model of the Antwerp Bourse; when the sun shines, his grasshopper still glitters above the present building. Elizabeth had much for which to thank him. He helped to restore the currency her father had debased. According to himself, his mastery over the rate of exchange saved the Crown tens of thousands of pounds. No doubt he boasted, perhaps exaggerated his achievements, possibly was no abler than that other wily financier, William Paulet, the jealous old Marquis of Winchester, who tried to undermine him at Court. The knowledge that such powerful voices were whispering against him could have made it necessary to blow his own trumpet all the louder from the distance. 'Rough and ready'[32] his reckoning may have been, by present-day standards, but few others were capable even of that; and voices in the wilderness usually have to repeat themselves to take effect.

He was used to secrecy and dissimulation and needed both. The hollow ring of Elizabeth's coffers must be muted for foreign ears. Barely a month after her accession she was instructing him: 'ye shall repayre over to Antwerp and at your coming, with all manner spede and as secretly as ye can possible, borrowe and take up as muche money to our use as ye may, to the somme of two hundred thousand pound for one whole yeere.' She enjoined him to let the banking community in Antwerp know about the impending currency reform, but again in secret. Three contributions to the conspiracy in Scotland were expected of him, and secrecy was essential to them all. He must supply arms, he must raise money, and he must discover the intentions of the King of Spain. In all three respects he already was or soon became highly practised in deceit.

*

During the rose and pomegranate days, while the King of Spain was still the husband of the Queen of England, Sir Thomas had enjoyed exceptional privileges in the Spanish Netherlands. Things were different now. The new Queen's brief flirtation with Philip had ended, and Gresham had turned from the agent of an ally into that of a potential foe. In September 1559 the Regent (now Margaret of Parma, Philip's half-sister) refused foreigners passports for horses, powder or munitions, until Spain's own needs had been provided. Challoner protested to Cardinal Granvelle. Granvelle was charming but adamant; it had become common talk that the French would soon take control of Scotland and the Pope excommunicate Elizabeth, whom many considered 'like to lose her throne'. In January 1560 an edict banned all movement of men, armour or provisions either to French or English. So Gresham took to shipping from ports out of the King of Spain's supervision and jurisdiction, notably Emden and Hamburg. He also resorted to smuggling.

He had been authorized to smuggle during Queen Mary's reign. Elizabeth not only gave him similar orders, but instructions how to execute them. He was to bribe the customs officials, '. . . so ye exceede not ye summe of five hundred crownes'. Of course he had also bribed before; modestly, as a New Year's gift, at Gravelines, where 'all tymes of nyght the gates of the town were open to my servants . . .' But what he was now to undertake from Antwerp, and in quite altered conditions, involved him and his agents in terrifying risks. Even as he was leaving London a message reached him on the Thames that Margaret of Parma knew about his operations. The river traffic harboured spies. Spies were suspected at the office of the Royal Ordnance in the Tower, to which his consignments were delivered. A certain Mr. Bloomfield was the official who received them. 'Great charge' for secrecy must be given him, Gresham begged Cecil, and Frenchmen were forbidden the neighbourhood even to sleep. No deliveries must be entered at the Customs House, since there were spies among the searchers. He devised some method, obscure to us now, for shipping bullion by concealment 'in the stone-work'. He requested a cipher and begged Elizabeth to keep what he was doing to herself, 'for, yf yt shoulde be knowen or per-ceved in Flanders, it were as moche as my liffe and goodes were worth . . .'

It cannot have been difficult for foreign spies to corrupt the English officials who unloaded Gresham's supplies, if we are to believe an interesting comparison, compiled about this date, between the ways things were managed on the Scheldt and on the Thames. We owe it to Richard Clough, the shrewd pageant-loving Welshman who was chief of Gresham's agents. Clough had managed to worm details about Antwerp out of Christopher Pruen, the City Treasurer. Antwerp employed only one or two searchers; London, employing five or six, known to be dishonest, amidst a host of hangers-on 'and other powlyng officers', had 'more custom stolen in one month than is here in Antwerp in one whole year, which cometh because they here do the things in order, and we out of order'. Clough questioned whether anybody on the Privy Council had any inkling of the tricks played almost under their noses. Ten days might pass before a searcher appeared to supervise the opening of merchandise; if the importer failed to give him a present of four or five groats, he might delay longer still. Meanwhile a package might remain in the importer's house, and merchants, not being 'the simplest kind of people', did not scruple to open it themselves; if it happened to contain silks, they substituted fustians, on which they paid a lower duty. People thought this was impossible, because the searcher had sealed the goods. Not at all, Clough replied, for a man who could make the searcher's true seal could also make a counterfeit. The searchers excused themselves for expecting bribes on the old grounds that they could not live upon their pay, and people said that things of this kind had been going on for ages. In Clough's view it was high time to do them differently.

Such conditions were a compost-heap for spies. Yet Clough's rosy comparison of Antwerp must have been overdone, for Sir Thomas Gresham found enough palms outstretched there to nullify the espionage against him in London. Among others he had the chief searcher in his pay, '. . . all my doer', he informed Sir Thomas Parry, 'and yff it were perssevid, there ys no other waysse but deathe with the serchers and wythe hym that enters yt in the customs house.' He found it prudent now to use a rudimentary code; one piece of double Genoese velvet pile meant a thousand-weight of corn-powder, a piece and a half of velvet pile meant the same for serpentine powder, and other kinds of cloth stood for other kinds of arms. The Queen instructed him to communicate with no one else on the Council apart from her two part-Welsh compatriots, Cecil, whose family began on the Welsh Marches, and Sir Thomas Parry.

Desperate appeals reached the Duke of Norfolk after Lord Grey had invaded Scotland and encamped in front of Leith. Wages were unpaid and all great and small shot 'utterly spent'. Money and munitions in the quantities needed could only come through Gresham, and during the vital spring of 1560 his own difficulties grew acute. A Flemish nobleman, the Sieur de Glajon, left Antwerp to expound to Elizabeth the outcome of King Philip's cogitations upon affairs in Scotland. Although inclined to favour the Reformed cause, Glajon, as Master of Armour and Ordnance in the Low Countries, had not been endeared to Gresham by the knight's purloining the previous Christmas of two thousand Spanish corslets 'which bye practise I fetched out of his armoury at Mechlin, for the which there hath been no little ado . . .' Once in London, Glajon began to get a little of his own back, joining forces with the Spanish Ambassador '. . . and there is nothing done at the Tower [Gresham wrote] . . . but the Bishop of Aquila hath good advice thereof.'

One evening the chief searcher of Antwerp came to warn Sir Thomas that a strange Englishman had just been at the Customs, demanding a search of all ships; if made immediately, the Englishman asserted—and he was quite right—it would uncover 'a great booty' ready freighted for the Thames. A meeting of all the customs officers was convened for early morning. Gresham was on tenterhooks all night, but next day he could write that the searchers had decided against an investigation, considering 'how beneficial' Sir Thomas had always been to them; and at ten o'clock a convoy loaded with seven 'pieces of velvet' and 'forty ells of crimson velvet' sailed unimpeded down the Scheldt. Another cargo of arms was appointed to leave on the night-tide, but the wind came about and the ships could not set forth. If searched now, their cargo would be discovered and 'the parties that shipped this gear for me must flee the country'. No search was made, however, and a week later a fresh batch of 'velvets, crimson velvets, black damasks, and crimson satins' got safe to London, there to be stored, distributed among the shires, or hastened north to the English soldiers besieging Leith. 'Well fares that penny given that saves one hundred,' Gresham once wrote, and it is a law more typical of him than the academic one that bears his name. During those critical months, licence or no licence, he sent Elizabeth munitions worth over £100,000.

*

Finally, Challoner and Gresham had to observe the movements of the Spaniards. The King of Spain had remained in the Low Countries longer than he had either intended or desired. Heresy, emerging even in Valladolid, demanded his return home; and he had his great palace to build in honour of St. Lorenzo, on whose day he had fought the battle of St. Quentin. Meanwhile money had to be raised somehow for his journey. In 1554 his father's cash deficit in Spain had been estimated at 4·3 million ducats, and arrears of debt were increasing at 2 million a year (twice the country's normal gross revenue at the beginning of his reign).[33] Credit was costing 43 per cent. All receipts for six years ahead had been pledged and the money spent in advance. In 1557 Philip had suspended all payments to his

creditors. The Flemings were restive, almost insubordinate; there
was that powder-keg in Scotland, and Elizabeth behaving in so
provocative and ungrateful a manner. Philip's advisers thought he
ought to stay in the North, so long as hope lasted of his presence
having some effect. It was not until August 27, 1559 that he set sail,
never personally to return; and all along the English Channel coast,
crews, garrisons and dignitaries had stood by to greet him with due
ceremony, should storms compel him into port.

Sir Thomas Challoner remained at the Court in Brussels. He
would rather have been in Antwerp. In Brussels everything was
formality and ceremony and the Court kept its counsel close. Still,
he had people to watch, and men with whom to watch them. The
Count of Feria, once Ambassador to Mary and a favourite of Philip's,
had stayed behind while his adored English bride recovered from a
difficult childbirth. Their house became a natural haven for refugees.
'Full of spies', somebody called it. The Catholic trek out of England
was beginning as the Protestants wound homeward, and in this new
emigration were hidden the seeds of new conspiracies.

Sir Thomas Challoner was a great believer in spies and pined at
Elizabeth's reluctance to support them. What about a man in France,
in the suite of the Venetian Ambassador? She could have someone
he knew for two hundred ducats a year and the promise of a benefice
in England. The man would report through Antwerp; a very good
man too and 'avisours, alias spies, look to be well feed'. Challoner
suggested a year on probation, but we hear no more. His first interview with Cardinal Granvelle was a model of precise and stately
skirmishing, at which not a tone, not a gesture, must be lost.
Delicately Challoner let it be understood that he knew more than he
chose to say, from his correspondents at home 'and elsewhere'. The
Bishop could improve on that. 'I also, quod he, for my part have had
sundry advices . . . both from my brother in France and owte of
Allemaigne (as in dede, for myne owne satisfaction . . . I enterteigne
of myne own purse some such abroad as weekly write me newes)', and
he pointed to a letter on his desk.

When Challoner returned to his lodging and sat down to compose
his dispatch, the interview began to rankle. He too paid correspondents out of his own pocket; but he was not wealthy and obviously
the Cardinal's was much deeper. 'Who ever heard of an Ambassador
allowed no special money?' he demanded in his first draft. '. . . I
have heard say it cost Cardinal Pole, for such manner of folks to

write to him from all parts, above 3,000 ducats a year. And to say truth, without sure and manifest advertisement, a Prince is destitute of the remedy in time against secret practises.' This message of Challoner's is criss-crossed with amendments. Perhaps he remembered that Elizabeth had detested Pole even more than she did John Knox; in his final draft he did not mention the late Cardinal and toned down his protest.

A little later he called on Feria. The Count knew every English personage of importance from the Queen downwards. From his familiarity with her Court, especially her ladies-in-waiting, had once come a report out of which pages of speculation have sprung: 'If my spies are not lying, which I do not believe,' he had written to Philip, 'I understand she will not have children.' Feria gave Challoner a banquet, sent for his luggage, put him up for the night, and opened his mind, revealing towards Elizabeth that blend of outraged anxiety with scandalized and uncomprehending disdain that characterizes the dispatches of all the Spanish Ambassadors who ever met her, and in Mendoza was finally submerged beneath passionate disgust. What did she think she was doing? His master, and he himself, had protected her during her sister's reign, but she could not expect protection to continue if she persisted in provoking France in Scotland. 'Is Arran's or Throckmorton's persuasions worth such an adventure?' She was a heretic, the country was not behind her, she had no arms, no money, no husband, and . . . but Challoner forbore to repeat what Feria had to say about Lord Robert Dudley. The report he sent Elizabeth of this interview left her, according to the Bishop of Aquila in London, *'assumbrado'*, and the Bishop so rubbed it in that he believed she had been ill for two days.

Challoner noted, perhaps was meant to note, that Feria's household was 'a world of letters', and 'in a princely order'. It was also frequented by two valuable informants. Both, like the Countess of Feria, were English; and both illustrate the shifts to which men may be driven, or willingly turn, when the government of their country undergoes a violent change.

The first was a certain Sir John Leigh, a Catholic patriot of considerable wealth, and uncle to Henry VIII's unfortunate Queen Catherine Howard. Much travelled and now nearing sixty, he had occupied such heights of favour under Queen Mary that so illustrious a person as a Papal envoy could only obtain an audience through him. Like many Englishmen of the old faith he had hoped

she would not marry Philip. He learnt of the project while it was still
a close secret and told the French Ambassador, who at once began
plotting to prevent it. Antoine de Noailles used him regularly afterwards, and found him the most dependable among his many sources
of intelligence.[34] Sir John's familiarity with the Queen also enabled
him to help Protestants he approved of, who might have been disgraced, or worse. Among them was Sir Thomas Gresham; Gresham
described him as 'the man that preserved me when Queen Mary
came to the crown: for the which I do account myself bound to him
during my lyfe'.

On Elizabeth's accession Leigh in his turn needed help. In the
summer of 1559 he was passing information to the Bishop of Aquila.
It was he who had (incorrectly) reported Arran to be in London by
July 1. Next day he was due to leave for Italy. By August he had
reached Antwerp, and sent a supplication to the Regent Margaret.
English enemies, he said, and English merchants especially, were on
his heels. They wanted their revenge for the orders which Mary had
given him, and he presumably had obeyed, to report on people
disaffected to her. His servants had been threatened with death and
he himself with violence, and he asked the authorities in the Netherlands to protect him.

A few months later he approached or was approached by Sir
Thomas Gresham, and in the following year sent Elizabeth a long
letter. It contained news about the Count and Countess of Feria,
with whom he had been on close terms in the old days, and about the
movements of Catholic émigrés. Most of it was no more than useful
gossip; but at the end he undertook, asking for secrecy, 'to write you
matters of more importance'. He thanked Elizabeth for her good
opinion of him, which 'I perceive by Sir Thomas', and declared
himself ready to spend his life in her service. It did not take him
long to earn his passage back to England, where in 1566 he died,
wearing on his breast the cross of St. John of Jerusalem and for-
tunate not to survive into the days when Catholicism ceased to be
merely a risk and became a major crime.

The other Englishman informing on the Feria household was
called Robert Hogan. We can read some of his life-story over the
shoulder of William Cecil's ghost. He offered intelligence to the
Secretary, not for the first time, in the autumn of 1559, from
Antwerp; the letter is sealed with Sir Thomas Challoner's seal. He
had spent many years soldiering, he wrote. Having done Mary some

service at the beginning of her reign, he had obtained a recommendation to Philip. His reward, whatever it was, so displeased him that
he took arms in the Italian wars under the Duke of Alva, returning
home in Feria's suite after the fall of Calais. After Elizabeth's
accession he had seemed so promising but questionable an agent
that the Queen herself had a talk about him with Sir Thomas
Gresham. She tended to mistrust him, as a sworn servant of the
Spaniards, but Gresham argued in his favour. Elizabeth needed
operators 'that must seem greater affectionated to them [in other
words, to Spain] than to Her Majesty, or else the perfect intelligence
. . . of Princes will not be obtained'. To Sir Thomas Parry Gresham
praised Hogan as a man of few words, who brought in all the intelligence he could lay his hands on and asked for none in return. He
ought to be paid the same pension as he had received from Philip;
otherwise he would be without a livelihood.

Hogan's first contribution had been somewhat sensational. Philip
had been warned that, if he did not soon do something to help the
English Catholics, they would turn to the King of France. Jealous
also of the ambitions in England which Henri II and the Guises were
using Mary Stuart to advance, he had secretly begun to sponsor an
English pretender of his own. This was Lady Catherine Grey,
grand-niece of Henry VIII and a younger sister to the late 'Queen
Jane'. Elizabeth could not abide her, and she had harmed her position
at Court by loud rude language in Elizabeth's hearing. Her own
family disliked her and she led a wretched life. Philip laid plans to
kidnap her. Hogan was to arrange to be attached to the Bishop of
Aquila at the Spanish Embassy (Durham House in the Strand), and
Philip would pay for a ship to await Lady Catherine in the Thames.
The plot would have failed, since Hogan passed it all on; besides,
Cecil had appointed an English gatekeeper to Durham House, who
reported every entrance and exit by the river stairs, and had also
bought the Ambassador's Italian secretary. In fact the plot never
went forward, since Henri II died and Philip felt less anxious about
François II. Gresham thought Hogan 'a very meet man to serve . . .
wise and secret and experimented in the wars, and speaks good
Italian and Spanish'.[35]

Sir John Leigh, Hogan, Gresham's agents in the customs-houses,
all joined their useful threads to Cecil's web. But none, unless by a
great stroke of luck, was likely to tell him what he most needed to
know in the spring of 1560. What would King Philip do in Scotland?

Granvelle and Feria could make it quite clear what they were all beginning to think about Elizabeth. But what, if anything, would their master do?

The likeliest clue lay in the movements of ships and soldiers. Philip still retained 3,000 (the number varies) of his best troops in the Low Countries; the 'culled choice', Sir Thomas Challoner called them. They should have gone home long ago. The Flemings clamoured to be rid of them. Why were they still there? Because of local unrest? Or were they destined for Scotland and, if so, on whose side? Or were they to be expected some misty morning in East Anglia? The Bishop of Aquila had already advised that King's Lynn would be a convenient landing-place. At the end of February 1560 Gresham was told of ships being rigged in Zeeland to take the '6,000' Spaniards aboard. He did not like it, and had the ships kept under close observation. They were rigging all right, but by the middle of April still had no munitions aboard. 'My man in Holland' reported that victuals would be provided from there, and Gresham promised Cecil to send 'perfect intelligence' from every harbour in Holland or Zeeland.

We see here the advantage the great banker then possessed, and has possessed often since, over a mere Ambassador. To transact his financial and commercial affairs Gresham had collected a little squad of highly trained subordinates, who were on close terms with skippers of ships and authorities in ports. They had mastered, like Francis Edwards in Normandy, those exact dry statistics which, removed from business routine into a great political crisis, sometimes impart far more than records of gorgeous tournaments or back-chat about royal love-affairs. Gresham knew he could trust them. They were almost part of his family.

At their head, with a roving commission, went Richard Clough, who was later knighted, made a fortune in Gresham's service, built himself two mansions in north-west Wales and married the much-married Catherine of Berain. There was Richard Payne, sited so usefully at Middleburg on Walcheren Island. There was John Waddington at Amsterdam looking over the Zuyder Zee and covering as far north as Groningen; Edward Hogan at Seville, John Gerbridge at Toledo; and John Brigantyne at Emden, reporting on the Scandinavian countries. There were couriers and forwarding agents. Gresham had made sure of his communications. (His riding and posting-charges for three and a half years ending April 1562 totalled £1,627 9s.) At Dunkirk he had Thomas Gerbrand. He obtained the coveted job of Royal Post at Calais for Francisco de Tomaso, 'so necessary a man for divers good services', and employed him and John Spritwell, the Post at Dover, for many years. Spritwell had been born at Calais and Gresham had promised him the Post there when Tomaso retired or died. Far more important than all these, Gresham had formed a close friendship with Jasper Schetz, the Flemish Treasurer-General of the King of Spain for the Low Countries.

Schetz came of an old Maestricht family. For some time he had been buying land in order to retire from business and Philip had agreed to appoint him as 'the most sufficient and qualified person' on condition he gave up business entirely. He spoke several languages and wrote verse. His three brothers, Balthasar, Melchior, and Conrad, were all like himself extremely wealthy. We have a glimpse of Melchior at a pageant, wearing a purple velvet suit embroidered with silver worth at least £300, and of Conrad outdoing him in green velvet so thick with gold and silver 'that no prynsee might be any costlyer'. Gresham had been Jasper's guest from the days when he first came to Antwerp, before he took his own house in the Langenieuwestraat, and he could safely recommend Schetz to Cecil during the Scottish crisis as 'one that favours Her Majesty's religion and her proceeding'. Schetz's daughter had in fact married a Scotsman called John Fleming.

Schetz had lent money to the English Crown as far back as 1536 and received rewards later at Gresham's request, 'for that it will serve the Queene's Majestie's turne, dyvers and sundrey wayes, more than I will molest your Lordeships withall'. His services were at first financial and made possible by his membership of the Council of Finance; Gresham wrote that he 'ruleth the whole Bourse'. In February 1560, however, we hear a slightly different note. Cecil was asked to pay Schetz 1,000 crowns; this time he had informed Gresham of the plans laid by Granvelle and Feria to prevent Elizabeth obtaining ready money. The Treasurer-General had begun to put friendship, religion and avarice before his duty.

During April the Bourse at Antwerp lost its head. The delirium, like others since in other capitals, was part induced by people interested in creating it, and part self-generated. The French had been doing their best to persuade themselves and others that the King of Spain would take their side in Scotland, and a chance

SIR THOMAS GRESHAM
AS A YOUNG MAN

SIR JAMES CROFT

occurred when M. de Glajon left Antwerp for England with Philip's instructions at the end of March. The King, he was to say, was concerned for the peace of Europe and wished to mediate. Elizabeth must be asked to withdraw her reinforcements from the Border and stop all support to the Lords of the Congregation. Philip, in order to help France extinguish the Protestant rebellion, would supply troops to bring the total force up to 4,000, all to be paid by France. If this was not enough, he would send a further 3,000. These would be paid by Spain. The French must agree not to bring in any more and refrain from threatening gestures. The King trusted that a Spanish presence in Scotland would give Elizabeth sufficient guarantee against a French invasion; but he took care not to commit himself to any action on her behalf if the French did invade, observing that she would not have become so embroiled if only she had listened to his advice.

The offer came far too late, and its disinterestedness was doubted. As soon as it became known, both French and English made propaganda of it. The French exaggerated the parts that suited them, omitting the moderating clauses, and their Ambassador in Brussels hurried off to ask Margaret of Parma how many men, ships, and arms she had ready. Meanwhile letters from the King of France to his Ambassador in London were intercepted in the Channel by pirates passing themselves off as Scottish, but in fact English, and were taken to Elizabeth. They contained a French version of Philip's proposals, and their tone so alarmed her that she assumed herself to be on the verge of war with both France and Spain. All ships and couriers in English ports were immediately detained so that a secret warning could be sent through to the English merchants in the Low Countries. Alarm in the Palace became panic on the Bourse. Cecil later disclaimed responsibility, but it is clear from Gresham's correspondence that Cecil had warned him, in a letter of April 13, which Gresham received on the 16th, that Philip might be preparing to help the French.

In the North the Duke of Norfolk expected a Spanish landing and asked if the Spaniards should be treated as friends or foes. The English merchants at Antwerp rushed to send their money home. The foreign merchants to whom the English owed debts rushed to be paid. Everyone expected all English ships in the Low Countries to be detained in retaliation, and Elizabeth's credit dropped to zero. Gresham went soothingly amongst her creditors, trying to defer instalments due to them, and used Schetz to spread tranquillizing rumours, for which he had not the slightest evidence, that Elizabeth had agreed peace terms except for one point and that her armies would be home from Scotland within a fortnight. And as head of Cecil's intelligence in the Low Countries he sent his agents spurring to the ports to discover whether or not the Spanish garrisons were on the move.

Waddington and Spritwell were in Zeeland before April 18 with orders to report the number of ships and warships, their state of preparation, 'as also vitallers, sowldyers, and ordenans'. At three in the afternoon on the 20th Spritwell galloped back with a list of seven ships and almost all Gresham needed to know about them, tonnage, names, skippers' names, everything except destination. They were victualled for three months, but so far carried little ordnance. Six of them, the largest of 1,000 tons, were to carry in all 3,300 soldiers and the chief captains would go in the seventh. They had been instructed to be ready to sail by the 22nd, but none of these soldiers had so far arrived, and Gresham sent Spritwell to keep watch.

On the 25th he received news from Amsterdam: no provision was visible there either for warships, crews, or soldiers. But on the 30th there arrived a report from Richard Payne, which Gresham sent on that day to Cecil, that an advance-party of thirteen Spaniards had taken up billets in Zeeland to prepare the soldiers' embarkation. The Regent was awaited in Antwerp to raise money to pay off 3,300 men. People said they were going back to Spain. Gresham did not believe it. It was a ruse; once at sea, they would make for Scotland. But before he had closed this letter Schetz came to see him. Schetz believed from all he had heard that the men really were going home; if not, 'it is marvellous secreat'. Gresham remained sceptical.

On May 2 Waddington arrived from Amsterdam. Certain Frenchmen had been there, 'gentilmen lyke', and had hired six ships ostensibly to fetch coals from Newcastle to Dieppe. If any soldiers came aboard, each master had been made to swear that he carried no French cargo. Their freight was masts, cables, bacon, 'gunpowder and suchlike', and they were to sail in a week by way of Texel, 'which is the waye into the mayne see, and from thence to take what waye they will, I thynck for sertayne towards Skotlande . . .' Gresham at once bought up all the powder that could be found or made until the end of June to prevent the Court at Brussels getting hold of it.

Day after day, letter after letter, Clough reported from Hamburg, Payne from Middleburg, Waddington from Holland, Friesland, Gelderland. Jasper Schetz, 'my friend that the Queens Majesty gave the chain of gold unto of 500 crowns', had managed to have Elizabeth's debts deferred until August at only 10 per cent, for which he earned a personal letter of thanks from Elizabeth and at least another 500 crowns. All the money the States Assembly had raised, Schetz declared, was for pay to send the Spaniards home. Waddington found no further preparations for war. And that, Gresham hoped, would scotch the 'vain rumour, which surely came first out of England'. All the same, a week later (June 3), when news reached him from Zeeland that the seven ships (now become eight) were ready victualled to embark the soldiers, Gresham was again not sure and warned London they might still go to Scotland.

Three weeks later the men were still in their garrisons. Jasper Schetz, now referred to by a cipher, made a special journey to Brussels at the end of June to investigate the Papal envoy's mission. Writing back to Antwerp, he hoped that Elizabeth would exploit the Guises' troubles with the Huguenots in order to do as she pleased in Scotland, and asked Gresham to burn his letter. Gresham sent it on to the Queen and humbly besought the same. On July 3 Schetz returned with emphatic information that the Spaniards would be withdrawn to Spain, once the States-General had agreed to pay their wages.

The mass of information which Gresham received from Schetz and others less powerful, coupled with his own, made possible his reiterated assertion that the Low Countries would refuse to let Philip drag them into war with England. '. . . King Philip can by no means annoy Her Majesty this year [1560], for that he is wholly unprovided of money, ships, men, as well as of all kinds of munitions and armour. . . . The Queen's Majesty is marvellously beloved of all nations [he meant, upon the Bourse], and hath here as good friends as King Philip hath any . . .' When news came of a vast cargo of gold arrived safe from America in Spain, Gresham did not worry; it would not pay Philip's debts in Antwerp. He knew the score. A year later several of the best houses in the city went bankrupt because the Kings of France, Spain and Portugal could not repay their loans. Even the Fuggers were in peril; and by 1572 the Schetz brothers were themselves driven to borrowing from Genoa at 30 per cent.

Gresham had great physical as well as mental energy. In middle age he still carried many of his own messages, braving the buffets of the North Sea and the perpetual threat of pirates, galloping to and from the ports and once taking a toss that broke his leg. Though he did not himself like strong drink, he understood its disinhibiting value. 'What cuppes of wine went round!' he wrote to Parry after a banquet at which the Germans had toasted Lord Robert Dudley, Parry himself, Cecil, and even Lady Cecil, adding virtuously that he would say no more about it, since 'it ys not so commendable in Ingland as it ys here'. Once he even made the Prince of Orange, William the Silent, drunk, and drew a valuable indiscretion out of him.

In misadventure he showed promptness and resource. During the fighting in March 1566, with a battle raging outside the walls of Antwerp, turmoil within, and 50,000 people in arms, he conveyed his report under the town-gate for an agent outside to carry to Gerbrand at Dunkirk. He pretended to stand outside politics. When Elizabeth began openly to support the Huguenots in France, Giles Hoffman the Flemish timber merchant (who had lent her money) asked if she would do the same for the Protestants in Flanders. 'I am no counseller,' Gresham replied, 'nor never dealt with such great matters.' It was quite untrue. His letters abound in political counsel and economic and financial counsel amounting to political. The same militant note rings through his immense correspondence that we hear from Sir Nicholas Throckmorton, with whom he was closely in touch. England must set up her own powder-mills, make her own munitions, extract money from her own merchants. He told Elizabeth—and made clear that she owed it to him—that her reputation in the Low Countries had never stood so high. Like Sir Nicholas, he did his best to turn the intermittent chicken in her into a permanent lioness. When he heard of an army being raised in Gelderland, he begged her to make it hers for the recovery of Boulogne and Calais, and of 'that creadit that Ingland haythe had in tymes past, and that was, that Ingland had the best men of war both by land and sea that was in all Christendome, for the wyche all prynssis fearrid England . . .'

Gresham died in 1579, the owner of many acres in several shires and a fistful of great houses. He left legacies, apart from his famous foundations, to several charities; large debts and claims, which Walsingham's brother-in-law at the Exchequer, Sir Walter Mildmay, spent months resolving; and to his litigious widow a colossal income of nearly £2,400 a year, out of which she subscribed £100 to the defeat of the Spanish Armada.[36]

ii. The Tightening of the Rings

Such was the intelligence during spring 1560 about the King of Spain's intentions. Could France then, unsupported, find the military and naval strength in time to break Admiral Winter's blockade of the Firth of Forth and land reinforcements?

The Privy Council had advised increased expenditure on spies in France. Once more the merchant Francis Edwards cantered up and down the coast of Normandy, observing, listening, counting, and reporting home to Cecil. The Marquis d'Elbeuf had not been drowned; on the contrary he had come safe home and was actually lodged in Edwards's house in Dieppe, making preparations to set out again. The spy posed as a French sympathizer and passed him titbits of information which Cecil authorized. He sent his own secrets in a curious doggerel and a code which seems to us today transparent, translating the warlike plans of the French (like Gresham) into the vocabulary of commerce. Soldiers became 'lively merchandise', but the King of France was 'the clouds', and Elizabeth 'the laurel-tree'.

On March 4 he reported that a letter from Marie de Guise to d'Elbeuf had been intercepted. The news from Scotland had so agitated the 'Chief Justice' (the Cardinal of Lorraine) that he rose from supper and called for 'fruit' (probably also soldiers) and was handed 'apples ribalds' (Jean Ribault) and a 'pomme rosse' (Captain John Ross). The French merchants all opposed the Cardinal's policy of war and wished him bound like a bear at the stake 'with all the dogs of Paris Garden on his back'. Edwards could obtain no certain date for the Scottish expedition. 'The partners cannot get their merchandise together . . . and may discharge part'; everything pointed to indefinite postponement.

Sir Nicholas Throckmorton returned to France at the end of January. The Court was still on the Loire, refreshing itself with balls and fêtes and water-pageants at beautiful Chenonceaux. Warning reached him that he and his retinue were about to be 'sequestered', in which event he would have no means left of communicating with London except through the dubious graces of the Spanish Ambassador, de Chantonnay, who was Cardinal Granvelle's brother. War might break out at any moment; he asked that on the day the English crossed into Scotland and attacked the French, all ships in English ports might be stayed except the one bearing the Queen's courier, so that he would receive the news exclusively and in time.

A month passed before the Cardinal could find leisure to receive him. His retinue's acquaintances 'utterly estranged themselves'; people who had been used to entertain them shrank away and even refused to return their greetings. After the Huguenot rising at Amboise in March the woods were no longer safe for hunting, the château courtyard became a bloody scaffold, the walls the gallows for scores of captured insurgents, and Court turned into camp. The Duke de Guise, who had narrowly escaped assassination, compelled the young King and Queen to witness several days of executions, and in Madrid the French Ambassador did his utmost to convince the Spaniards that the rising had formed part of a plot, with its roots in England, to Protestantize the whole of Europe. The Venetian Ambassador, like many French historians since, was inclined to accept this view and thought it the greatest conspiracy that had ever been known.

Isolated and highly nervous for his own safety, Sir Nicholas also worried about security at home. Somebody told him that one of Cecil's cipher-clerks was a French spy. He wanted to know how a certain John Combes, against whom he had warned the Council, had heard of the warning a short time afterwards; and he besought the Queen to keep to herself the private intelligence he received from de Chantonnay, to whom, by means unknown, it was coming back from London. 'Nothing can more serve France than to have intelligence from Scotland', and the amount that still reached the French dismayed him. On the very eve of the invasion a captain managed to travel straight through England with details of Lord Grey's dispositions. Messengers slipped through by way of Flanders, by way of Cornwall, by fishing boat from Dunbar, and returned through Flanders to Montrose, Dundee, even as far north as Aberdeen. Couriers disguised as scholars or merchants had arrived even by way of Dover; were the watchers all asleep?

At the end of April a certain Battista de Favori came to see the Ambassador at Amboise. The Guises were sending him through England to beleaguered Leith, but he was willing to serve Elizabeth, to whom he had 'certain weighty matters to impart'. He must speak to her in private and urgently, he said, since the weighty matters included a list of French spies in her service at Court, and news of a 'pestilent and horrible device'. The Guises had lately sent to Germany another Italian, called Stephano, 'a burly man with a black beard, about forty-five years old'; from Germany he was to travel to London, offer the Queen his services as an engineer, and poison her. Not a gullible man, and used to all the tricks, Sir Nicholas inclined to believe Favori's story. He gave him thirty crowns, trusted him with a letter, and recommended that Cecil should add another hundred crowns on his return from Leith; Cecil, who must see him alone, would soon be able to judge his value as a spy. Cecil did not think much of him. But one item the Italian did let fall, which was almost certainly correct: the Guise network in London included the Bishop of Aquila, who sent the French Ambassador's mail with his own by way of Flanders—and the French Embassy now had a dangerous new occupant.

In February the Guises withdrew Gilles de Noailles and put in his place the Chevalier de Seurre, a creature of their own, trained in at least six capitals. 'The enchanter is come to the land,' wrote Sir Nicholas, '. . . a select vessel, to be employed in such a time as this is, to be a maker of a dissembled friendship and a soon broken peace.' In March there followed as a special envoy the rusé old Jean de Monluc, Bishop of Valence, sent via London to Scotland ostensibly to negotiate a treaty, with promises to withdraw French troops and pardon the rebel lords. Throckmorton knew him of old; years ago James Melville had attended Monluc as a page on a secret mission to subvert the Irish. Elizabeth attached the dogged and prosaic Henry Killigrew to him, officially as escort, in fact as spy. 'Believe nothing that shall be said unto you by any of these Ministers,' Throckmorton begged the Queen. Spied on as much as spying, surrounded by fear, rumour, French anger at setbacks and gloatings over success, he began even to wonder if the Queen and Cecil intended him to become so discredited in France that he would never again be accepted for a post abroad, and his career be ruined. In May he was so sick and weak he could 'scarcely creep off my bed', and renewed his plea to be recalled.

*

While the Guises drew one ring ever tighter round Sir Nicholas, in Scotland the other had been closing round their sister.

In December they had dispatched to her the young Sieur de la

Marque, officially to ascertain the state of her health, but also with other instructions so important, Throckmorton informed Cecil, that nothing would be done in France until de la Marque had returned. De Noailles arranged an audience for him with Elizabeth on his way through London. This time she received the two Frenchmen during a ball in the Presence Chamber. She gave them her usual cheerful denials and evasions and made light of the Dowager's illness; the poor woman had so many worries, she said, one could not wonder that her family inquired about her health. However, she issued orders that de la Marque should receive a passport to go to Scotland and return, and off he went.

Horsemen coming from the direction of Berwick surrounded him just after he had crossed the Scottish Border and compelled him to ride to Dumbarton. Although no state of war yet existed, he was treated as a prisoner. Thomas Randolph, who had met him in France, thought it prudent to remain in the background while the Congregation cross-questioned him. He gave offence by keeping his hat on and staring idly at the walls during a Calvinist service; but no papers were found on the fashionable and bewildered youth other than some 'very Papistical' books of religion, some love stories 'to recreate his spirits', and the prophecies of Nostradamus. Later Randolph intervened and, posing as a Scot, managed to draw him into some lighthearted conversation; but unfortunately the Earl of Arran entered and called Randolph by his correct name, whereupon de la Marque appeared to recollect something he had heard about Randolph in Paris and closed up. Nothing more could be got out of him; but he was kept where he was, despite angry protests from Marie de Guise, and whatever verbal instructions he might have been carrying never reached her.

Another of her envoys suffered a fate even more unfortunate for her. In London William Cecil discovered that one of two Livingstones who had travelled south with James Melville carried information about the help Elizabeth had given to the Earl of Arran (it was in that packet which d'Oysel had twice reopened), and was taking it back to France. Cecil warned Sir Nicholas, who kept his ears and eyes open accordingly.

In February the Ambassador advised Cecil that Livingstone would soon be returning to Marie de Guise by way of London; he had been instructed to pose as yet another Scot dissatisfied with the French, and secretly to convey alluring offers to the Earl of Arran, if only

Arran would return to France. At all costs, Sir Nicholas wrote, Livingstone must be stopped. Cecil passed on the tip to the Duke of Norfolk, and when Livingstone reached Newcastle he was told he could not proceed. He handed over a letter in cipher to another Scotsman, who carried it north not to Marie, for whom it was intended, but to Lord James Stuart on the other side. No one in Scotland could decipher it. It was returned to London, where again nobody knew the code. Cecil sent it to the Paris Embassy, where John Somer, formerly confidential secretary to Dean Wotton and now working with Throckmorton, managed to penetrate it. It turned out to be a letter written from Vendôme on February 19 by the Duke and Cardinal to their sister. Throckmorton reciphered it into English and sent it back to Cecil.

It revealed the fact that, when the French protested to Elizabeth that they sent troops to Scotland with no aim except to defeat a rebellion, and sincerely desired peace with her, they used these phrases merely 'to amuse' her and keep her from becoming suspicious. They were not in the least disarmed by her pretences, and continued the diplomatic charade merely in order to gain time. It was of great help to Cecil, poring over this twice ciphered and twice deciphered piece of parchment, even though he did not have it till April 6, to learn Marie's instructions. They were: so long as things went badly, to offer the rebel Lords a pardon; express her willingness to withdraw all French troops; and put it about that Elizabeth did not seriously intend to help. The letter also invited her to send M. de la Brosse with news of the way things stood at Leith; and it had been deciphered in time for Cecil to stop his passport.

Another letter from her brothers, sent a month later by way of Flanders, fell into English hands. It contained an assertion that Philip sided with France and had promised King François 'as many vessels, men, and victuals as he wishes'. At the moment, with the eastern approaches blockaded, the Guises did not dare risk dispatching money to their sister; in the previous letter they had already asked if they might safely send by the western route to Dumbarton. A week later the English acquired a whole package of replies to the Cardinal and Duke. From these they learnt which western route Marie suggested; also, that the garrison at Leith had victuals left for two and a half months; also, that of the powder sent in the autumn only a third remained.

Marie had to endure one specially exasperating exposure. One of her agents had managed to acquire two blanks sealed by the Duke of Châtellerault, who had declared for the Congregation soon after his son Arran arrived home. At the end of January Marie had the far from new idea of filling in one blank with a letter to her daughter and François II, in which the Duke appeared voluntarily to ask pardon for past crimes against them in Scotland, offered his submission, and promised to send his children back to France as hostages. It had been Marie's intention that this missive should be shown to Elizabeth either secretly by M. de Candalle, one of the French hostages for the Treaty, who got on well with her, or by de Noailles, but that nothing official should be made of it.

Unfortunately de Noailles was withdrawn about this time and de Seurre, unprimed, chose to boast openly to Elizabeth of the Duke's 'repentance'. The Duke had changed sides so many times that she immediately ordered Norfolk at Newcastle and Randolph in Scotland to investigate, and demanded that the Hamilton children left in Scotland should be sent to London. Outraged, Châtellerault sent de Seurre a denial and challenged him; the least of the Hamiltons was his equal in rank and only waited for him to put aside his diplomatic status to fight him. 'The Ambassador has very evil understood the blank,' Marie had to confess to her brothers. 'Having sought every means to reduce the Duke,' and seeing that he was about to come to terms with Elizabeth, 'in order to bring him into suspicion, the said blank was sent and a letter filled up, whereof the said Duke has no manner of knowledge . . .' Equally unfortunately, this confession was also intercepted; thus her ruse not only failed, but became known to both Scots and English, the Duke of Châtellerault was absolved, and the Hamilton children stayed where they were.[37]

At the end of March Marie shut herself into Edinburgh Castle with a small entourage of faithfuls, while two miles away d'Oysel and the remnant of the French army hung on to Leith. As the stranglehold tightened, the English intercepted more and more of her messages and at the end of April one courier of d'Oysel's reported that he dared not risk bringing in the mail at all. Sir Nicholas Throckmorton had broken into most of the channels from Paris. At the beginning of April he wrote to Cecil that a monk from Newbottle called Harvey would soon be on his way from France, with a 'changed coat', speaking ill of the French and cordially of the English, and bearing letters 'good for the Queen's service' and money for Marie hidden 'in the thigh of his hose'. During

Passion Week, while the Cardinal of Lorraine preached to large congregations in his Abbey of Marmoutier near Tours, his splendid diction and vivid gestures arousing enormous admiration, Sir Nicholas was busy uncovering a line of secret communication between the Cardinal and Edinburgh Castle. The Guises had fitted out a small boat and put it in charge of somebody described as a 'cannonier', to whom François II had paid 1,500 crowns for the voyage from Scotland and back again. On April 12, Sir Nicholas wrote to Cecil that the cannonier had arrived with letters of the highest importance. Security at Amboise had become so strict that he had failed to obtain a sight of them; however, 'by great practise . . . and at some charge to the Queen', he managed to lay his hands on the ciphered reply from the Cardinal and Duke. Invaluable Mr. Somer deciphered it. It was only three days old and contained two precious statements: the first that the French Armada would not now be ready until the end of July; the second, a reiteration which Sir Nicholas advised Cecil not to believe, that Philip would come to Marie's aid, indeed was now the only hope the French had left.

The filching of this reply seemed at first to be a coup for the Ambassador; but not many days passed before it caused him great worry and his staff began to suffer. It had been handed over by one of the Cockburns, known in France as Beaumont, a gentleman archer of the King's Guard enjoying a French salary and estate, whose wife was a lady-in-waiting to Mary Stuart. Cockburn had instructions to ride to Dieppe with it; either Harvey, the Newbottle monk, or David Hume, a servant of the wavering Lord Home, would take it on across the Channel and so to Scotland. Cockburn let it out of his hands for two hours, long enough for John Somer not only to decipher it, but 'cunningly to make it up again'. Handing it back, Sir Nicholas pretended that, since the letter was in cipher, he could make no use of it.

About the same time he learnt that one of his couriers had been attacked on the coast and killed. He asked for Cockburn's influence at Dieppe to obtain shipping for another of his servants, Stephen Davis, so that Davis could cross in the company of Hume and Harvey; Davis was carrying a packet addressed in French to Queen Elizabeth. To the Ambassador's horror Cockburn-Beaumont handed the deciphered reply not to Hume or Harvey, but to Davis, and Davis was refused a ship. Thoroughly alarmed, the English courier started off towards Boulogne; but at Rue the French Governor arrested him, seized all he carried, and threw him into prison. Thence Davis sent Sir Nicholas a message that he was being so badly treated, he would probably die.

The reply now began to look like a plant. Sir Nicholas dispatched John Somer to the Cardinal with a protest. He was to demand the immediate return of Davis and his mail, so that it could be re-directed to the Queen with another courier. The Cardinal received Somer with 'countenance and gestures . . . so demure and grave, mixed with a kind of pitiful plaint, that they would have persuaded a man that did not well know him . . .' He wanted the courier's name. He could not bring him back, he said, since he was already so far upon his journey. He pretended ignorance that the mail had been addressed to the Queen. The courier had been seized, because he had been travelling off his route in the company of heretics involved in the insurrection at Amboise, and had also been spying on the fortifications at Rue; however, he would now be allowed to continue. The Cardinal reminded Sir Nicholas that some French mail had lately been violently purloined in Dover harbour, and a Frenchman killed.

Open war on couriers would render diplomacy impossible. Sir Nicholas warned the Cardinal that the Queen might retaliate. Suddenly he heard that Cockburn, who had said he was going no further than Dieppe, had arrived in London. It became imperative to test the man's honesty and, if possible, to use him. Throckmorton asked Cecil to have him watched, keep him from the French Ambassador, and give him a hundred crowns on top of the 'charge to the Queen' he had already received. Sir Nicholas also sent a transcript of the vital letter, suggesting that Cockburn should be sent on with it to Leith, where Lord Grey must 'wink at' his passage through the lines. He must be allowed to see Marie or d'Oysel, and Cecil must instruct him what news he could betray to give his story colour. To any French queries about the condition of the letter, Cockburn should reply that he had had to cut away all superfluous paper to conceal it. With any luck he would return with full information about the state of Leith.

Had Beaumont been cheating Sir Nicholas? On June 10 he was at Dieppe. On the 22nd he turned up in Antwerp in the suite of the French Ambassador. At eight o'clock in the morning he went to see Sir Thomas Gresham and gave him the names of two French agents in the town. His master, he added, had come there 'to practisse wythe some Schottyshe man' to take the Earl of Arran a message

from the King of France; all Frenchmen would be withdrawn from
Scotland, and the whole government of the country handed over to
Arran, if he would only agree to cease all dealings with Elizabeth.
Gresham appears to have known 'Mr. Bewmownte', for in reporting
the visit he wrote of him as a friend of Henry Killigrew, recommended
to him by Cecil; he also forwarded a letter to Sir Thomas Parry from
Beaumont's wife, lady-in-waiting to the Queen of Scots. So Beau-
mont-Cockburn and family were well-connected in London, to say
the least.

All in all, Throckmorton could be proud of his work. He recommended John Somer to the Queen and Cecil, and also his secretary
Mr. Jones, for their 'great and continual pains'. The deciphering of
the Guises' letters had been 'the crabbedest piece of work I ever
saw'. During his visit to London the Queen had given him licence to
speak his mind. He continued to speak it from France, over and over
again, and on the same note: 'strike while the iron is hot.' His own
intelligence from the ports and elsewhere confirmed that of Francis
Edwards and the Guises' letters; the French were not yet ready and
every conciliatory move was made only to gain time.

Failing both immediate reinforcements and Spanish support,
what hope then had Marie finally left but treachery in the English
camp? An extremely highly placed personage had indeed come
under grave suspicion. The case offers an example of the mist that
hangs about so much of espionage, obscuring the difference between
the spy and the man who is merely well-intentioned. Motive is so
easily misinterpreted, and in making up our minds about a man
accused, we must bear in mind the character and motives of the witnesses. Sir James Croft's first of a succession of accusers, that continued until his death, was his Commander-in-Chief along the Border;
and it is just possible that Thomas Howard, 4th Duke of Norfolk, had
an axe to grind.

iii. Sir James Croft: an Enigma?

Throughout its course the 16th century had continued to point the
Howards to glory or the block, or both. Two cousins of Thomas,
Catherine Howard and Anne Boleyn, had been Queens of Henry
VIII and lost their heads. His father, the poet Earl of Surrey, had
dared to quarter the royal arms and been beheaded, and only Henry's
death had saved his grandfather. The family had been attainted and

their possessions confiscated, and in February 1547 his mother had
led a melancholy procession out of the great house at Kenninghall.[38]
The Norfolk store of salted fish had had to be surrendered to the
royal household, but 'one hundred cod and three ling were charitably reserved for the Countesse of Surrey', as well as her imprisoned
father-in-law's 'night gowne of black satten . . . much worne and
furrid with conny and lambe . . . to put about [her] in her charet'.[38]
She took with her to a temporary refuge at Mr. Gawdy's house at
Shottesham four children, of whom Thomas had been one, then aged
eleven. Such a winter seemed, according to the violent political
meteorology of the age, to qualify some Howard sooner or later for a
summer. Mary Tudor reversed the attainder and the family returned
home. The fourth Duke now hoped that under Elizabeth the solstice
would be his.

He was twenty-four years old, suffered from rheumatism, and was
ambitious but not particularly bright. He was the last Duke decapi-
tation had left in England, the natural leader of the old nobility, had
power in the north and east, and passed for Protestant. He had not
wanted command on the Border, which the Privy Council now
offered him. His second wife had just died, and the Queen might
marry him. If not, he was closely in touch with the Spanish Ambassador and shared his belief that her problems could all be solved by
marriage with Philip's Catholic cousin, the Archduke Charles of
Austria. The Archduke's outsize head could be ignored and concessions made to his religion, and the Queen would then have Spain
and the Empire as her friends, and France think many times before
attacking her.

There was another powerful argument against going North, and it
was not rheumatism. If he went, he would leave Lord Robert
Dudley behind, and Lord Robert was a rival for the Queen. Twin
stars of her first Court, one by birth, the other by physical attraction,
the two young men detested one another and lately had almost come
to blows. Having agreed to take the Border command, the Duke
knew he must return with laurels. He was conscious of his inex-
perience. Edward Randolph, returning from Berwick in March,
informed the Bishop of Aquila that there were not three English
captains fit to command 200 foot, and the Bishop commented to
Philip, 'I do not think the Duke of Norfolk is among them.' Norfolk
wanted no followers of Dudley's near him to tell tales. Sir James
Croft, at that time, was one.[39]

At first Norfolk reported politely on Sir James's services, but occasions soon arose for censure. Nobody liked to answer for Berwick. He allowed that the most that could have been done with the means available had been done, but denied credit to Sir James. He considered that in their present unfinished state the fortifications would be less help than hindrance, and as for the garrison, the Queen had been so robbed by cheating on the muster-rolls that she would lose less by assuming twenty dead men's pay in every hundred than by letting things continue as they were. 'To be plain with you, I think there is not one Captaine of Berwicke . . . but that doth rather serve for gaine than for any good Will of Service.' He contrived to exonerate Sir James Croft in words that indirectly damned him: 'I thinke hym rather deceaved than otherwise; for he, being a very Wise Mann . . . would (as I suppose) wishe, that the Captains had rather more than less.' The faint praise was not lost on the Privy Council, and Sir James received a reprimand.

Part of the truth was that the 16th-century revolution in the science of warfare had rendered the defences of the fortress obsolete. Cecil sent up an Italian Protestant exile and engineer, Jacopo Aconcio, whom he had coaxed to England, and Aconcio found much to criticize. The new mobile cannon familiar to him on the Continent could hurl flat-trajectory missiles which soon crumbled the curtain walls of the Middle Ages. Modern European defence consisted in jutting arrow-headed bastions set at intervals, from which an enemy attacking the curtain wall between them could be raked and decimated. A start had been made with them at Berwick in Queen Mary's reign, but who would take responsibility for completion? The cost would be enormous and any day, in the middle of the work, the French might attack.

Norfolk could not get a firm opinion out of Croft and asked the Council for an arbitrator. Elizabeth did not 'disallow the circumspect answer of Sir James'. Six years previously another of his circumspect answers had possibly saved her life; but the Council did not think much of it, expressed confidence in the Duke, and promised to send him Sir Richard Lee, the foremost English engineer of the day, who had been absent fortifying Portsmouth. Thus they wrote on February 20.

The previous day Lord Grey had announced that he must have a second-in-command to take over in Scotland, should anything happen to himself. He nominated Croft. Cecil approved. The news struck horror into Croft. Something was highly likely to happen to Lord Grey, who had exhibited a spectacular penchant for risk and injurious heroism wherever he went. At the battle of Pinkie a pike had slashed his cheek, knocking out several of his teeth and piercing the roof of his mouth. At Guisnes in the Pale of Calais, limping with a wounded foot across mounds of corpses, he had taken the Duke de Guise a refusal to sign any surrender that did not permit his soldiers to march out with colours flying. His soldiers decided to surrender, colours flying or no, 'since they for his vainglory would not sell their lives'. Taken prisoner, he had been kept by the Count de la Roche-foucauld in a turret eighty-seven steps up, guarded day and night within and without, and had had to sell his castle at Wilton on the Wye to pay his ransom. This grim fire-eating Reformer was now returning to attack the Lowlands, which he had already once laid waste, with revenge for defeat, disgrace and ransom burning beneath his armour; and when d'Oysel and his captains in Leith heard who was on the march against them, they resolved that if yield they must it would not be to Lord Grey.

Sir James Croft was not of this mettle. At first he could not think Lord Grey serious. The appointment was all too sudden; he would have no time 'to furnish himself'. He was poor, an expedition into Scotland would ruin him. He compared himself to an overburdened horse. The Council assured him that the brusque translation implied no doubts about his patriotism. Elizabeth wrote personally to her old friend; the notice was short, she recognized, but go he must, and the Duke must make him a suitable allowance. Lord Grey and his army entered Scotland at the end of March, and Sir James had no alternative but to accompany them, out of Norfolk's way, but into worse trouble.

The military invasion of Scotland, unlike Admiral Winter's naval expedition, was an act which not even Elizabeth could represent as other than it was. No royal mummery of surprise or anger, no histrionic coquetries in the Presence Chamber, could persuade the Bishop of Aquila or de Noailles or de Seurre that Lord Grey had moved 6,000 troops across the Border merely to satisfy a personal caprice. Elizabeth began therefore to belittle their importance, turned from hawk into dove, and talked about a settlement by negotiation. It had not yet fully dawned on all her servants that they had exchanged a female fanatic on the throne for a female Janus, and the old distrust, that she had never seriously intended to help the Scots, revived.

Lord Grey found in his instructions 'such contrary matter as I know not which way to turn'.

Indignation centred on Sir James Croft, summoned to a parley with Marie de Guise almost before a blow had been struck. He took Sir George Howard with him. They were not a pair likely to allay suspicion of an arrangement. Only six years ago Croft had been conspiring hand-in-glove with d'Oysel. Knox had always thought him lukewarm in the cause, and Howard had once been a page to the Duke de Guise. Since Lord Erskine, Governor of Edinburgh Castle, was trying to preserve a difficult neutrality and would allow neither French nor English inside, the talks took place with the dying Dowager on the ramparts of the Spur and Croft and Howard standing underneath. Knox felt sure she had bewitched them. Maitland wrote to Cecil that 'the whole nation mislikes it'; if the English were now to pull back, he wished he had never had anything to do with the whole affair. The talks came to nothing, Elizabeth issued reassuring explanations, and the dust settled; but some of it was left sticking to Sir James.

His own attitude appears from a letter he wrote Cecil on April 24. He was by now at siege headquarters in the priory of Restalrig between Edinburgh and Leith. The Scots, he said, were insisting on too much, and would use the Queen's money to promote their private feuds. Ignoring the Treaty lately signed at Berwick between Queen and Congregation, and the Scottish hostages already on their way to London, he accused the Scots of continuing to fight only in order to make Elizabeth marry their Earl of Arran and share the throne of England with him; when the war was over, that would remain their only pledge of friendship. Report after report from the militants Thomas Randolph and Henry Killigrew contradicted this opinion, which Norfolk sent on with a copy of his own reply, acid with comment on the defeatism of its author, a man 'so desperate that nothing proceedeth'. To Croft he began to hint at cowardice. It was high time the second-in-command left the shelter of Restalrig and presented himself in the tents and trenches, which by the end of April had been dug close under the very walls of Leith.

*

Marie de Guise had become almost a prisoner in the Castle. Knowing now that her letter from home of February 19 had been intercepted, she sent d'Oysel in Leith a summary of everything she had written to him since the English invasion. Intercepted, this too went the usual way to John Somer to be deciphered. It gave away that someone in the English camp was keeping her well posted; well enough, indeed, to advise d'Oysel that Lord Grey hoped to make the final assault at daybreak on Tuesday or Wednesday, May 6 or 7. It began at 3 a.m. on May 7.

Over 3,000 men were detailed to attack the fortress on the landward side, and another 3,600 to make a breach seaward, of whom 900 were under the command of Croft. No breach was made, and the assault became a fiasco. The English lost over 1,000 dead and wounded and met with such hostility on their retreat to Edinburgh that the wounded were left dying in the streets. They were out of powder, men were 'stealing away in heaps', and Sir Ralph Sadler dreaded a counter-attack.

From the maze of recriminations and counter-recriminations and reports to London emerged an order to Norfolk from the Queen. Croft was to be brought back to Berwick under pretence of being put in charge again. Once there he must be sent on to Court, while Sir Peter Carew investigated and reported back from Leith. Marie de Guise, her spirits renewed by this disaster for the English, consented to receive the Lords of the Congregation and even William Maitland, officially to negotiate, but in her private mind hoping for a delay during which she could restore communications with d'Oysel. The Lords had requested audience with this Regent they had deposed, so that if by some unlucky chance the war went against them, she might not later be able to accuse them of ill-will. But since they again demanded withdrawal of all French from Scotland, and she again refused, these talks also came to nothing.

In her account to d'Oysel, intercepted as usual, Marie wrote that she was acting as her own doctor and surgeon. She gave him detailed information of the mines the English were digging under the walls of Leith and warned him that he could expect no help from France until July. If he was in grave danger, she would go on working for delay. She had sent Bothwell with an 'ample dispatch' to France, and another by a Mr. Wilson, who had just returned. 'For the love of God,' exclaimed Throckmorton, as these missives landed in his net at Blois, 'provide by one means or another that the Queen Dowager were rid from thence, for she . . . hath the heart of a man of war.'

Cecil now decided that the moment had ripened to negotiate a favourable peace, and set out north with Dean Wotton. The news came as a relief to the Duke of Norfolk. Now there would be no 'dilatorye handling'. Now he would be able to inform Mr. Secretary, verbally and in private, of 'those Cases . . . which had not been untold, if wishing could have furthered my desire'. Sir James Croft had been sent for and 'I shalbe hable to shewe you Things touching him, which peradventure will cause the Quene's Majestie hereafter to take a vigilant Care, howe she trusteth . . .'

Croft was not included among the Commissioners appointed to negotiate the peace. Of the northern officials only Sadler and Sir Henry Percy were to join Cecil, Wotton, and Sir Peter Carew from the south. Elizabeth feared that Croft might 'attempt some dangerous enterprise'. Might it not be better, she asked Cecil, to include him? Twice more she asked urgently for his opinion about Croft. Cecil would not commit himself until he had heard the facts, but Norfolk took the bull by the horns and wrote to her direct: 'the abomynable Robberie of your Garrison of Barwycke hath infected your Country Bandes [troops levied in southern counties for the Scottish war]. And your Garrison was first encouraged to robberye by the unsatiable pillinge and pollinge of your Capten Sir James Croffts, who has used himself so suspiciouslye in this your Majestie's last Servyes . . . I durst doo non other . . . but delyver hym your Lettres, for his repayring to the Courte: whose disordynatt Doings, if they may skape unpunysshable, lett your Majestie ever thinke heereafter rather to be worse served, than better.'

With Cecil within three days' ride of Berwick, Norfolk promised him strange stories. Sir James would pass him on his way to Court to answer for himself, '. . . the Bell-Wether of all myschyff . . . whose Companye I am sure you cannot mysse, an if it were for half a score Myles . . . I never had so much adoo, as to use Temperaunce with hym; He saw I did no way like his Doings, nor greatly his Companye; and yet I could never be rydd of his inquysytiff Hed.'

Cecil had reached Berwick by June 8. Early the same morning the Duke of Châtellerault, Lord James Stuart and others of the Lords went to Edinburgh Castle to take their leave of Marie de Guise, whom they had alternately served and fought so long. Her tongue and wits were failing fast, her lips, hands, and legs very cold. She never learnt the instructions of the new French envoys, which would have told her that French help must now be postponed till August. Some nameless person with her sent a suggestion to d'Oysel that, since the English had his cipher, he should use it to write a favourable but false account of the state of Leith, which would be intercepted. The true state he was to indicate by fires: near St. Antony's Church, if he had provisions to last till July 15; near the Citadel, if till the end of the month; near both places, if between those dates; and three fires, if he was desperate. The suggestion was intercepted and, if fires were ever lit, Marie de Guise never saw them. She died between midnight and one o'clock on June 11.

Sir James Croft had reached London the day before and Elizabeth was 'making fair weather' with him. By the 15th Cecil had seen Norfolk and formed conclusions. 'The old Captains had been guilty of abominable robberies.' Their bands were not merely half, but three-quarters short, and their venal example had indeed spread to the raw reinforcements from the south. 'It hath bene no small Fault of Sir James Croft . . . both to gyve Example and to nourrish them therein . . . whereof I am sorry.' Sir Peter Carew confirmed that Sir James had failed to make a breach wide enough for an assault, that his men's ladders had been too short, their covering fire inadequate, and their instructions so vague that they had never even approached what breach there was. Carew also discovered from the accounts that, although the Queen was being charged with pay for 8,813 foot soldiers, the total of live men on parade could not in fact exceed 4,500, 'wherebi I gather that your Majestie is marvelousli robbed'.

For the next three weeks the leaders on all three sides occupied themselves with the bluff, counter-bluff and steely courtesies of the peace talks. At the last moment Elizabeth tried to have restitution of Calais slipped in as a condition, but her letter luckily arrived too late. Norfolk heard rumours that Maitland and some of the Lords had pleaded for Sir James and even that he might be back in Berwick soon; if this were true, the Duke promised himself never to make such hasty judgments again, since no one in his view 'could have gone nearer a traitor and missed than Sir James'. But Sir James did not come back; whatever influence he had tried to muster with Elizabeth or Lord Robert had not availed. Norfolk presented a fresh catalogue of accusations, and Sir Henry Percy remembered an affair a little while ago of a French ship wrecked off the Northumbrian coast. Thomas Clavering of Norham had been accused of looting it and had pleaded that Sir James's Berwick soldiery had arrived there first; and Sir Henry backed him up by witnessing that 'Sir James Croft

. . . had had more than any ten there, though his finesse could well enough put the matter off'.[40] Sir James now found himself a prisoner in the Fleet and unable to share the rejoicings of the peace.

The Treaty of Edinburgh, agreed on July 8, and the subsequent departure of the French, provided one of the greatest successes of the reign. Despite intrigues and scares in later years and generations French dominion in Scotland was ended for ever and the threat removed to the 'postern gate' of England. The Treaty established the Protestant religion and cleared the ground for that ultimate union which many Scots now wish to loosen or sever totally. When the Cardinal of Lorraine heard the terms from Sir Nicholas Throckmorton, he could not believe them. Mary and Francis refused to ratify them, and Mary had still not ratified them at her death.

Success must be attributed partly to the weather, partly to the great advantage the English enjoyed in operating on interior lines of communication, partly to the troubles of the French at home. It must also be granted that English Intelligence had been admirably organized. Able men had occupied crucial positions with remarkable rapidity. Immediate use had been made of the conflict in men's minds. Gresham in Catholic Antwerp with his staff of business spies and Schetz, the Reformer Treasurer of the Catholic King; Sir Nicholas in Paris with the English exiles, the discontented Scots at the French Court, and Francis Edwards up and down the coast; Sadler 'secretly' on the Border, Thomas Randolph 'secretly' in Scotland with Kirkcaldy, Maitland, and the smuggled Earl of Arran; how well they fitted the new age, how efficiently they had kept in touch with one another and been kept in touch with and controlled from London!

The whole operation had been a triumph for William Cecil. He would serve Elizabeth nearly forty years longer. Though rather a dull person and in some ways unpleasant, the Great Minister had the gifts of a great head of Intelligence: enormous industry and application, a cool head, voracious curiosity about almost all things, scepticism, scholarship. Neither Leicester nor Essex possessed his patience or precision or carefulness with money. The intelligence services of this showy fascinating pair never had a chance against William Cecil nor against Robert, who inherited his father's gifts. It is interesting, in parenthesis, that two contemporary spies, Richard Sorge and Molody-Lonsdale, wrote that in different circumstances they would have liked to have been scholars. Curiosity, many-sidedness, exactness, are qualities of high value in the game, and a legacy from the Renaissance.

*

Sir James Croft must be excluded from the panegyrics. Certain anxieties beset him in the Fleet. His administration of Berwick was being audited. A sum of £100 'espiall money' was on his mind, at the same time as the new authorities there were asking Cecil to send up 'for the government of the spies . . . some true and diligent man who will not use corrupt means to enrich himself'. Thomas Randolph wrote in amazed regret about Sir James, than whom he had 'found no man franker to set forth the purpose'. But the Spanish Ambassador had his own private reason for being less surprised; he wrote to Margaret of Parma that people held Croft to be a Catholic 'and he was one of those who held a pension from our Lord the King'.[41]

Croft had three charges to answer; first, he had falsely told the Scots that Elizabeth intended to withdraw her naval and military assistance (which was also the story Marie de Guise had been instructed to spread); second, that without a word to Sadler, he had held talks with the laird of Blanern, a French supporter, and only discontinued them on learning that Blanern had tried to bribe the Master of the Ordnance at Berwick to blow up all the powder; third, he had arrived late for the assault and directed his men so badly that most of them were killed.

He switched the blame for this last charge on to others, but Lord Grey attested that when the assault began he had been unable to find Croft, whose troops had been compelled to wade ashore through deep water, and then uphill, to a point 'where they could not choose but to be slain'. To the second charge Croft agreed that Blanern had come to him from Marie de Guise about a truce, and claimed that he had listened with Lord Grey's permission. Lord Grey's version was that he had turned up one morning at Croft's billets in Restalrig Priory and, after knocking two or three times, found an unknown Scot with him. Croft asked him to leave. He returned after half an hour to find the Scot still there. The man left on Grey's insisting, and Croft explained that he had been offering money from Marie for a truce. Cecil had a note to add to this. A Scot had indeed come to Leith with an offer of 200 marks, but delivered them to the wrong man. They ought to have gone to someone with a black beard. Should we now assume that the white beard shown in the portrait of Sir James at Croft Castle had not yet turned?

To the first charge about misrepresenting the Queen's intentions Croft replied with the massive understatement that 'he understood the Queen's disposition sometimes to alter', and 'according thereunto he used speech with the Scots, meaning no harm therein'.

He remained in disgrace for a time. In 1562 the Dominican Father Black, formerly confessor to Marie de Guise, was talking about events in Edinburgh Castle during the siege of Leith. Marie, he boasted, 'had from time to time true and perfect intelligence of all the proceedings and devices in the English camp, by one chief of the Council there, Sir James Croft, who gave intelligence to the laird of Blanern'.[42] Three years later Don Diego Guzman de Silva, who succeeded the Bishop of Aquila as Spanish Ambassador, was writing to Philip II. He described Sir James as 'the most experienced soldier in the country. Your Majesty will know of him, because, although he has not visited me for fear of arousing suspicion, he is strongly attached to your service. His sister married Randolph, the captain of artillery . . .'; and when Randolph was killed next year in Ireland de Silva wrote, 'The Catholics are sorry . . . as he was a faithful one.'

Years passed, and gradually Sir James found his way back into favour. He became a Privy Councillor and Comptroller to the Queen's Household. Watching the widening rift between England and Spain, he became yet more 'strongly attached', if secretly, to Philip's service. He severed himself completely from the patronage of Lord Robert Dudley. Lord Robert, created Earl of Leicester in 1564, moved further and further to the militant left. By the 1580s he had joined Walsingham as a friend to the Puritans at home and a champion in foreign policy of all that was anti-Spanish, whether it might be the revolt in the Netherlands, or Huguenot against Guise in France, or adventures on the high seas and in the New World, or ultimately open war. Both Leicester and Walsingham were friends of Drake and had invested, as had the Queen, in his marauding journey round the world. Both were also nominally grantees in the charter of privileges to the Merchants of Spain and Portugal, incorporated in 1577; but the appointment signified little to them and took precedence well below their contradictory interest in Drake. Sir James was also a grantee, and it meant much to him.

When Don Bernardin de Mendoza, the last Spanish Ambassador to Elizabeth, reached London, he made it his business to keep the English merchants trading with Spain in constant dread that their ships and cargoes would be confiscated in retaliation for any plundering by Drake. They in turn put pressure on the Privy Council not to provoke Philip, and Sir James Croft became their spokesman. Thus the man, who some thirty years ago had rushed to Wales to raise a rebellion against Mary Tudor's marriage with Philip, had now become one of the leading Hispanophils and a pillar of conservatism and a quiet time. He had also become, in Mendoza's phrase, 'my first informant', and for money.

Once again we hear of his chronic indigence. 'Without money,' Mendoza told Philip, 'want will drive him from the Court, and whoever represents Your Majesty here will be without any assistance at all.' For services rendered up to June 1581 Philip allowed Mendoza to pay Croft a lump sum. The Ambassador recommended the same again 'with further Hope held out', arguing Sir James's zeal in 'advising me instantly of whatever happens', and adding that he was reputed a Catholic at heart and therefore shown no favour by the Queen. He had just given Mendoza details of an expedition being prepared to intercept the Spanish treasure-fleet from the West Indies; two of the ships would be the Queen's, and Leicester and Walsingham were among the chief financial backers.

Drake dropped anchor in Plymouth Sound in the autumn of 1580 after a voyage of two and a half years. He brought the Queen, Leicester, Walsingham, and the other investors in the *Golden Hind*, a profit of 4,500 per cent on their capital. Mendoza at once demanded restitution of the colossal loot. Leicester and Walsingham opposed restitution entirely, Cecil and Croft favoured it on terms. Privately Croft suggested to Mendoza that Philip could best put a stop to Drake's maraudings by sending 2,000 soldiers to Ireland 'under cover of the Pope's name'; this would compel the Queen to keep her men and ships at home. In July 1581 Philip sent Mendoza a fresh credit for 2,000 crowns, 'so that the absence from Court of your valuable informant should not be necessary'. Mendoza pretended to Sir James that the King had sent nothing, but having heard that Sir James was trying to negotiate a loan elsewhere, offered to advance him 1,000 crowns, with the hope of more. 'This is the only way Englishmen are kept faithful, for if they do not actually see the reward before their eyes they forget all past favours . . . we shall keep him longer by giving him the money in two payments.'

Relations with Spain grew steadily worse. The Ambassador was ostracized at Court and Croft no longer dared speak 'except upon very rare occasions to the person through whom he was in the habit of communicating with me'. By the following July he had been 'almost dumb for some months past', because, according to Mendoza, Leicester had set the Queen against him. By November Leicester had 'quite terrified him', and Mendoza declared that 'he must again make himself useful for some years before Your Majesty makes him another grant'. But the story does not end here. Put charitably it is possibly the story of one among many men who have entered into secret relations with a foreign Power in the belief, or on the pretext, that what they were doing was in the interest of peace. Looked at less charitably, he did it for money.

He remained in want, and in the summer of 1583 asked Cecil to intercede for him with the Queen, 'knowing my unskilful manor of delyng for my selfe . . . having my sonne so farre in dette as for a time he muste leve the realme, my plate and wyves jewells layd to gate, and I presently selling of lande to releve my necessyte . . .' The following autumn Elizabeth granted him lands worth £100 with the reversion of a lease worth £60, and on his own initiative he embarked on the last of his ill-fated secret ventures. He got in touch with Alexander Farnese, Duke of Parma, the son of Margaret of Parma and Philip's great captain and Governor-General in the Netherlands.

By 1585 Parma had brought the southern Provinces back into subjection. The next task the King had allotted him was to prepare a vast flotilla of flat-bottomed barges in which, covered by a victorious Armada, his soldiers were to cross the Channel and invade England. The Queen went under great nervous strain during the three years that preceded the arrival of the Armada. From Walsingham's account of the Babington plot in 1586 she had cause to think that any day she might be assassinated, as William of Orange had been in 1584. The following year she had to take responsibility for the execution of the Queen of Scots, and every month more and more of her treasure, her arms, and finally her men were being forced and wheedled out of her to support Protestants overseas. Leicester set out on his expedition to the Netherlands, by her ill-supplied, by himself ill-conducted. The war with Spain which she had dreaded was upon her. The traditional markets for cloth were closed, the weavers without work and beginning to starve. More than ever she alternated between hawk and dove.

Playing upon the dove, Sir James started negotiations for peace with Parma through a merchant kinsman of his in the Netherlands,

William Bodenham. Bodenham had lately been a merchant in Spain, spoke Spanish, and had supplied Walsingham and Leicester with information about Spain. He now communicated through a servant of Sir James's called Morris,[43] whom he had sent over to the Spanish port of Dunkirk on the pretext of buying horses. Croft, and Cecil with him, also made use of a Dutch merchant in London called Andrea de Loo. He instructed these go-betweens that, in return for peace, Elizabeth would keep Drake off the high seas, return to Philip the towns the Dutch had handed over to her as pledges for the money she had lent them, and refrain from insisting on religious toleration for the Netherlands Protestants as a condition of a settlement. Parma seemed receptive and promised that if peace resulted he would give the credit to Cecil and Croft.

All this was done with the connivance rather than the authority of the Queen, and kept secret from Walsingham and Leicester. But in the spring of 1586 Walsingham got his hands on the correspondence, and he and Leicester had to be told. Walsingham wrote to Leicester: 'I have let Her Majesty understand how dangerous and dishonourable it is for her to have such base and ill affected ministers used therein. Morris, the Comptroller's man, is both a notable papist and hath served . . . heretofore as a spy.' The Queen herself had constant doubts and flew into a rage when the negotiations began to give her the air of a suitor for peace; all her life she had been the one accustomed to be sued.

After changes of mind that become almost impossible to follow, she sent over Commissioners to treat with Parma. Sir James Croft, now seventy years old, but full of hope, was one. He left his colleagues behind and rode off on his own, to their great suspicion. From Dover he wrote to the Queen, accusing Drake of 'being animated to maintain a war' and of representing her efforts for peace as fraudulent, and soon afterwards: 'Those that recommend war recommend it . . . some for war's sake, as I should do perhaps if I were young and a soldier; others for religion; others for spoil and robbery, whereof Your Majesty feeleth too much. They are all inclined to their peculiar interests, caring nothing for the Prince's treasure, the impoverishing of the subject and the overthrow of trade.'

He crossed alone to Dunkirk, and his good reception by the Spaniards increased the suspicion of his colleagues, whom he joined for a week or two at Ostend, only to ride off alone again for a private

interview with Parma at Bruges. Elizabeth demanded to know why
he had dared to act independently of the other Commissioners, and
to send the report of his talks with Parma 'in an open writing by a
man of no better reputation, or more secrecy, than John Croft', his
second son. Finally, after Croft had had another *tête-à-tête* with
Parma in Ghent and offered him terms of peace on no authority but
his own, there came a stinging blow from the old swan's wing. She
thought it strange 'that you the Comptroller, being of such years
and bringing up as you are, should take upon you, without either
direction from us, or the assent and privity of the noblemen and
others of your associates, to enter into such particular dealing of so
many several matters, and those of such weight'; and she summoned
him back to Court, as she had from Leith twenty-eight years before,
to answer for himself. This letter went to him the day after the
Armada sailed from Lisbon.

Sir James asked pardon with the customary abjectness, but
declined to return on grounds of health. Even more surprisingly, the
Queen instructed Walsingham to send him a pardon and to 'persuade
yourself, that she holdeth you in as high degree of favour and grace
as ever she did . . . albeit your earnestness of zeal to further Her
Majesty's service took not that good success which you desired . . .'

Throughout the weeks during which the Armada was approaching
the Channel, and even while the two fleets were fighting their way
towards the Straits, Croft and his colleagues remained near Ostend
solemnly negotiating terms of peace with the man whose troops were
waiting to link up with the great galleons and invade England; and
solemnly they returned to Dover within days of the final battle
off Calais, within sight of the burning ships.

Sir James's pardon was not confirmed on his return to London.
He was sent to prison in the Tower, as previously in the Fleet.
Leicester died a few days later, and Sir James's eldest son Edward
was summoned before the Privy Council on an extraordinary charge
of having caused his death by witchcraft. Perhaps the departure of
this man who had long ago been Sir James's patron and turned into
so virulent an enemy rescued Sir James. Perhaps it was Elizabeth's
old friendship. Perhaps it was something else. So far as is known, he
kept his Comptrollership and died without further accusations in
1590. The charge against Edward Croft was dropped, but we hear of
him in 1596 'a banished man through debts of my father' begging to
'serve anywhere than spend my days in forgetfulness'. Edward's son

Sir Herbert Croft married, but later became a Benedictine monk. Sir Herbert's son in turn changed his faith, took orders in the Church of England, and was thirty years Bishop of Hereford. With him the religious ambiguity of the Crofts seems to have found an end.

The story of Sir James's odd relationship towards Spain during the 1580s bears close resemblance to the story of his odd relationship towards Marie de Guise in 1560. There are the same accusations of disloyalty, the same strange forgiveness by the Queen, the same fury roused among the militants. Indeed in 1588, just before Croft left England for his talks with Parma, one of them was angrily reminded of the earlier occasion. The Lord Admiral, Lord Howard of Effingham, wrote to Walsingham: 'There never was, since England was England, such a stratagem and mask made to deceive England, withal, as this is of the treaty of peace. I pray God we have not cause to remember one thing that was made of the Scots by the Englishmen; that we do not curse for this a long grey beard with a white head, witless, that will make all the world think us heartless. You know whom I mean.'[44]

Lord Howard might have been the Duke of Norfolk, writing from Berwick twenty-eight years before; except that then, of course, the Croft beard had been black.

*

One cannot but wonder, considering not only the peculiar story of Sir James Croft but the whole story of Intelligence throughout the reign and even before the Queen's accession, whether she did not employ some private secret service of her own. She took a close interest in Intelligence, and it is beyond doubt that she was well informed. She once interrupted an envoy's report with 'Tush, Brown, I know more than thou dost'. Henri IV of France's Ambassador at the end of the reign said, 'She knows everything', and William Cecil declared that she knew before her ministers informed her. She had plenty of hawks around her. Is it possible that she used Sir James Croft as her dove, conniving at 'betrayals' to Marie de Guise while her armies fought under the walls of Leith, or at 'secret' talks with the Duke of Parma while her navy battled in the Channel? Her public fury with Sir James would then have been a mere blind, her pardons easier to understand. Perhaps she was merely sorry for a rather foolish old friend, with whom once thirty-five years ago she may, or may not, have conspired while she was still Princess. But it is speculation only, like so much else about her.

Part Two

DOMESTIC INTELLIGENCE

Chapter Six

SECRET SERVICE AGAINST THE LEFT: BANCROFT AND THE PURITANS, 1585–90

i. Richard Bancroft

THE conspiracy in Scotland occurs near the middle of the Tudor period. The Intelligence history of that period begins with the Queen's grandfather, Henry VII. Francis Bacon called Henry and his contemporaries, Louis XI of France and Ferdinand of Aragon, the three Magi. One can imagine many more cheerful kings to summon to a birth; but wise they were, if the use of espionage for the maintenance of power is a sign of wisdom. Thomas Wolsey learnt State affairs under Henry, and himself apprenticed Thomas Cromwell, who in turn employed Sir Ralph Sadler; all three became masters of Intelligence. The nephew of Thomas Cromwell was that Richard Williams who took his uncle's name and became great-grandfather of the Lord Protector; and of Oliver it was said that 'he carried the secrets of every Prince in Europe at his girdle'. On Robert Cecil fell the mantle of his old father William; they dominated the English secret service for more than half a century. Francis Bacon and his younger brother Antony, who for a time supplied the Earl of Essex with intelligence, were nephews of William Cecil and first cousins of Robert; it was Francis who, after Walsingham's death, brought his sinister cryptologist and confidential secretary, Thomas Phelippes, into the service of Essex.

Members of the Kentish family of Wotton occupied themselves professionally with intelligence during three generations, and inherited the papers of Sir Nicholas Throckmorton. Sir Nicholas was an early patron of Francis Walsingham. Walsingham, another Kentishman, was cousin by marriage to Thomas Randolph. Randolph received the Mastership of the Posts, an office that put into his hands, and through his into Walsingham's, one of the commanding heights of secret service; he was also an overseer of the will of that skilled decipherer John Somer.[45] Sir Thomas Gresham's role as secret agent and paymaster of spies passed to another great financier, the Genoese Sir Horatio Pallavicino; and Sir Horatio married into the ancestry of Oliver Cromwell. Only one important operator in the later Elizabethan underground, Richard Bancroft, has no obvious personal link with those who contributed to the conspiracy in Scotland; and Bancroft, the foeman of the Puritans, is worthy of consideration.

*

Bancroft emerges in the 1580s, a generation after the business in Scotland. The small war fought there has widened, and the religious divisions on either side of the walls of Leith become the divisions of all western Europe. In France there is civil war. Philip II has allied himself with the Guises at the head of the Holy League, Elizabeth with the Huguenots and, in the Low Countries, with the Prince of Orange and the provinces in revolt against Spain; promises have become money, money will become men and arms. William Cecil is Lord Burghley and Lord Treasurer. Sir Francis Walsingham is Secretary of State.

Among those who played their leading parts in the Scottish conspiracy, there have been labyrinths of plotting, strange changes of policy and affection, and some violent deaths. Thomas Percy, the suspect Earl of Northumberland, has been reconciled to Rome, put himself at the head of the rising in the North, been defeated, betrayed, and executed. Sir Henry Percy has succeeded him as eighth Earl and become suspect in his turn. Sir Nicholas Throckmorton has fallen out with Cecil, taken admiration for the returned Queen of Scots too far for safety, and died in some disgrace. Mary herself has ruled for a few years in Scotland, married and seen the end of Darnley, married and seen the end of Bothwell, and spent some fifteen years as the guest and prisoner of Elizabeth in England. The Duke of Norfolk has conspired with her and followed his ancestors to the block. William Maitland and William Kirkcaldy, despairing like Throckmorton that Elizabeth will ever recognize Mary as her successor, have turned against the English party in Scotland and even thought of bringing back the French. Besieged in Edinburgh Castle with the last remnant of Scots lords holding to the captive Queen, they have at last surrendered to the Regent Morton, and Kirkcaldy been hanged and Maitland died or committed suicide in prison.

RICHARD BANCROFT

SIR FRANCIS WALSINGHAM WEARING A
MEDALLION OF QUEEN ELIZABETH

James Melville has returned with Mary from France, served her faithfully as long as possible, and is now a faithful servant of her young son James. Lord James Stuart has been murdered by the Hamiltons. The Duke of Châtellerault has died in 1575; the Earl of Arran has survived, but mad. John Knox has died in his bed, the hero of the Scottish Reformation. Henry Balnaves has died, making James Melville his heir. Sir Ralph Sadler lives on in his Hertfordshire palace, emerging now and then as an elder statesman, and for a time an exasperated guardian of the Queen of Scots.

Scotland was likened earlier in this book to a 'powder-barrel connected to two fuses leading into England, one French-Catholic, the other Scottish-Calvinist'. In 1562 reformism had so many powerful friends in England that, had Elizabeth died of her smallpox that October, 'a second Scotland might have developed south of the Tweed'.[46] Elizabeth survived, conservatism triumphed, and Scotland had to meet troubles of its own. But twenty years later, while Council and Court were mostly preoccupied with the Jesuit 'invasion' and rumours of fleets gathering in Spain, Richard Bancroft sensed that the old attack from the Left might again be maturing among the Puritans in the shires and Colleges at home. This man did far more than set spies upon the Puritans. He was one of those masters of Intelligence who have understood the importance of things written and said quite openly. Filing libraries and computers would have been bliss to him. As his great enemy John Field amassed his monumental Register of misdemeanour and inadequacy against the conforming clergy, so Bancroft assembled his counter-catalogue of subversion against the Puritans, and out of it erected a compelling bogey-man.

Born in 1544 of a Lancashire family, he had been educated at Cambridge at the expense of his great-uncle, Hugh Curwyn, Archbishop of Dublin, and ordained priest in 1574. He became chaplain to the Bishop of Ely, Richard Cox, and in 1575 was one of the twelve University preachers. He acted as Visitor to the diocese of Peterborough in 1576 and of Ely in 1581, thus coming to know a number of neighbourhoods rife with nonconformist thought and preaching. A tradition that he was good at games, especially boxing, wrestling, and quarterstaff, has been enlarged to represent him as one of the founders of muscular Christianity. John Whitgift, Archbishop of Canterbury by 1583, in whose steps he trod like a sturdy page behind a rather irascible Wenceslas, praised him because he was 'not tyrannous, but mild and kind and persuading'; most of his enemies described him as a bully.

From College and Close he came to Court and attracted the favour of Sir Christopher Hatton, favourite of the Queen. It is possible that he assisted the grubby deal by which Hatton acquired Ely Place, Bishop Cox's house in Holborn. By 1579 he had become Hatton's chaplain, with a room in the residence of his former master; by 1586 Canon of Westminster, Treasurer of St. Paul's, and rector of St. Andrew's, Holborn, enjoying a town house of his own, and by 1587 chaplain to Whitgift. It is a steady rather than a meteoric rise, impelled by solid fuel and relentless purpose and ambition. One day, he must have known, the Queen would make him Bishop. One day, he could have guessed, James I would make him Primate.

After Cambridge there seems never to have been the smallest question where he stood. It was well to the Right. Cambridge, that nursery of Puritans, sent Bancroft the opposite way. Whitgift, who had been the battle-axe of University conservatives in Bancroft's youth, wrote of him that 'he ever opposed himself against all sects and innovators'. By the middle 1580s he, Whitgift, and Hatton had formed that tough no-nonsense trio whom Whitgift's first biographer styled 'the little faction' of the Right. The Right at Court badly needed someone. The Left had Lord Robert Dudley, long since Earl of Leicester and the Sir Lancelot of the Puritans, as he had once been briefly of the Catholics. The Left had the Queen's cousin, Sir Francis Knollys. The Left had Walsingham and his restless coterie of radical Reformers. William Cecil was neither Left nor Right, but in-between, hearing from everybody, listening to everybody, by now both ear and oracle. People have justly attributed charm, devotion, eloquence and hard work to Sir Christopher Hatton, but never intellectual brilliance. Whitgift was overworked, Bishop Aylmer of London no courtier, and both prelates ageing, a little suspect for their grandeur, and distrusted for their intolerance. Bancroft was someone fresh.

He knew how to remain in the background. Elizabeth had made up her mind against 'further Reformation' ever since her accession. Religion, her marriage, the succession, were the three matters she would not let Parliament discuss; in regard to herself as both a spiritual and a carnal body, she stood adamant on her prerogative. In front and at her side, spokesman and support alike, went Whitgift and Hatton waving their banners of obedience, and behind them trod Richard Bancroft, 'employed in sundry matters for the Queen's service'. At the rather late age of forty-three, he had reached the ear of Majesty.

He made Puritanism his speciality, as Sadler's had been Scotland, and Throckmorton's France, and Cecil's remained everything. He wrestled with his enormous brief for years, setting himself to read all that radicals had written, and so to know his enemy: in our own age he would have read *Das Kapital* and *Mein Kampf* and taken them more seriously than many, who should have, did. He translated Walter Travers's first formulation of the Puritan Book of Discipline from the Latin, and pored over the work of the Huguenots and of those dangerous evangelicals in Scotland. Nor was it all reading; he met the enemy in the field as well as from the study. Sent from Cambridge to preach at Bury St. Edmunds against Robert Browne, father of Congregationalism, he had dared to face inflamed crowds whom 'hardly anyone else could be got to oppose', and with his own hands tore down a placard mocking the Royal Seal.

During his Visitation of East Anglia and later on Whitgift's behalf in the diocese of Canterbury, he became ombudsman and pugilist for outraged conformers. Protests poured in to him. Vivacious satire in one of his early tracts depicted the court paid to Puritans preaching in a country town: Amens greeted onslaughts upon the Establishment; when the preacher descended from the pulpit, the gentry rushed to embrace him and invite him home to dinner; but for the conforming preachers there was 'neither good morrow nor good speeches, neither Brother, thankes, nor dynner, but after a few disdainful looks they may goe walke'. All, read, reported, or personally observed, went to wait its time in Bancroft's indefatigable, sifting, commemorative mind.

It must be said that he became a master not only of Intelligence, but also of the smear, and not for nothing has been likened to the late Senator Joseph Macarthy.[47] He was conducting a witch-hunt; indeed he once compared the Puritans to witches, because 'though by great distance of place they be severed . . . they knew by reportes one another'. He had the propagandist's talent for daubing many-coloured issues with a violent monochrome, of missociating moderate men he desired to discredit with extremists, and of giving highly complex questions falsely simple answers. Exactitude went by the board whenever he needed to obtain conclusions that would frighten people, and frighten them he did, beginning with the Queen herself.

ii. Security and Spite

Bancroft found engines of law and order at hand, whose efficiency in maintaining internal security varied with local and individual willingness and ability to work them. The Queen, supreme head under God in all matters temporal and ecclesiastical, had two sets of eyes and ears at her command. The Privy Council, under the Queen, governed, rebuked, goaded, rewarded, and punished Church and State alike, as it thought fit or had the time. On the civil side, the shires were controlled through the Courts of Session and Assize, the Sheriffs, the Justices of the Peace, and their deputies and underlings down to the Dogberrys on the village green. The Church operated on a national scale through the Court of High Commission, whose members possessed inquisitorial authority to summon whom they pleased, administer oaths, ask what they chose, detain, imprison, fine, and suspend or dismiss from the right to preach and teach. Bancroft became a member in 1587 and remained one till his death in 1610. Discipline was exercised through the Visitations of Archbishops, Deans, Archdeacons and Bishops, and through the Church courts and officials down to the smallest unit, the parish. The task of all was to ensure obedience to the Acts of Supremacy and Uniformity passed in the first year of the reign; the former had re-abolished the authority of the Pope, the latter re-established the use of the Book of Common Prayer.

As the Puritans grew bolder, and, most of all, after the influx of Catholic missionaries from Rome, Douai, Rheims, and Spain during the eighties, increasingly severe Acts of Parliament rounded off the ramparts of internal security and put them in battle array. But from the outset one particular order had given the Government, in theory at least, a perfect view over the allegiance or disaffection of the entire nation. The Act of Uniformity had ordered every householder to attend church in his own parish every Sunday and Holy Day with his family, children and apprentices, on pain of a 12*d.* fine for each absence. Sundays and Holy Days thus became occasions not only of worship, but also of surveillance. The churchwardens, chosen by minister and parishioners, watched the minister for divergences from the approved rule of service, doctrine or apparel, and the parishioners for unseemliness of conduct and non-attendance, and were in turn themselves observed.

Of course this ideal system did not work ideally. Churchwardens were often men of lowly origin. They might themselves be on the side of deviation. A certain Higgins, for example, churchwarden of Guiseley, summoned before the Archbishop of York, and so poor that he had to come in a borrowed cloak and his wife's hat, stood up for his Puritan minister, Robert More, and said he would rather lose his head than agree that More had called the Archbishop 'an olde doteinge foole'. Parts of Lancashire and the North long remained Catholic at heart. Parts of East Anglia, Northamptonshire, and London moved openly into Puritan observances and privately towards a form of government by deacons, presbyters, and elders, disregarding all hostile bishops except for convenience and 'safe standing'. Both sides had powerful supporters among the nobility and gentry.

But the system was there, and, on the whole, did work. The parish officials became in effect 'N.C.O.s in the army of the New Divine Right of Kings'.[48] They served in the 16th century the same purpose as, in later centuries, the intendant, the concierge, the janitor of a block of flats, the secretary of the party cell. Custodians of 20th-century faiths have been as fearful of dissent as were the old, and since the populace no longer conveniently assemble once weekly at a place of worship, we have seen supervision shifted (so far only in Europe) to their factories, their offices, and their homes.

Such a system created many opportunities for the spy and the delator, but its comprehensiveness and competence modified the need. It served, moreover, a government which enjoyed a large measure of consent. Although Bishop Aylmer might ask for a network of espionage to be built into every diocese, on the whole prelacy, magistracy, Court of High Commission, and Privy Council, managed well enough with less drastic means. They could draw on a fairly general indignation against dissenters, which sprang from an authentically grateful sense that Elizabeth had brought the country peace. Nonetheless over-zealous Puritans must always expect suspension from preaching, loss of livelihood, or long imprisonment. We have only to read the diary of Richard Rogers, preacher in the quiet little village of Wethersfield in Essex, to detect the fear in even a brave man, 'stayed on God', as he hears of brother ministers arrested, and gathers up his holy thoughts and memories to strengthen him 'even till my lif be taken from me also, as well as credit, countenance, and all hope of maintenance'.[49]

Finally the authorities, and Bancroft especially, in the role he had set out to play, disposed of the everlasting human springs of jealousy, avarice, vengefulness, busybodiness, and spite. Spies draw constantly at these poisoned wells. The odious qualities released under a government which seeks, as the Elizabethan did, to regulate its subjects' lives down to the smallest detail, present as sad a sight as the noble qualities suppressed. For every group of men or women who exercise a claim to differ, there will be others with an equal desire to get their own back and denounce. Love of sneaking is as deeply ensconced in human nature as love of liberty. Some among the sneaks may most sincerely believe that their victims endanger the security of the State and harm public morals, and they may be right. They bear no private grudge. But others there always are, to whom the State's resolve to discover and punish certain opinions gives a longed-for chance to satisfy bitter personal resentments, often quite unrelated to the opinions themselves. Such men do not have to become spies. On the contrary, the law encourages them to take to the open, and offers them the name of patriots. It is vital to understand not how much, but how little, given such a climate, any government need be driven to depend on spies.

Here then, to convey something of the atmosphere within which Bancroft went to work, are a few samples of information lodged against nonconformists of the Left.

Thirty witnesses deposed that Robert Johnson, minister of St. Clement's in London and domestic chaplain to Lord Keeper Bacon, had not reconsecrated the Communion wine after it had been finished, baptized without the sign of the Cross, and married Leonard Morris and Agnes Miles without using a ring or the words 'with this ring I thee wed'. John Farmer, a High Church curate at Barnstaple, complained of the maimed Puritan Eusebius Paget, minister of Kilhampton, who was often in trouble. Farmer wanted to give eighty people Communion on All Hallows' Day. Paget, on the ground that All Hallows' Day was not one of the four 'grand Communions', threatened to throw Farmer out, and when he arrived to make the attempt preached for two hours and a half, and instructed the churchwardens to refuse bread and wine and hide the chalice. Later he accused Farmer to the Bishop of Exeter of 'an infirmitie infective and too odious to mention' as well as of Papistry; while Farmer counter-accused Paget of calling the Queen's late sister Mary a Jezebel.

There is clearly a vendetta behind the denunciation of Sanderson, minister at King's Lynn, by the alderman cornmonger Francis Shaxton, a very powerful and shady citizen, and three confederates called Smith, Makins and Blaseby. They had accused Sanderson of 'charging the Established Church with papistry'. To this he replied that Shaxton, while Mayor, had been 'put to silence' for falsely reporting a sermon of his, and since then 'he could never abide me'; and he counter-accused Smith of usury, Makins of whoredom 'with Puckering's wife', conjurations and fortune-telling, and Blaseby (a churchwarden) of having been 'taken in Church with a whore', for which he had gone unpunished, 'these things being so buried with money that no man can justly prove them'.

John Wilson, preacher at Kildwick-in-Craven in Yorkshire, presented two parishioners before the Council of the North, whereupon they informed Archbishop Sandys that he had been preaching without licence. Robert More, the rector of Guiseley, had presented Mark Hoppaye for fornication and his brother Matthew for not attending church; it was those two who countered by accusing him of nonconformity and calling the Archbishop 'an olde doteinge foole'. Higgins, the brave churchwarden in his wife's hat, may have brought on the bitterness himself by over-zealously rebuking the parishioners for swearing; some of them told him 'they hoped to see him hanged'.

John Stroud, minister of Yalding in Kent and printer, was first delated in 1567 by another minister to whom he had lent a Puritan book, and who 'somewhat blushed' when asked to witness, and also by a Mr. Storer 'for distributing seditious books' and other errors. Although his sidesmen and churchwardens backed him, Archbishop Whitgift deprived him of the living. In 1576 we find him minister at near-by Cranbrook and again in trouble. This time some two hundred people petitioned to have him restored to liberty of preaching, protesting that he had been 'sharpely beaten and whipped with the untrue reports of slanderous tongues'.

Turbulent Giles Wigginton, in whom some have seen a precursor of the Quakers, was the eager victim of a life-long feud with the Archbishop and, despite his sufferings, as cantankerously self-righteous. The feud began at Trinity College, Cambridge, where Wigginton was a Fellow when Whitgift was Master. Denunciation to Whitgift, according to Wigginton, had started even then; a certain Master Backhouse, 'a scholar of his own', accused Wigginton of

dancing ('which was when I was a child') and not washing his hands
enough. In 1585 Whitgift was Archbishop of Canterbury and
Wigginton vicar of Sedburgh in Yorkshire, where, an extreme purist
among the pure, he refused even to acknowledge the greetings of conformist ministers. According again to him, the Archbishop accepted
the denunciations of Edward Middleton, 'notorious for unchastity,
hard dealings with tenants, swearing and popery, atheism . . . neither
he nor his wife come to Church', and sent a Mr. Colecloth to take
the living. It was given to Edward Hampton, a cousin of Colecloth's,
who slandered Wigginton 'saucily and continually . . . in the churchyard, streets and alehouses of Sedburgh'. Wigginton was summoned
to London and imprisoned, and Hampton cited 140 parishioners to
appear at York, Manchester and Chester for listening to his sermons.
Wigginton described Hampton as 'a swashbuckler and roysterer
with a narrow-brimmed hatte with crosse garters, greate ruffes and
paunch-bellied coate, and other sucklike unseemely apparel for his
calleinge and so jetteth up and down . . . with the vilest persons and
most notorious sinners'.

Allowance must be made for the exceptional propensity of the
godly to be shocked, and for the vehemence of Elizabethan church-
men's language on all sides. But evidence abounds to support the
complaint of a Puritan Minister, who taxed the Chapters and Con-
sistories with 'inciting and animating underhand some devilish
instruments of his owne congregation, to give the first onset to bring
him to their judgment seat, and then to tosse him like a tennis ball for
a stage plaier'. Even William Cecil had found Whitgift's articles 'so
curiously penned . . . as I think the Inquisiters of Spain use not so
many questions . . . to trap their preyes'.[50] We do not have to think
ourselves back into Elizabethan times to picture the exploitation by a
State of personal and local rancours. They render spies unnecessary
up to the point where, behind the people and the views denounced, a
secret illegal organization comes to be suspected or imagined, and
has to be proved. We shall see how that point was passed, and how
Richard Bancroft in particular set about his proof.

iii. Dangerous Subversives

The Queen of Scots was beheaded at Fotheringhay on February 8,
1587. Ten days later the Puritan member for Banbury, Sir Antony
Cope, confronted the House of Commons with a Bill, of which Sir

John Neale has written that 'never had such a revolutionary proposal been made in Parliament before', and Dr. Collinson that it 'was perhaps the most immoderate measure ever to come before the House'. Its promoters demanded a clean sweep of all ecclesiastical legislation since the beginning of the reign and the substitution of a Form of Common Prayer based on the liturgy of Geneva. Sir Christopher Hatton, leader of the House and the Queen's spokesman, delivered a tirade against the Bill which Bancroft had drafted, and dismissed the members with a list of inflammatory Puritan tracts for homework, also prepared by Bancroft. The Queen sequestrated the Bill and sent Cope, Peter Wentworth, and three other of its supporters to the Tower. So much for Puritan attempts at legislation. There remained the campaign in the parishes, outside Parliament, to persuade, to infiltrate, to penetrate, and even, where possible, to introduce their Discipline in practice.

One of their chief weapons was the printing-press, and the chief counter-weapon was the official censorship. Mary Tudor had employed one and Elizabeth had set up hers in the first year of the reign. In 1586 Archbishop Whitgift reinforced this decree of 1559. No book might now appear that had not first been perused by himself or the Bishop of London, an authority that was later delegated. Printing of anything deemed contrary to the form or meaning of any Statute, Injunction, Ordinance, etc., carried a sentence without trial of six months in prison and total destruction of the press. There were some twenty licensed printers in London, owning about fifty handpresses. Two of them belonged to the Puritan Robert Waldegrave. By 1588 he had been seven times imprisoned during the five years since Whitgift went to Canterbury. Those whose works he now brought illegally into the light included two young rebel scholars, John Penry, the Welsh evangelist, and the Englishman John Udall, whom James of Scotland was later to call the greatest scholar in Europe.

Penry had first come under the frown of authority with his '*Humble Supplication . . . on behalf of the country of Wales*', published by licence and presented to Parliament in 1587. Its innocent frankness about the almost total lack of dutiful preachers in Wales ('not twelve in all') and its backhanded excuses for the Queen, had angered the Archbishop; the book was seized and Penry hauled before the High Commission and imprisoned for a month without a charge. Udall, a friend of Penry's from Cambridge days and author of a Hebrew grammar, had for some years been substituting at Kingston-on-Thames for the non-resident vicar Stephen Chatfield. John Cottington, Archdeacon of Surrey, had called the Kingston parish officials' attention to certain nonconformist observances Udall had encouraged, including the singing of psalms and the reading and interpreting of Holy Scripture in private houses. He had also dared to censure a wealthy money-lending parishioner, called Harvey, for usury, oppressing the poor and buying houses 'over the heads of those that love the gospel', including Udall's own house. Chatfield, who appears to have borrowed money from Harvey, was ordered to take up residence so that Udall might be silenced.

Early in 1588 Waldegrave, without licence, issued two vigorous Puritan polemics. The first was John Penry's signed *Exhortation*, again demanding attention to the lack of preachers in Wales and attacking the Bishops. The second was a satirical conversation on 'The State of the Church of England laid open', usually known as the *Diotrephes* from the name of one of the characters. The author's name did not appear.

On April 16 Mr. Coldock, Warden of the Stationers' Company, Wolf their beadle, and two others, raided Waldegrave's premises in London. They seized the press, several copies of the *Diotrephes*, and two cases of pica Romana and pica Italian type. Wolf rode out the same day to Croydon to solicit the Archbishop's further orders. Waldegrave went into hiding. Fellow printers offered to buy his equipment and give the money for the relief of his wife and six children, but early in May he issued a second printing of the *Diotrephes* in the type supposed to have been seized. The Archbishop gave orders for the timber of his press to be hewn to pieces, the ironwork battered, the type head melted, and the tools defaced. This Wolf supervised for a fee of sixpence. (He was a printer himself and later published one of Bancroft's most celebrated anti-Puritan pamphlets.) Waldegrave retaliated from his hiding-place by issuing second and third editions of Penry's *Exhortation*.

A certain Thomas Draper now informed the Stationers' Company that the printer might be found at Kingston, for which Draper received a handsome present of five pounds. Off to Kingston by boat went Mr. Coldock, other officials of the Company, a pursuivant, and Wolf the beadle. They searched the wrong house, for which they paid two shillings compensation to the 'poore woman' they disturbed, had supper for 10*s*. 6*d*. and came home late by link-light, having found no one and nothing criminal. Thomas Draper was sent to prison for misleading them.

The Armada reached the English Channel that July. In mid-October, as the remnants limped back to port, and their sick Admiral was being jolted home in his litter to the orange-groves of San Lucar, and London made ready for thanksgiving, nonconformity leapt suddenly into a blaze of limelight. This time it was not a Bill, or a Godly Exhortation, or a Learned Discourse, or a Lamentable Complaint. It was a Tract, certainly; but what a Tract! Never had the Bishops been so slashed. Not for a long while had there been such rumbustious muck-raking and mud-slinging, such a letting-out of skeletons and opening-up of manholes, not perhaps since *Piers Plowman* such ferocious satire. It was the first Epistle of an unknown rebel, styling himself Martin Marprelate, 'to the right puissant and terrible Priests' of the Elizabethan Church, printed in a fine new black-letter type.

Who was this Martin? Who had printed him? Who was behind it?

*

The Queen, between sorrow for the death of Leicester (September 4, 1588) and rejoicing for the defeat of Philip, sent for Cecil; and on November 14 Cecil wrote to Whitgift. The authors, printers and distributors were to be sought out by 'all privy means'. We have Whitgift's authority that Richard Bancroft now became 'by his diligent search, the first detector of Martin Marprelate's press and books; where and by whom they were printed'. Interior evidence cast the first suspicions on John Udall. Waldegrave had already printed his sermons. Stephen Chatfield, now dutifully fulfilling his parochial duties at Kingston, offered to make a deposition, and a fresh batch of sleuths rowed up-stream to receive it. He declared that Marprelate's *Epistle* was being sold at two places in the town. Other citizens added that Udall had had 'someone' in a house near-by at Richmond, copying out a book for him; but whose the house was, they could not or would not say.

A fortnight later out came Martin's second blast, the *Epitome*, to which the *Epistle* had been an overture. It lived up to the rollicking satire of the first. Pursuivants rushed to Waldegrave's London house one November night in the small hours, but he was not at home. They broke in, removed his books, and sold them to nightwatchmen and anyone else found stirring. On November 30 Walter Rogers, conformist non-preaching minister at Richmond, gave away the house at which Udall's scribe had been working. It belonged to one Horton, a man 'addicted unto Puritanisme'; the information came from Horton's servants. Parson Rogers had a particular complaint. He had gone at Michaelmas to collect his tithes, whereupon Horton had lost his temper and shouted that he hoped to see all of Rogers's profession 'pulled out of the churche by the eares'. Neighbours deposed that Udall had often visited Horton. Neither neighbours nor servant, however, could declare what the book being written had contained, nor who had been the 'someone' writing it. Udall made himself scarce. He was welcomed in Scotland by the ministers, whom he had welcomed four years ago in their English exile, and preached before James VI. Then he returned to his native North Country, finding a temporary refuge and pulpit at Newcastle under the patronage, like several colleagues in trouble, of the Puritan Earl of Huntingdon.

Archbishop Whitgift's own suspicions darted to his *bête noir*, Giles Wigginton, who had just emerged from one of the London jails and was staying in the Aldermary house of Mrs. Crane, a well-known protector of the Puritans. On December 6 the Archbishop summoned him to Lambeth and ordered him to take the oath and swear what he knew about the 'seditous foolish and intollerable booke' by Martin Marprelate. Wigginton asked to see his accusers, but there was none. He suggested that, since 'many Lords and Ladies and other greate and wealthy personages of all estates had been receiving Marprelate', Whitgift should examine them 'and not poor folk only as you are used to do'. He personally 'liked well' of Marprelate, but would say no more. On January 9 the pursuivants spent two days and a further 6s. 2d. hunting vainly for the hidden press. Suddenly the search was extended to the Midlands.

Northamptonshire was an obvious place to look. It 'swarmed with sectaries', lamented Sir Christopher Hatton, who had built one great mansion there and restored another and, as Lord Lieutenant, should have known. So too should Richard Bancroft, not only as Hatton's chaplain, but as rector of Cottenham near Northampton, to which living his patron had presented him; presented, it has been suggested, in order the better to watch the Puritans. On January 29 a pursuivant called Walton raided the house of Penry's father-in-law, Henry Godley, at Northampton, and ransacked Penry's study. All he found was a new tract of Penry's in manuscript and a copy of the illegal and anonymous *Demonstration of Discipline*. After vainly trying to persuade the Mayor to arrest Penry whenever he should return, Walton departed, taking the documents with him.

Parliament reassembled the following month and on the first Sunday of the session Richard Bancroft preached a thumping sermon at Paul's Cross. Secure in the support of Whitgift and Hatton and of Cecil too, on whose and Hatton's directions the sermon was at once published, Bancroft could now demand for the Elizabeth settlement the authority once accorded to the Pope. 'Notwithstanding many Blemishes, Imperfections, nay divers and sundry Errors', it must now be acknowledged as 'the Mother of the Faithful and the House of God . . . out of this church, *nulla salus*, there is no salvation'. He took his text from I John iv. 1: 'Believe not every spirit, but prove the spirits if they be of God, because many false prophets are gone out into the world.' The Puritans were the false prophets now. Individual judgment, that was their canker . . . 'always seeking and searching . . . they wring and wrest the Scripture according to their fancie'. No wonder they were hopelessly divided. It was not the way. Not every man could judge, but only 'those who are well experienced and exercized', in other words the Bishops. Bancroft claimed that an episcopal system of Church government had existed from early Christian days, accused the Puritans of seeking further reform merely in order to obtain the Church's wealth for themselves, extended his attack to the highly placed laity who backed them, and demanded for the civil magistrate the same unfaltering obedience as for the Church.

He also made a rash first entry into international affairs. A domestic plot is always likely to alarm a nation more if it can be shown to have its roots abroad. It was Bancroft's original contribution to discover or invent a European Calvinist conspiracy, originating in Geneva but channelled into England via Edinburgh. He was soon to involve himself in attempts at espionage in Scotland. He read, with his usual thoroughness, the works of Scottish preachers and historians; and he ferreted away at any warrens that might be shown to link Puritans at home with Presbyterians in the North, using information so acquired as Walsingham used his about the English Catholics' links with France and Spain. The most sensational passages in his sermon concerned Scotland, where King James VI, now in the thick of his prolonged struggle against the Ministers, had lately been compelled to give in to them. Bancroft contended that the King was only biding his time to restore Episcopacy; and he asked his hearers to believe that if the English Puritans had their way Elizabeth would soon be in the same boat.

The 'incomparable' sermon, this massive cornerstone of Elizabethan conformism, sank into place with a thud ominous to all who disagreed. A few days later the Queen herself pronounced. By a Proclamation dated February 12 she declared Martin's books 'schismaticall, seditious and diffamatorie'. Anyone who possessed a copy must surrender it within a month, or lose all hope of pardon. 'What then will become of me?' exclaimed the young Earl of Essex at Court, plucking a copy from beneath his cloak.

Three days afterwards the hounds belatedly picked up a scent. It had occurred to someone that, all the while they had been sniffing around Kingston and Richmond, Giles Wigginton's hostess Mrs. Crane owned another house a few miles away at East Molesey. Richard Cosin, Dean of the Court of Arches and one of Bancroft's most vigorous colleagues, examined a servant of Mrs. Crane's called Nicholas Tomkins. He confessed that the pica type had survived, because Waldegrave had rescued a case and Mrs. Crane had hidden it. Penry and Waldegrave had spent several weeks at East Molesey the previous autumn. The unlicensed *Demonstration* had been printed there, and either Waldegrave or Wigginton had given him a copy of Martin Marprelate's *Epistle*. People, he could not recall who, had named Wigginton as the author, or Penry, or John Field, or the Puritan Marbury. He thought Udall to have been the author of the *Diotrephes*. Since both the *Diotrephes* and the *Demonstration* had already been deemed felonies, this deposition was tantamount to Udall's death-warrant.

On March 9 there appeared, from some place and press unknown, a *Supplication* to Parliament signed by John Penry. It was the first time his hidden voice had been heard publicly since his study had been raided; and he emerged now as champion not only of a true preaching Church in Wales, but of the right of 'all the subjects of this kingdome' to bring their petitions to, and receive redress from, the House of Commons. The demand for religious freedom had led to the demand for political freedom, as Queen and Bishops had always known and feared it must.

In the same month Martin Marprelate published two more broadsides. But scared accomplices, strong drink, and accident, those perennial enemies of secrets, now began to play their part. At the end of March a London ale-house yielded a clue among some very great personages. A country servant of one Sir Richard Knightley blabbed that he had come to town with a little packet of books for his master's brother-in-law, the Earl of Hertford, who refused to have anything to do with them. The books were the works of Martin Marprelate, printed (the servant said) in Sir Richard's house. Martin himself might be seen there, 'apparelled in green'.

This was appalling. Sir Richard Knightley was one of the richest landlords in Northamptonshire, Deputy-Lieutenant, Member of Parliament, and a close friend of Sir Christopher Hatton. He had taken as second wife Elizabeth Seymour, daughter of Protector Somerset, and Hatton had stood godfather to his son. And during Easter week a Puritan bookbinder of Northampton called Henry Sharpe heard that the High Commissioners were looking for him. They had imprisoned him before, but the Privy Council had judged their handling of him to be 'against lawe and conscience', and set him free. This time he feared he might not be so lucky. He went into hiding and sent his wife to Court to obtain him a remission from Hatton; for what errors, or on what terms, we do not know. It was refused, and about midsummer Mistress Sharpe came home to her husband with news that the Court were taking the Marprelate business very badly.

On July 22 and 29 two more brilliantly scurrilous and defiant tracts appeared. The first pretended to be the work of imaginary Martin's imaginary younger son and was ironically dedicated to 'Master John Kankerbury'. The second, dressed up as a *Just Censure and Reproofe* by an imaginary elder brother, contained a hilarious parody of Whitgift's instructions to his pursuivants,[51] and one other gibe that later brought disaster. The author's satirical fantasy was freewheeling round an imaginary retinue for the Archbishop. Bancroft was to be one of his yeomen of the cellar, and Antony Anderson, vicar of Stepney, 'should make room before him with his two-hand staff, as he did once before the morrice dance at a market-town in the edge of Buckingham or Bedford shires, where he bare the Potter's part'. The reference was to a pagan game, and fairly harmless. But a note alongside accused Parson Anderson of robbing the poor men's box at Northampton and begetting a maid with child in Leicestershire; and four years afterwards Parson Anderson remembered.

That summer half a dozen Puritan sanctums were raided. One of the hard core of preachers, Edmund Snape, rector of St. Peters,' Northampton, managed to hide his stock of banned publications, but the searchers got hold of a written declaration that he did not consider his ministry derived from ordination by his Bishop. The studies of pastor Edmund Littleton and others yielded a copy of the Book of Discipline, with names of the Warwickshire ministers who had subscribed it; the minutes of a secret synod held in Warwick in 1588; and a document, which Bancroft later styled the 'Decrees', indicating how the Puritans were to infiltrate and ultimately take over the Established Church. This was a real haul, and gave Bancroft the sinews of a major trial.

And on Friday, August 8 a man called Hodgkin, accompanied by two assistants called Valentine Sym and Arthur Tomlyn, drove a cart into Warrington in Lancashire, loaded with hay and other objects which had nothing to do with farming. As they were unloading, some of these other objects spilled. Hodgkin told the bystanders that it was 'shot', and that he and the other two were 'saltpetre men', engaged in the gunpowder trade. Somebody was curious. Somebody recognized, or gave away on interrogation, that the 'shot' had been type, and a week later the three saltpetre men were caught in a house at Newton Lane, a mile outside Manchester, in the middle of printing Martin's latest broadside. The brief audacious game was up.

iv. Weaker Brethren

The three prisoners reached London on August 23. Next day, Sunday, Cecil, Hatton and others of the Privy Council, interrogated them. They gave nothing away, and were committed to Bridewell. If they continued obstinate, they must be tortured; a memorandum from the Queen to Cecil on September 2 noted: 'the examinacyon of Martin Marprelate to be thoroughlye persevered in', and by September 11 Hodgkin was in the Tower. Whitgift and five other Privy Councillors issued a warrant declaring Penry an enemy of the State and exhorting the entire country 'if they can by enye means apprehend or lay hould on him, they shall therein do her Majesties good service'.

The young Welshman fled across the Border, but Whitgift and Bancroft had kept close connexions with the anti-Puritan party in

Scotland, and Bancroft made an attempt even to infiltrate the Scottish Ministers. He asked Robert Naunton, attached to the English Embassy in Edinburgh, to provide him with their confidential correspondence with Beza and other prominent European Reformers, so that he might use it to discredit their sympathizers in England; Naunton's most fruitful ruse, he suggested, might be the old one of presenting himself among the Presbyterians 'as one desirous to embrace their thought'. It was not difficult for him to have Penry watched.

Penry had fled just in time, for now evidence came thick and fast. A carrier whom Hodgkin had employed admitted to moving 'a printinge presse, two boxes of letters, a barell of incke, a baskett and a brasse pott', from a gentleman's house at Wolston, near Coventry, to Warrington. This gentleman, Hodgkin had told the carrier, 'did often harboure him a fourte-night together, and relieved him with meat, drink and money'. It could only be a certain Roger Wigston, since no other gentleman owned a house at Wolston. The authorities pulled in Sharpe the bookbinder, whom their bailiff actually found at Wolston hiding at his father-in-law's. Roger Wigston was foolish enough to threaten the bailiff, who happened to be his tenant, and thus became further incriminated. Some time before September 22 Sharpe divulged that tracts had indeed been printed at Sir Richard Knightley's great house, Fawsley. One person unnamed deposed that he had been invited to Fawsley to see Martin himself, 'but he did not, because he could not staye'. Had he but stayed, he might have saved volumes of speculation. Not all Bancroft's spies, nor all the scholar-spies of the centuries since, have yet established beyond doubt who Martin really was.

Hodgkin and his two apprentices told little that was not by now already known. They denied seditious intent against the Queen. Hodgkin protested that his apprentices' confessions had been 'violently extorted' and, as for his own, he 'was forced thereunto by racking and great torments'. None of them had strength to sign his name. Perhaps the poor men did not know much. Perhaps they did, and kept just enough endurance not to tell. It did not matter, since in Henry Sharpe the authorities found a witness who knew a great deal, and on October 15 all too gladly told.

Although the controllers of the secret press had used Sharpe, and although Penry had spoken of him as a man who had suffered much for the cause, they had never entirely trusted him and had refused to allow him into Fawsley House while the press was there. He had been far too inquisitive; once Penry had seen him following and had to beckon him to go away. It is an odd story, that sending of his wife to Hatton for a 'remission', and an odd accusation had been laid against him by a Coventry Puritan called Pigot, who had known about the printing of the tracts; Pigot declared that Sharpe had been the cause of his house being searched and 'had done wickedly in taking his oath before the Lord Chancellor'. Moreover, the book-binder possessed a strong mercenary streak, and the profits from Martin Marprelate's works had not been what he had hoped. The conspirators had perhaps made a mistake in removing so many copies for sale independently of Sharpe; he had particularly resented the large quantities carried off for sale by the cobbler Humphrey Newman, 'for which I did chide with Newman, for that he was loth to have any to gayne but himself'.

Terrified by his arrest, Sharpe now described how he had seen Waldegrave print the first tracts at Kingston-on-Thames and Nor-thampton on a press belonging to Penry. The scandalous material against the Bishops had come, so Penry had told him, from notes found in the study of John Field; on his death-bed Field 'had willed them to be burnt and repented for collecting them'. Udall had corrected the proofs. Udall had indeed written the anonymous *Demonstration*, and had it printed at Mrs. Crane's. Worried about the searches at Kingston, Penry and Waldegrave had gone to Nor-thampton to obtain the help of Sir Richard Knightley, using a county muster as their cover. A tenant of Sir Richard's son Valentine, called Jeffs, had been paid 50s. 6d. to cart the press to Fawsley. There the second tract had been printed. This time Penry corrected the proofs, and Humphrey Newman took the books to London.

After a few days the presence of the press at Fawsley had become common gossip. Steven, one of the Knightley servants, moved it to a lonely house near Coventry belonging to Mr. Hales, a poor relation of Sir Richard's. The search now became 'very hot', and Steven had to be 'conveyed out of the way'. Sharpe went to earth at his father-in-law's at Wolston, where Waldegrave arrived one day looking 'palely', to say that he was giving up. Sharpe himself had begun to crack and thought of surrendering to Sir Christopher Hatton; he had even asked advice of Knightley, who dissuaded him from going to Court since people there 'were presently so moved, as surely they wolde hang him'. Penry had invited him to take Waldegrave's place, but he had declined unless Hatton refused to give him his remission; it was at this point that he sent his wife to Hatton, 'with a Supplication to that purpose'.

Penry had tried twice more to enlist him after Mistress Sharpe's return. The bookbinder had equivocated and, thinking the press gone north, again fled to his father-in-law's, only to find Hodgkin printing away there at Roger Wigston's, 'for the which I was sorry'. Nonetheless he consented to bind the new lot of tracts for delivery by the Warwick–London carrier 'to one Lawrence Wood, a Taylor dwelling at the end of Fish Street', and that had been his last service to Martin Marprelate before his apprehension. Flashes of incident authenticated the bookbinder's grim but eager tale. Once a cart conveying the press had stuck in a gutter, and the carter never passed the place again without shuddering. Mrs. Wigston had pretended to her servants that she employed Hodgkin as an embroiderer, and Sharpe had bound the tracts in a bedroom. His long detailed confession was disastrous to the conspirators. Those he had named were arrested and made depositions which led in turn to others. By November 16 Knightley, Wigston and Hales were in the Fleet, and spent the winter there.

But to Richard Bancroft the hunt after Martin Marprelate was no more than a sensational, totally unexpected hue and cry, heightening and exhilarating his wider and more plodding purpose. He spent most of the winter of 1589–90 questioning Puritan ministers and preachers, as well as more pliant parishioners and servants. Stephen Chatfield at Kingston deposed that two years previously Udall 'talking one day in the fields' had declared that, if the Bishops did try to silence him, he would 'give them such a blow as they never had'. In January 1590 Udall was brought from his refuge at Newcastle, and examined before the High Commission, 'after a journey I would not wish mine enemy'. He admitted the previous year's visits to Horton and Mrs. Crane. Penry he had last seen three months before, when he had called at his door in Newcastle for a few minutes on the way to Scotland, but 'neither came in neither did he so much as drink with me'. After refusing to say anything that would incriminate himself or anybody else, Udall was sent back to jail.

Next month Sir Richard Knightley, Mr. Hales, and Roger Wigston and his wife, appeared in the Star Chamber 'for maintaining seditious persons, books and libels'. Hatton presided, but Richard Bancroft was 'the special man that instructed the trial'. Knightley pleaded that Penry had cheated him into allowing the use of Fawsley by feigning to reprint a tract already licensed, and begged forgiveness of the Queen. The judges were at pains to extenuate the offence of this powerful landlord; 'yet notwithstanding you be beloved of all of us,' said Hatton, 'justice must be done.' Hales blamed Sir Richard for involving him, and Penry for deceiving both. Roger Wigston said that his wife had asked a room at Wolston for the printer, 'which he consented unto, knowing the purpose . . . and that was all'. Mistress Wigston displayed more courage than the men. Zeal of reformation, she declared, had been her motive, and she asked the judges 'to spare her husband, who was not privy, but only by her means and request'.

All the Lords sitting concurred that Martin's tracts 'took away Her Majesty's regal power, disinherited noblemen and gentlemen, took away all property . . .' apart from abolishing Bishops. It was a silly answer of Wigston to plead that he had obeyed his wife, 'and she passed the modesty of her sex to rule him'. They fined Sir Richard Knightley £2,000, Mr. Hales 1,000 marks, Roger Wigston 500 for obeying his wife 'and not discovering it', and Mistress Wigston £1,000. According to Camden, all the fines were remitted at Archbishop Whitgift's intercession.

It is now that we begin to glimpse the role that spies played in all this detection. Professor Trevor Roper has called secret intelligence 'the continuation of open intelligence by other means. . . . The greater part of it must always be acquired by open or official methods. Only a relatively small area requires secret penetration or espionage'.[52] The small area vital to Bancroft consisted of the plans and discussions on which the Puritan Ministers engaged in private, and it was penetrated by spies who brought him page upon page of their confidential correspondence. Who were these spies?

They have no names, unless Antony Munday, who is best known as a spy upon the Catholics but also arrested Giles Wigginton, was among them. There is a strange tale of a visitor who arrived at Fawsley unbidden while the hunt was at its height; his servant proceeded to get the Knightley servants drunk, while he himself, feigning an interest in architecture, attempted an inspection of the house. Martin Marprelate indicated how spies operated, and where, in that tract in which he parodied Whitgift's orders to his agents. The Archbishop was displayed bidding them: '. . . a six or seven of you . . . watch me Paul's Churchyard [the booksellers' quarter] . . .

especially have an eye at Boyle's shop at the Rose. And let some of you that are unknown go in thither, and if there be any strangers in the shop, fall in talk with them of Martin'. Others were given mock instructions to attend places where Puritans habitually preached, 'and there see if you can draw by speech anything from any Martinist . . . have a watch at all common inns, to see what carriage of paper either goes from or comes to London . . . and mark if any Puritan receiveth anything. Open his pack . . . we will direct our warrants so that you may search all packs'.

It was spies and snoopers and agent-provocateurs of this kind who put into Bancroft's hands that secret correspondence, stretching back at least to 1582, which became the foundation of his case against the Puritans and proved so telling later in his published exposés. It betrayed not only the Ministers' aims, but also the issues that divided them, and which men took which sides. For they too, like their enemies, had their zealots and their moderates, their fanatics and fainthearts, their autocrats who had given offence to colleagues and parishioners, and Bancroft saw to it that some of the offended talked. Under interrogation cracks appear even in monolithic organizations, which the skilled investigator is trained to widen, and Puritanism was far from monolithic. Some private grudge, some inner compulsion in a man to get his own back even at the cost of the cause, is enough to start with; the rest is coaxings, promptings, inducements, threats. By the spring of 1590 Bancroft had found at least one of the godly disgruntled enough to turn Queen's evidence. This was John Johnson, rector of All Saints, Northampton, the church in which John Penry had been married.

His more fervent colleagues had specially antagonized Johnson by their sanctimonious ritual of mutual censure, nowadays called self-criticism, and by their exaggerated displays of penitence for past conformity. When, for example, they had met at Northampton to subscribe the Book of Discipline, 'there was such ripping up of one another's Life, even from their Youth, as that they came unto great Bitterness, with many reviling Terms among themselves, one growing thereby odious to another, and some did thereupon utterly forsake those kind of Assemblies'. Johnson himself had been several times privately censured for refusing to elect elders who would put the Discipline into practice, until, threatened with more severe punishment, he had complained to a Justice of the Peace.

He was first interrogated some time before April 7. On the strength of what he gave away, the High Commission summoned Edmund Snape, Johnson's militant neighbour-minister at St. Peter's. Snape started off defiant. He refused the oath, demanding first to see the articles against him. The articles being based on Johnson's disclosures, the High Commission found it convenient to break with usual procedure and let him see them. Some of the members stood by while he read, and watched his face. He was sent back to prison, where (though he himself describes it as 'close') it had also been found convenient to permit him a visitor or two. Through one of them he sent out a letter, 'which course taken by him', Bancroft was soon to claim or admit, 'was not without the great Providence of God: For thereby their whole Plot, and all in effect that was laid to their charges, was discovered. His Letters were intercepted'. They were intercepted by Bancroft, and published by Bancroft three years later 'for the private satisfaction' (or so he said) 'of some few especial Persons'.

'Reverent and Beloved', Snape wrote, 'this day, April 7, I have been again before the Commissioners . . .' He described the articles against him: 'many . . . and very large, some Twelve, some Twenty Lines long . . .' with their details of place, time, and persons, 'by all which . . . it is most evident, that they have manifest and certain knowledge, not only of Generals, but also of Specials and Particulars'. Four days later he wrote a second letter 'to forewarn and forearm', which was also intercepted. 'Beloved. I have twice appeared before the High Commissioners. . . . Touching the Conferences, those of our Country' (meaning the Midlands) 'are yet more particularly discovered. . . . I would judge John Johnson to be the man; because, to my remembrance, Persons and Things of his Time being mentioned, he only is not named. . . . They will not, they cannot be any longer concealed. Now whether it is better and more safe that one man, with the Consent of the Rest, should boldly, freely and wisely confess and lay open, etc., or that some weak or wicked man should, without Consent, and in Eveil sort acknowledge, etc., Judge you. The thing they aim at is a Conventicle. It must come to tryal. In the cause of murther, etc., it is wont to be enquired, whether the Party fled upon it. Consider and apply . . .' He asked them to send for Thomas Cartwright's advice 'with all speed'. The High Commission also had Cartwright much in mind, and a pursuivant had already gone for him to Warwick; but they were not quite ready to arrest him, and the great Puritan leader had powerful friends at Court.

A month later Johnson gave away the organization of the Northamptonshire cells, their method of reporting upward to secret assemblies, their procedure, and their tactics. Tactics included pressure on Parliament as part of a concerted national plan, and preparation of the famous Register of all Ministers whom the Puritans disapproved and would have ousted. Parliament having failed them, every member of a cell (or *classis*, as the term was then) was to persuade as many parishioners as possible to obey the Discipline in secret. The Church established 'by human laws' in 1559 was merely the 'Church of England . . . which is ruled by an anti-Christian government'; but their own congregations were 'the Godly Churches, or the Church of God in England'.

Johnson betrayed more places, dates and names, listing some twenty members of the Midland cells. Penry and Snape had represented Northamptonshire. At the Northampton assembly, consisting of two members from every cell, Snape was 'a chief man'. In the writing of letters to brethren in London and the Universities, Snape 'was commonly the man', and most of the answers came back to him. The tactical instructions for lobbying Parliament and preparing the Register 'were penned by Snape'; it was Snape who had registered the Northampton minutes in a book 'and always kept the same'. Snape's parishioners were brought to London to quote his own words against him. They gave evidence too of secret assemblies in Cambridge and London, which had used the great Stourbridge and Bartholomew fairs as cover; somewhere apart from the booths and sideshows the godly had gathered together and agreed to teach one pure doctrine, and to work for one true Christian government 'by pastors, doctors, elders, and deacons'. No place at all for Bishops. What place then even for the Queen?

On the same day as Johnson's unburdening of himself, the Commissioners examined Thomas Edmunds. Twenty years before, a young radical just down from the University (Oxford this time), Edmunds had come under the influence of Field and Thomas Wilcox, authors of the first Puritan *Admonition to Parliament*. Appointed to a London living, he had been imprisoned during Archbishop Parker's campaign against the Puritans in 1573. But gradually he had taken against the un-Christian snobbishness of the godly, which went so far 'as the rest of the Ministers, who and wheresoever, that do not join with them . . . are altogether excluded . . . insomuch, as they will avoid the Company of all other, as much as they can possibly, refusing either to buy or sell, or to eat or drink with them'. When the militants began to take over, urging the cells onward from lesser controversies to question the entire government of the Church and 'the handling of the Discipline began to rise', Edmunds decided he had had enough and 'misliking of these courses, departed out of their company'. He now became almost as voluble as Johnson.

Some of the Ministers examined refused to give the names of those who had subscribed the Book of Discipline at Warwick, but the Commissioners had only to confront them with the Book itself and all the names, written in a 'Note taken with Mr. Littleton'. The subscribing had been done in Edward Lord's vicarage at Wolston, within easy walking distance of that manor-house of Roger Wigston's, in which the three 'embroiderers' now in the Tower had printed Martin's tracts.

In July the Commissioners, Bancroft among them, delivered the ecclesiastical sentence against Edmund Snape. He was removed from all his offices and rendered incapable of holding any title in the Church; this was commuted later to suspension for ten years. While he lay in prison awaiting his State trial on the charge of sedition, John Udall, chained among felons and denied counsel, was brought to the dock at Surrey Assizes, held for the occasion in Whitgift's manor-house at Croydon. The indictment charged him with authorship of the anonymous *Demonstration*, 'a slanderous and infamous libel against the Queen's Majesty'. John Puckering was one of the judges; the drafts of his speeches include insertions in Bancroft's handwriting. A Mr. Daulton gave evidence for the Crown in a long speech, which contained little precisely to the point. Stephen Chatfield was summoned from Kingston, but did not appear. One of the judges told Udall he must be pleased. 'I wish heartily he had been here,' Udall replied. 'I have heard and can prove it to be true, that he is very sorry that ever he made any complaint against me, confessing he did it in his Anger, when Martin first came out.' At the end of the Assizes he was remanded back to prison.

The pursuivants brought Thomas Cartwright to London in October, but he was not at once imprisoned. Time was given him to be decoyed to a conference which several of the leading Puritans still at large held, as they hoped, secretly, in the Whitechapel rectory of Richard Gardiner. Then he was taken to the Fleet. The Clink and other London prisons closed round the other seven Puritans against whom it had been finally decided to concentrate the case: Andrew King, William Prowdlove, Humfrey Fen, Daniel Wight, Edward Lord, John Payne and Melancthon Jewel. They remained in custody for some six months before their trial. Liberty was restricted, but not so sternly as to prevent them sending out messages, most or all of which were intercepted. In midwinter Snape and four others wrote to their parishioners to organize petitions for their liberation. Petitions were loyally written and presented, and this fact was added to the indictments now being prepared as evidence of seditious conspiracy. Those who had signed them had to appear before the Privy Council and put their names to a submission.

v. 80 per cent Study, 20 per cent Spies

The great trial of the Puritan Ministers opened in the Star Chamber on May 13, 1591. It lasted a month. Richard Bancroft was almost certainly one of the two expert counsel chosen to advise the Attorney General; some time before, on Hatton's orders, he had written Whitgift a letter for Elizabeth, informing her 'how far the Puritans had gone'. The Crown called Johnson, Edmunds, Stone of Warkton and Littleton, as well as other Ministers. They repeated their depositions made already in front of the High Commission, and added more. Stone's evidence, given first, lasted from six in the morning until seven at night, and now included details of the 'secret' meeting at Gardiner's Whitechapel rectory a fortnight before the arrest of Cartwright. Expecting the arrest, the assembled Ministers had discussed whether Cartwright should or should not 'reveal all or any of the matters . . . in any of their former assemblies'. Writing a little later Bancroft regretted that, either through negligence by the officer who examined Stone, 'or Mr. Stone's Perversness', he did not know what resolution had been reached. But his gift for drawing the conclusions he desired from evidence he did not possess came to his rescue, and he declared that, since Cartwright did in fact refuse the oath, this must have been the instruction given him at Whitechapel; and perhaps it was.

Thomas Edmunds's change of heart so delighted Bancroft that afterwards he could commend him as 'then of that Faction, but now a very honest man'. Richard Holmes, one of Snape's parishioners, repeated an almost lethal spasm of thinking aloud by Snape in 1589: 'How say you if we devise a way whereby to shake off all the Anti-Christian yoke and government of Bishops, and will jointly erect a Discipline and government, and that in such sort, as they that be against it shall never be able to prevail to the contrary? But peradventure it will not be this year and a half or more.' Edmund Littleton was examined about the documents discovered in his house. What precisely had been meant by the undertaking to advance the Discipline 'so far as the peace of the present state of the Church will suffer'? It meant, he replied, 'till the magistrate did inhibit him to the contrary, and force them to leave it'. Then what would happen, Bancroft inquired, if 'by their secret practises' the ministers drew away so many people that the magistrate would be unable to suppress them? 'I do but ask the question.'

It was two years later, in a pamphlet, that he asked it at length, and answered. Somehow the trial did not develop as he and the Archbishop had desired. The crime in which we must assume he believed, which from early manhood he had steadily been compiling mountains of evidence to prove, was a revolutionary conspiracy. If he had managed to prove it, the accused would have been doomed. But he did not manage. They maintained steadily that they had never sought more than to persuade, to prepare, to petition, and to introduce the new form of Church discipline by legal means; there had never been any intent of violent overthrow by any of them. All, witnesses and accused alike, firmly denied that the Queen's title had ever been called in question; indeed she was their one hope, the female Hercules who would one day arise and cleanse the Augean stables of the Bishops. Many of the common lawyers were on their side against the prerogative courts of Star Chamber and High Commission. They still had highly placed friends close to the Queen, and among their sympathizers, though wavering, cautious, and reluctant to go too far, may be counted William Cecil.

So there were no convictions in the Star Chamber. The Ministers were set free by stages, though never totally discharged. John Udall had been separately sentenced to death. The Turkey Merchants pleaded through a series of mediators with Whitgift and the Queen to let him go as their chaplain to the Guinea coast. Pardon came, if it came at all, too late. Udall was dead in prison before it could avail.

Penry remained with the Scottish Ministers a year, despite protests from the English Court and a perfunctory writ of banishment by James VI, which was a dead letter from the start. Though he could, he said, have spent the rest of his life there 'privily', he returned south to take up his mission on behalf of the people of Wales. In London he joined a separatist group and was arrested at a secret service in Islington woods, escaped, and went into hiding further out. He came back to town to join his wife and children. On March 23, 1593 Antony Anderson, the same vicar of Stepney whom Martin Marprelate had once satirized as a thief and seducer, recognized and denounced him. Pursuivants took him to the Counter prison near London Bridge, and while he was there the Separatist leaders Henry Barrowe and John Greenwood were hanged.

The indictment against him was built in part upon scraps of paper stolen by Bancroft's agents from his room in Edinburgh.[53] They were nothing more than notes, never intended to be published as they stood, but unfortunately could be interpreted as insulting to the Queen. He pleaded in vain to have other notes produced, with much material from his published works, which would bear witness to his loyalty. He appealed to William Cecil, who received him at Cecil House and advised him to write to Elizabeth herself. But Whitgift saw to it that his trial was rushed through, and the Court of King's Bench condemned him to death. He was dragged hurriedly to the gallows on a May morning, aged thirty, after a mission of six years.

Despite the failure of the trial, Bancroft could be satisfied with his own work of those six years. During the rest of the reign Puritanism as a political force was dead, killed by the death of its great patrons and by him. Its message sank more quietly and deeper into the souls, minds and hearts of the English people and within three generations would for a brief spell sweep away both sovereign and Church. This he could hardly have foreseen. He himself had taken such pains to know his enemy that he could have argued for them as powerfully as he did against. Human weaknesses of course had helped him, such as Sharpe the bookbinder's panic and financial disappointment, Johnson's resentment of Snape's arrogance, and Edmunds's feeling that the militants had taken things too far. Torture had helped. So had accident, and the fear or garrulity of servants, and spies had given the alleged conspiracy an air of life. In 1593 Bancroft put some of the story together in his two celebrated little books, *Dangerous Positions* and *A Survey of the Pretended Holy Discipline*. They

were his compensation for failure to secure convictions and his
justification and vaunt of all he had done, and are still a monument to
his mastery of Intelligence and propaganda.

John Johnson's Queen's evidence is there. So are extracts from
Penry and Marprelate, all neatly mortised with the confessions of
Edmunds, Stone, Littleton and the rest. There too is the principal
trophy of Bancroft's secret service, the stolen correspondence of the
Puritan Ministers, written mostly to or by John Field. Reading
through the information furnished by these letters, and assuming
that they helped to frame the articles shown to Edmund Snape, we
understand Snape's consternation. What secrets they betrayed! 'A
Bill endorsed with Mr. Field's hand' about the Wandsworth conference in 1572, the election of eleven elders, names, rules; an account
of a great welcome in 1584 for those firebrand Scottish Presbyterians,
temporarily refugees in London, and injunctions to debate the ever-
crucial issue whether or not 'to tarry for the Magistrate'; pastor
Gellibrand, noting the fear of the godly 'to testifie anything with
their Hands, lest it breed danger before the time'; a Minister
boasting that he preached every Sunday without any reference to
the Book of Common Prayer; directions how to turn churchwardens
into elders; warnings about a woman apostate who had gone to
London to betray the secret meetings; a pastor begging Field's
forgiveness for some unknown offence, 'and if it may not be passed
by without a further Confession . . . in London will I lie down and
lick the dust at your feet'; and finally, among much else, Mr. Lord
contemplating a day when the 'archbishops, Bishops, Chancellors,
Deans, Canons, Archdeacons, Commissaries, Registers Apparitors
etc. . . . must be thrust from their livings' and somehow 'provided
for, that the Commonwealth be not thereby pestred with Beggars'.
For a mind like Bancroft's, not too scrupulous in determining what
all these words had exactly meant in practice, they may well have
seemed a blueprint for revolution; and balked of a like conclusion
by the Star Chamber, revolution is what he made of them in his
books.

Many reformist movements of either Left or Right, having once
come to power and carried out certain changes, find themselves
harried by extremists of their own side, who accuse them of not
having gone far enough. The resemblance in this respect can hardly
have been missed between, on the one hand, Protestantism and
Puritanism at this period, and, on the other, Social Democracy and

Communism today. During Mary Tudor's reign everything hostile to the Roman Catholic Church had been forbidden, and most of the Reformer leaders went to prison, exile or the stake. So in many parts of Europe, until quite recent times, was everything that seriously jeopardized capitalism either forbidden or kept in severely restricted opposition. In 1559 the exiles returned. The Pope was expelled, the Book of Common Prayer established. Some of the exiles became Deans and Bishops. Within months these one-time sufferers for change were being assailed by Puritans-to-be for having betrayed 'true religion', as Social Democrats in power have been assailed by Communists for having 'betrayed the working-class', and Russian Communists by China for having 'betrayed the international proletariat'.

Bishop Aylmer, who in the fifties had escaped from Mary Tudor in the false bottom of a wine-vat, became to Martin Marprelate in the eighties 'a furious and senseless brute beast . . .' who had 'bidden farewell to the sincerity of religion', as British Labour leaders became 'capitalist lackeys' to the British Communist Party. The extremist group that thinks itself betrayed divides in Parliamentary countries into two wings, one open and outwardly constitutional, the other penetrative and clandestine. Until 1587 the Puritans centred their efforts for 'further reform' on Parliament. After the failure of 1587 the main thrust came from outside Parliament, and hope rested with the clandestines. The Puritan penetration of the parishes may fairly be compared with Communist penetration of trade unions, the battlefield shifting over the centuries from Church to factory, from congregation to economic group. Language is similar. Exclusiveness is similar. Organization into cells is similar. Tactics of attack are similar. And so are the Establishment's tactics of defence: to penetrate the penetrators, and infiltrate the infiltration. Little in these respects has altered save the original source of inspiration and the names.

*

Six years passed after the great trial before the Queen rewarded Bancroft with the see of London. Whitgift's much-quoted recommendation[54] of his protégé reads more like a reference for a Chief Constable than for a prelate. It contained very little about learning, and nothing about saintliness, but a great deal about Bancroft's endowments as a hunter-down of sectaries. The new Bishop found St. Paul's a pigsty and purged and scourged it with a Visitation lasting the whole winter of 1598–9, the record of which is seventy pages long. In 1600 he took a lead in the suppression of the Earl of Essex's abortive rebellion; indeed the Earl might have succeeded in capturing London, but for 'a company of pikemen and other forces gathered together by the wise and diligent care of the Bishop of London'. Bancroft primed the preachers against Essex the following Sunday and 'sent diverse up and downe the Citie' to seize ballads published in his favour. This was the old trail, the old enemy again; Essex had become the Sir Galahad of the Puritans and after his execution took his place in their hagiography . . . Essex, Leicester's stepson, who had once flourished a copy of Martin Marprelate at Court.

Elizabeth died three years later, with an exhausted Whitgift praying at her side. The following winter King James summoned his great conference between the Bishops and the Puritans at Hampton Court. Andrew Melville, leading the Scottish Presbyterians, shook one of Bancroft's pamphlets in his face and called him 'the capital enemy of all the Reformed Churches in Europe'. A month after the conference had ended Archbishop Whitgift caught cold crossing the Thames from Lambeth. He died at the end of February, and before the year was out the Great Detective had succeeded him in the throne of Saint Augustine.

Chapter Seven

SECRET SERVICE AGAINST THE RIGHT: THE CATHOLICS, 1578-1603

i. The Protection of the Realm

THE English Catholics contended that they were persecuted for their religion, and their religion only. The English Government contended that the laws penalized the Catholics as a danger to the State, and a far greater danger than the Puritans, because of their links with the Papacy, Philip II and the Guises. Philip remained the arch-enemy until his death in 1598. The massacre of St. Bartholomew's Night in 1572, laid first and foremost upon the Guises, blackened for ever in all Protestant eyes a name already dark and left a lasting dread of a similar night of the long knives in England. Fear for the Queen's life, and total uncertainty about her successor, kept the country in restless apprehension of the same kind of civil war as left a million corpses in its wake in France. Behind all these there was believed to stand a succession of Popes, each one holding a new Cardinal Pole in leash to sweep across to Dover, reconcile the God-forsaken English, and drag those who would not be reconciled to the stake.

An engine of savage enmity had been set in motion, to which an alternation of Acts of Parliament and events at home and overseas gave almost continual momentum. The wheels began to turn with the Acts of Supremacy and Uniformity in 1559. The penalties they had provided were extended in 1563, the oath of Supremacy now being demanded of many classes of private individuals, instead of only the chief servants of the State, and a second instead of a third refusal to take it being made punishable with death. Five years later Mary Stuart crossed Solway Firth and threw herself on Elizabeth's protection. There followed the rising of the Northern Earls, the execution of Norfolk and Northumberland, and the flight into lifelong exile of the Earl of Westmorland. Two months after the defeat of the rising, Pope Pius V excommunicated Elizabeth, declared her a heretic and her 'pretended title' to the Crown forfeited; her subjects were released from their allegiance and commanded never to venture to obey her laws. The Government replied by promising anyone who would give information about 'seditious books or Bulls' rewards so large that 'they should have just cause to think themselves well used'; any accomplice in such publications who turned informer was guaranteed protection. The following year anyone who brought any Papal decree into England was made guilty of high treason. Lists were drawn up of Catholics abroad, and all who had fled since the Queen's accession were condemned to loss of their entire property, unless they consented to return and submit to the religion of the State.

Return some did, but not to submit. On September 29, 1568 William Allen and a group of 'poor men without resources' founded at Douai in the Spanish Netherlands a college for the housing and training of English priests in exile. In 1572 Pope Gregory XIII granted a monthly allowance of a hundred gold crowns, and in 1573 the College sent home its first missionary for the recovery of England, Lewis Barlow. Philip granted an annual sixteen hundred florins in 1578, which he soon increased to two thousand. By 1579 fifty-two priests had been sent on the English mission. That was the year of the abortive Spanish landing in Ireland. More alarming to the English authorities was the secret arrival in London in 1580 of the two disguised Jesuits, Robert Persons and Edmund Campion, armed only with their faith. Persons returned safe to Europe and spent the rest of his long life overseas (chiefly in Spain) as a brilliant, tireless and at times disastrous organizer and polemicist of the English Counter-Reformation. Campion was betrayed and executed. His radiant example reconciled many to Catholicism and left the Government in little doubt that the old faith would not be allowed to die away from fear, indifference, or apathy.

So the Act passed in the following year aimed first of all at converts. It was proclaimed high treason to return to the Roman Catholic religion or to persuade anyone to return. The 1559 penalty against recusants rose from 12*d.* for every Sunday and Holy-day missed to the enormous sum of £20 for every month. Only one-third of the fines was now to be applied for relief of the parish poor, instead of the whole sum; one-third went to the Queen, and one-third to the informer. In default of payment the Queen might seize and enjoy all the offender's movable property and two-thirds of his lands and tenements. Many Catholics had made property over to family or friends in order to avoid the fines imposed in 1559 and retain a livelihood; all such conveyances were now made void retrospectively. Nonetheless, during the five years after the mission of the two Jesuits, 216 more priests followed them. During 1584 Francis Throckmorton, one of the Catholic branch of Sir Nicholas's family, confessed a project for the rescue of Mary Stuart and the invasion of England, part of which was to include a landing by the Duke de Guise in Sussex. The Pope now summoned William Allen to further tasks in Rome, and in 1585 a new Statute ordered all priests to quit England within forty days. Any who remained behind, and all who harboured them, were declared traitors. In 1586 Antony Babington and his companions confessed a treasonable correspondence with the Queen of Scots, aimed at invasion and the murder of Elizabeth and her principal advisers. Mary's trial and execution followed hard on his, and soon after receiving the news the Pope made Allen Cardinal. Allen had merited this dignity for services well apart from his political activities, but the English Government inevitably took it as a political retaliation.

As the Armada approached, Allen, though far from being one of the most bellicose of exiles, 'was induced to write—or to set his name to'[55] a long and vitriolic attack upon the Queen, which described her as 'an incestuous bastard, begotten and borne in sinne of an infamous curtesan', and violently denounced her public and her private life. The populace were adjured to rise against her. As for those who fought for her, 'you are sure to be damned . . . this is the daie of her fall . . . forsake her therefore betime . . .' The Spanish Ambassador in Rome sent this document to Antwerp, where it was printed ready for distribution in England, had Parma and his Spaniards landed. A number of priests were executed soon after the defeat of the Armada, and in 1593 all Catholics over sixteen, free, in prison, or abroad, who had been convicted of not attending the State Church, were ordered by Act of Parliament to return to their homes within forty days of the end of session and 'not any time after to pass or remove above 5 miles from hence'; the penalty for non-compliance was loss of all property of whatever kind, and could extend to death. In terms of Statutes the anti-Catholic arsenal was well charged. Elizabeth still had no declared successor. In 1594 Father Persons pseudonymously published a book examining a dozen possible heirs to the English crown and suggesting that in the Catholic interest it might be best allotted to Philip II's daughter, the Infanta Isabella.

Between 1577, when Father Cuthbert Mayne suffered at Launceston, and the death of Elizabeth in 1603, 182 English Catholics were executed, of whom 123 were priests and 54 had been converted. Many families were ruined. Men and women continued to leave the country; in all 44 English religious houses were founded in various parts of Europe during the half-century after the establishment of Douai. The English College at Rome began to send priests on the English mission in 1579 and the College at Valladolid ten years later. Douai sent 438 priests from its foundation until the year of the Queen's death.

Those Englishmen therefore who were responsible for recruiting men into Intelligence had fear first of all to play upon; and this fear cannot be conveyed without a word or two about the manner in which the laws were carried out. The picture is not one of that total desolation which strict literal obedience to the Statutes would have made possible. The number of those executed, even of those imprisoned, is extremely small in proportion to the whole population, and many priests were only banished. Families survived, and survive to this day, who were neither ruined nor apostatized. In the remoter country areas Mass was said regularly over long periods; Catholics gathered together at private houses even in the heart of London. Noblemen's houses were not subject to search, and Lady Montagu's residence became known as 'Little Rome'. Father Richard Blount managed to remain in the same house undetected for fifteen years. John Towneley of Towneley Hall in Lancashire passed years in prison and paid huge fines for refusing to attend a Protestant service; but several Catholic neighbours with big estates went unmolested, and even in the eighties a few Justices of the Peace remained Catholics.[56]

Conditions for the laity, and sometimes even for priests, also varied in the prisons. It was possible for an informer to denounce the jailer Gittens (who had had charge of John Penry) for extortion, but most of this crew expected and managed to make money out of their job. The Tower bills show considerable sums owing the Governor from well-to-do prisoners for fuel, light, washing, clothing, barbers, bedding. Some had a servant with them, others were allowed visits by doctor or surgeon. Captain Edmund Waynham received a physician 'who healed him of his sciatica'; further on we come to

William Stocks, London prentice, 'brought in for Papistry', who 'lay without a bed for 7 weeks'. Messages could be passed in or out for bribes, and priests managed to say Mass and hear confessions. But punctuating the privileges is always the grim phrase 'close prison'. Many Catholics spent years in prison separated from their families, and some died there.

After the Statute of 1581 the fear was always present of torture and a frightful death. Knowledge of the agonies endured by victims of the Spanish Inquisition, captured Englishmen among them, played its part in keeping Elizabethan England Protestant. In Spain the final execution was by fire, in England butchery. Horses dragged men condemned for treason on hurdles to the scaffold, over the mire and rough stones of the public highway. The sentence decreed that they should first be hanged, then cut down while yet alive, and that their genitals should then be cut off and their entrails torn out and burnt. By the scaffold stood the officers of State and preachers of the Established Church, offering pardon in return for apostasy, and huge crowds customarily attended every execution. (At the execution of Father Henry Garnett a place in one of the stands cost twelvepence.) The attitude of these crowds might determine how much or how little a doomed man was to suffer. In 1601 an onlooker ran out and supported the hanging body of Father Mark Barkworth, so that its weight might not choke him and save him from disembowelment alive; but Lord Howard of Effingham ordered the executioner to let Campion hang until he died.

To the priests all their recent lives had been only a prelude to this day. Murals of scaffold and torture-chamber covered the walls of the English College in Rome and once a year a group of students, set apart to observe the Spiritual Exercises laid down for the Society of Jesus by St. Ignatius Loyola, learnt to contemplate and ardently desire the bloody deaths of martyrs. Almost every record bears witness that the priests met death with incredible courage and forgivingness, even with joy. 'To be hanged, compared with torture,' one of them wrote, 'is not so much as to suffer a bad hiccup in Rome', and Father Robert Southwell cried out at his trial: 'I am decayed in memorie with long and close imprisonment, and I have been tortured ten times: I had rather have endured ten executions. I speak not this for myself, but for others, that they may not be handled so inhumanlie to drive men to desperation, if it were possible.'

Francis Throckmorton withstood his first racking in the Tower and gave nothing away. Strung to the rollers again, he confessed everything 'before he was strained to any purpose'. Antony Babington had become so terrified by the arrest of his companions, that he was on the verge of going direct to Walsingham and turning spy, when his own arrest intervened. Many priests were racked, some of them several times, and Campion, pleading Not Guilty at his trial, could not lift his arm. The names of the professional torturers, Richard Topcliffe and Justice Richard Young, are two of the most infamous in our history. The Privy Council granted them the right to take prisoners to their own houses and extract information from them privately in their own way. Topcliffe so used Father Henry Walpole that, trying to write from prison afterwards, his hands could no longer form legible letters.

Shortly before Christmas 1591 Father Robert Southwell wrote secretly from London to Richard Verstegan at Antwerp: 'From Topcliffe's house [a priest] is carried to Bridewell. There he is hanged up by the hands in manacles and examined. . . . In prison, if they have not relief, or be not able to pay, they are used like dogs, throwen in to dungeons . . .' Sometimes men were hung by manacles as long as nine hours, 'so that oftentimes they swound upon the torture . . . and are hanged up againe: . . . They whipp priests naked, as they did Mr. Beesley and Mr. Jones. . . . Topcliffe useth to keep them from sleep by watching them until they are almost past their senses . . . and then beginneth to examine them afresh.'

The following June Southwell himself was betrayed to Topcliffe, who wrote to Elizabeth that he had him safe 'in my stronge chamber in Westminster churche yard . . . if your highness pleasure bee to knowe any thinge in his harte, To stand against the wawle, his feet standinge upon the grownde and his hands put as hyghe as he can reatche . . . will inforce him to tell all . . .'. And in August Verstegan reported that on one occasion, after Southwell had refused to confess, 'Topclif left him hanging, and so went abrode. After he had been a long time absent, one of his servants, perceaving the father . . . in some danger to give up the ghoste, called him hastely home againe to lett him downe for that tyme.' Southwell did not yield; but in that earlier letter, while still at liberty, he had written, 'If some priests have fallen, yet can it not be much marvelled at.' Of those who did fall a small number became spies; with one or two, like Gilbert Gifford, the motive was something worse than fear.

ii. Remorse of a Spy

Thomas Bell, ordained in exile at Rome in 1572, went on the English mission six years later. He was caught and 'endured many kinds of torment'. Although a report to the English Government in 1586 could describe him as still 'a Romanist, a dangerous person for sedition', by 1593 he had apostatized and was busy betraying fellow-Catholics in Yorkshire and those who housed them. With him travelled the former priests Thomas Clarke, William Hardesty and Antony Major. Clarke, sent from Douai, had been caught at Newcastle soon after landing. Examined by the Bishop of Durham, he gave away the whereabouts of the Jesuit Richard Holtby, to whom he had been specially directed. Holtby was never caught, but on the night of September 30, 1594 Clarke betrayed the seminary priest Edward Osbaldeston, also from Douai, in an inn at Towlerton. Taken to York Castle, Father Osbaldeston wrote an account to warn his fellow-prisoners: 'I came to the inn a little before Mr. Clark . . . I knew him not fully, for I thought he had been in the South; but at supper I looked earnestly at him, and I thought it was he, and yet I still persuaded myself that he knew me not, and if he should know me he would do me no harm, which fell out otherwise. God forgive him for it. For when we were going to bed, he went and called the curate and constable and apprehended us . . .' Father Osbaldeston was hanged, drawn and quartered at York two months afterwards.

William Hardesty had been admitted to the English Hospice at Rome as a pilgrim and remained as a student at the College. He was one of those who in 1586 petitioned to keep the College in charge of the Society of Jesus. The petition he signed declared that he had been one of 'the sons of the Society for the full term of seven years, nor, by the help of God, will we ever withdraw from the duty of upright children towards their pious parents'. He was sent on the mission and by the summer of 1592 Verstegan heard in Antwerp that he had been captured in the North, 'brought to London and sent down again, but to what end is not known'. In fact he apostatized, and in 1594 betrayed and identified the seminary priest John Ingram, who had been with him in Rome. Ingram was several times tortured by Richard Topcliffe in London, and executed at Newcastle. Antony Major, ordained in France about 1587, apostatized in England in 1594, and accused the seminarist Father John Boste

while Boste was being racked. Boste went to execution together with
Father Ingram.

Unforgettable among these wretched stories is that of the one-
time priest Antony Tyrrell. The violence of his remorse after he had
betrayed his faith and friends and raped his conscience tore from
him what must be the longest and most excoriating self-revelation
of any spy in history. Even abridged, it occupies nearly two hundred
printed pages. It throws a piercing light not only upon himself, but
upon the methods of those who exploited him; methods used also by
Catholic inquisitors then and often before, and still in use in the
service of various creeds and States.

*

Antony Tyrrell came of gentry with land in Essex. His father George
Tyrrell went into exile for religion's sake, with his mother, a brother,
and a sister, who became a nun; in 1573 father and brother, almost
destitute, journeyed on foot into Spain and received a small pension
from Philip II. In all save religion Antony may be likened to those
Protestant sons of country squires, already described, whose
rebellious energy found an outlet at the beginning of Mary's reign in
joining Sir Thomas Wyatt. Frustration involved them in conspiracies like those of Francis Throckmorton and Antony Babington, part
of which was reckless and romantic fantasy. Sometimes they would
talk idealistically of retiring into contemplative life. Many fled
overseas to the seminaries and some returned to martyrdom.

In 1574, aged twenty-two, Tyrrell took his B.A. in England. He
joined his family abroad, but suddenly returned and lived on his kin
and friends, endeavouring to raise the £10 necessary for an M.A.
For a while he hung around William Cecil, who had once been
friendly with his father. That autumn he was caught in an attempt
to go abroad again, and put in prison. Cecil interceded for him, and
George Tyrrell wrote from Louvain in July 1576 to thank him 'for my
poor son, who if your honour had not extended your pitiful hand,
had drunk of the sour and bitter cup'.

After his release Antony did go abroad once more, first to the
seminary at Douai, and then to the English College at Rome. He was
ordained priest and sent on the English mission via Rheims on
October 29, 1580, with a blessing and 160 gold crowns from Pope
Gregory. In April 1581 a lay apostate called John Nichols recognized
him in the street in London and shouted that he was a traitor. He

was thrown into the Gatehouse prison, where he formed a catastrophic friendship with the priest John Ballard, soon to become an evil genius of Antony Babington and his companions. In January next year he escaped and spent some time at liberty. Early in 1584 he came across Ballard in London. Both of them got away to France, and in April Father Barret reported him again among the students of Douai (temporarily transferred to Rheims), 'little by little regaining strength after great hazards and labours'.

He went to Rome with Ballard that autumn and returned secretly to England with him at the beginning of 1586. They shared lodgings, and rode many journeys together in disguise 'following the company of young gentlemen'. Deciding it was time to attend to their function as priests, they planned to cross the Channel again 'to study and to retire themselves to a more strait life', but as Tyrrell had not the means Ballard went alone. He returned in June with a story that the Pope and the Kings of France and Spain had settled to invade England before Michaelmas. With Ballard, Tyrrell began to meet Babington's wild young friends and even paid a visit to the French Ambassador. He was playing with fire; and on July 4 he was again arrested and taken to the Counter prison in Wood Street.

His capture occurred at a deadly time. A few weeks earlier Walsingham had arranged for Mary Queen of Scots' 'secret' correspondence with Catholics in England and abroad to be reopened, so that Thomas Phelippes and his other agents could intercept it. Babington had used this channel in innocence to write to her a day after Tyrrell's arrest, and Mary sent her fatally incriminating reply a fortnight later. Both plot and counter-plot were near their climax, and Tyrrell became an important catch.

Examined by Young and Topcliffe and alternately offered promises and threats, he at first yielded nothing. On the night before the Assizes he was told that he would be tried next morning and executed. He prepared joyfully for martyrdom, but his captors denied him the satisfaction. Instead he was released from close confinement and with the help of friends procured freedom of the prison for £10; and when he had ripened into new hope of life, with 'the memory of my former pleasures and delights . . . by little and little sensuality creeping into me', Young sent for him again. He had returned, he flattered Tyrrell, from a talk about him with the Queen herself. Her Majesty recalled his father and wished Antony well, if he would tell all he knew. He was coaxed into taking an oath on the Book of Common Prayer and revealing a little about his journeyings with Ballard. On August 4 Ballard was arrested and accused with Babington and the rest of plotting the murder of Elizabeth . . . 'which when I did hear [Tyrrell wrote] did sore appall me . . . I should be a partaker of his punishment, though I deserved it not. From thence began the cause of all my ruin.'

Tyrrell had taken Ballard's talk about an invasion as braggadocio, but he had concealed it. He now disclosed it all, at which Young was much pleased, shook hands with him, and promised him the Queen's favour if he would write a full account that night. He sat up till ten o'clock in prison writing it, and incriminating his friend Robert Barnwell, to whom he had repeated Ballard's talk. The thought of this denunciation would not let him sleep. Early next morning he tore it all up, wrote another account leaving Barnwell out, and sent it away. His captors demanded more. A list came back from Young 'of divers gentlemen's names', about whom he must deliver information by the morning following. 'All night I was wonderfully perplexed what I should do, and in the end the devil getting the upper hand . . . I gave my consent fully to become a Judas . . . and in one moment of time to abandon myself of all grace and goodness that ever I had obtained before, and plunged myself headlong into the bottomless pit of hell.'

As a priest, he knew himself doomed; by remaining Catholic and betraying his friends, he would incur the disgust of Catholics without gaining favour with Protestants. So he decided to apostatize. He also resolved on an attempt to ingratiate himself with the Lord Treasurer, fearing that Young, having once milked him of everything he could betray and used it to his own advantage, would send him back to prison and forget him. He sent Young his letter abjuring the Catholic faith on a Sunday morning, making out that he had more to tell for Cecil's ears only, and was summoned by Young the same afternoon; 'and as soon as I was come hither he carried me up into his upper parlour all alone, and pinning fast the door did then embrace me in his arms, as who should say "welcome home, gentle brother".' Young inflated Tyrrell's sense of self-importance by telling him that his letter had gone to the Privy Council, 'and it is incredible what joy they have conceived'.

After more brotherly talk he gave Tyrrell a cloak, and the two men were rowed up-river to the gardens of Cecil House, where the Lord Treasurer awaited them. Tyrrell prostrated himself and swore that, though he might have been deceived in his religion, he had never been a traitor to the Queen. After voicing guarded pleasure at his 'miraculous' conversion and warning him to keep nothing back, Cecil asked questions about Babington and his fellows, now under torture in the Tower, to which Tyrrell answered 'as much as I did know and more, with hard and bitter speeches against each of them', and was just beginning to denounce others when the Earl of Huntingdon arrived and Cecil had no more time that day to listen.

Next morning Young sent urgently for him and showed him a letter from Cecil, in which 'for your father's sake, whom I loved entirely, as I am sure he did me', the Lord Treasurer exhorted the trapped man to reveal everything he knew about all Catholics in prison or still free. Tyrrell complied in a long letter 'which contained naught else but false reports, malicious inventions of mine own pernicious head'. This too was not enough. He received a demand from Cecil by return, under twenty-eight headings, for yet more detailed intelligence about all those he had spoken of meeting in England and abroad. In his reply, which occupies some twenty-five pages of print, he now proceeded falsely to denounce more than a hundred people from Pope Gregory XIII and the Queen of Scotland to Catholic noblemen like the Earl of Arundel, now in the Tower, and country gentry at whose houses he had been given refuge. Here and there were scraps of truth, on which he built 'a mount of lies', especially about secret meetings at which great men abroad and their instruments in England had plotted to assassinate the Queen. His fabrications concerning Babington and Ballard were enough to hang them twenty times. He was given a room to himself in prison, and explained his strange absences to his fellow-prisoners by sending them a message that he had been examined about Ballard and sent back into close confinement for refusing to give anything away.

During the week following he invented dozens more denunciations. At first he felt sure that Cecil must see through them; but often Cecil prompted him, repeating things which the prisoners now in the Tower had confessed, 'and I was very glad to hear him, hoping thereby that my own reports would carry the more credit'. On September 13 Justice Young had Tyrrell moved to the Clink. The Babington trial opened the same day. Ballard had been so racked that he had to be carried into the dock in a chair. The accused men were sentenced to death on September 14 and 15. On the day of Ballard's sentence Tyrrell was being rowed along the Thames with his keeper to make fresh confessions before Justice Young, 'and by the way it was my hap to meet the barge that carried the prisoners, and to come so near to it that I looked Mr. Ballard full in the face, and he earnestly beheld me . . .'

He now passed from false witness to sacrilege. Elizabeth and Cecil, through Richard Young, authorized him to carry out his duties as a Catholic priest in the Clink, the better to observe his fellow-prisoners. He said Mass, heard confessions, and himself made false confessions. Those he now spied on and betrayed included the priest John Adams, who had just returned from banishment, Richard Dibdale, and his own confessor, John Lowe, all of whom were martyred at Tyburn on October 8. Having done all the harm he could in the Clink, it was arranged that he should be set free to spy outside. On Young's instructions he persuaded another Catholic, 'my dearest friend', to intercede for his release, to which Cecil and Young consented after a pretence of fury at such a traitorous request. He spent the Christmas season visiting Catholic houses and other prisons and denouncing whoever came his way. Conscience was driving him distracted. 'I would sometimes when my candle was put out imagine my chamber to be full of devils . . . watching when they should carry my soul as their perpetual prey into eternal damnation.' In order to escape this nightmare double life he begged that he might be publicly declared a Protestant convert and began to write a book against Catholicism, as two or three lay apostates had done. The authorities, however, had more use for him as outwardly a Catholic and were preparing fresh assignments, when some time in the New Year events forced their hands. Father Lewis Barlow, then in the Marshalsea, confronted Tyrrell with some scraps of torn paper recovered from his room in the Clink, which had been gummed together and found to be part of his correspondence with Cecil. After attempts to lie his way out, he broke down, confessed his perfidy, and swore to finish with it and do whatever penance was imposed.

But courage failed him in the streets. He continued his visits to Justice Young and 'my foot was no sooner over his threshold than my heart began to quake'. So he continued his denunciations, while secretly composing a letter that acknowledged false accusations against at least fifty people, some lately executed, and two separately to Lord Windsor and the Earl of Arundel, imploring their forgiveness; the letter to Arundel was thrown into his room in the Tower.

He also wrote an extremely long letter to the same effect to Elizabeth, in which he detailed his treatment by Richard Young, 'a most cruel blood-sucker, a destroyer of your people, and a great abuser of your Majesty'. Finally he told Young that the Catholics had found him out. Though 'somewhat sorrowful', Young at last made arrangements for him to appear openly as a convert, the intention being that he would now abandon spying and begin afresh as a Protestant propagandist. Tyrrell gained a week's leave by a promise of returning with fresh betrayals, and went off to Yorkshire early in March 1587 with £5 and a passport.

Unknown to him, Sir Francis Walsingham took charge. The authorities had learnt from other prison spies that, apart from the letters, Tyrrell had compiled a document fifty sheets long, retracting his betrayals and accusing Walsingham and Leicester of engineering, through their own agents and agents-provocateurs, the deaths of Babington, his companions, and the Queen of Scots. Imprisoned priests had seen and approved this document and Catholics had collected £40 or £50 for Tyrrell to escape to France and publish it. Walsingham set two of his chief professional spies, Nicholas Berden and Malevery Catlin, to watch him. Catlin traced him to a remote house in Yorkshire, where he went under the name of White, 'about forty years of age, of an indifferent stature, and of an auburn hair'. Catlin advised the Earl of Huntingdon, as Lord President of the North, so thoroughly about the secrets of the house and the recusants living there 'that they cannot, I hope, escape'. But Tyrrell did escape. He got across the Border to Leith and took a boat to Hamburg, intending to do penance for the past in some Catholic community. Once again his will failed him. Walsingham's agents followed him and somehow, incredibly, he was persuaded to return to England.

The Government had him kept in close prison, while a great spectacle was prepared. Tyrrell was to appear at Paul's Cross as a Protestant Minister, there in a public sermon to recant his confession of having borne false witness against the Catholics and reassert that all his denunciations had been true. Outwardly he consented, but the Government failed to reckon with the other self that still struggled within him. Using the writing of his State sermon as a cover, he prepared the speech he had made up his mind to deliver, or at least begin, in which he would recant the expected recantation, again confirm that all his witness had been false, and declare himself a Catholic. He managed to arouse no suspicion in his jailers, who believed the pages he was so busy writing to be 'all in their favour and sound, albeit somewhat long', and on Sunday, January 21, 1588 he appeared before the people.

A Government preacher opened the proceedings with a long prologue, in which he introduced Tyrrell as an important convert with a dreadful tale to tell. Tyrrell followed. Putting aside the sermon, he began the speech. Within moments his intention had become obvious. Uproar ensued. He was torn from the pulpit and dragged to Newgate in the midst of an infuriated and cheated crowd shrieking for his blood, but not before he had had time to scatter copies. One of them fell between a young Catholic, Robert Ashley, and Richard Leigh, or Garth, a disguised priest, who had come to hear Tyrrell. Justice Young leapt into the pulpit and stormed against him. Later Young read a Royal Proclamation, making it punishable with death to possess a copy of Tyrrell's speech; but Ashley and Leigh kept theirs long enough to have others made, which were distributed in secret.

The mood of the crowd outside Newgate became such that within two hours Tyrrell had to be transferred to his old prison, the Counter in Wood Street, 'where none but Topcliffe and Young came to him'. He remained there six months, and steadfast for three, and then began once more to yield. The Armada was defeated that summer. Cecil again promised him his favour, and on October 14 the wretched man wrote thankfully accepting it 'upon any condition'. On December 8 he was brought back to Paul's Cross and this time delivered the sermon the authorities demanded. Four days later he again wrote to Cecil, hoping for his patronage and begging for a livelihood 'whereby I may the better serve God, my Prince, and my country in my vocation'. He was set free and officiated as a Protestant Minister for many years.

When he was an old man his brother Robert, who had gone into exile among the Jesuit community in Belgium, found means to persuade Antony to join him, and there Antony was reconciled to the Catholic Church for the fourth and last time. A list of apostates has against his name the words: *mortuus est poenitens*, he died penitent.

*

Tyrrell mentions at the beginning of his terrible story that Justice Young was first to have taken him for questioning by Sir Francis

Walsingham, had not Walsingham been too busy. Walsingham might have been less kindly, less paternal, than William Cecil. There would not have been the same regretful memories of friendship with Tyrrell's father in the old days. There would have been less show of intimacy with the mind of the Queen. Walsingham would have been less of a shepherd recovering a lost lamb than the Lord Treasurer. But essentially the treatment would have been the same, and Tyrrell could only have been confronted with the same alternatives: either spying, or the shambles. Walsingham had put these alternatives to so many others. He himself, subject to the anti-Catholic laws and responsible to the Privy Council for the Queen's protection, had no alternative. It was for the prisoner to choose.

Walsingham's is of course one of the great names for any History of Intelligence, if such an epithet may be used. Like other masters, he was also a great statesman, equally admired and abominated by those who have written about him. His secret service was indeed an adjunct of his statesmanship and probably the path by which, with Cecil and Throckmorton's patronage, he reached power. It was never his monopoly. He cannot be described as 'Head of the Eliza- bethan Secret Service', since no such office existed at the time. William Cecil had had many years of experience in such matters long before we begin to hear of Walsingham, and survived him by eight years. The Earl of Huntingdon ran a grimly efficient organization of spies and pursuivants and informers in the North.[57] But it so happened that most of the threads of espionage against the Catholics passed through Walsingham's hands, were even controlled by him, during a critical period from 1570 until his death in 1590. He re- ceived large sums for Intelligence from the State and spent large sums of his own, and he had a singular talent for such work.

His name is linked for ever with that of the Queen of Scots, whom according to some writers he trapped and according to others brought to justice. This part of his work has been the subject of many books. One observation is, however, worth making. All roads had ceased to lead to Rome by the 1580s, but no conspiracy could fail to lead to Mary Stuart. The Privy Council, and Walsingham especially, made ever more insistent representation to Elizabeth of the mischief and unrest Mary encouraged, as indeed she did, and the havoc which she might cause, as indeed she might if free. But in one sense Walsingham should have been grateful. Seldom, surely, before or since, has an Intelligence service held the one person on whom all trails converged so securely in its hands so long; they were bound to converge upon her by virtue of her religion, by virtue of her claim to the throne, by virtue of her character. Everything she wrote, everything written to her, every visitor she received, could be checked and traced through their links with the leaders of Catholicism in England and abroad. False sympathizers could be sent in to her in her mansion-prisons, as they were sent; communication could be cut off and restored at will, as was done. It is as if Napoleon had been granted political asylum in England after the Hundred Days, or Trotsky remained in Siberia after Stalin's victory in 1927. How much more difficult the 'Daughter of Debate' would have been to watch in France, how impossible in Spain! By coming to England she had given English Intelligence an ideal, a textbook situation; it held the one inescapable and central clue for nineteen years.

Walsingham's life-work, policies, and character are set out in three volumes of monumental biography. His whole network of spies was too wide even to be summarized here. He will be placed only in contrast to his most formidable opponent in London, Don Bernardin de Mendoza, the last Spanish Ambassador, and one or two of the situations and motives he played upon to secure his spies will then be examined.

iii. Don Bernardin de Mendoza: Priests as Spies

Mendoza was the first Spanish Ambassador in London for six years. He arrived in 1578, a year in which the Thames flooded and fish swam through the Palace of Westminster. The Spanish Embassy during his predecessor's tenure had been at Winchester House on the Southwark river-bank; if (as seems likely) Mendoza also occupied it, he could not have failed to see the heads of traitors spiked over the southern gate of London Bridge, whenever he rode or took a boat to Court. For several months the Queen refused to see him. Western Europe was narrowing into a stage for war between Elizabeth and Philip; and while the Old World fell into two halves, in the New the West-Country sea-dogs had been harrowing the Spanish Main for years, and Francis Drake had just set forth on his voyage round the world.

Mendoza and Walsingham give a first impression of being elementally opposed. Mendoza came of one of the most ancient, most powerful of Spanish noble families, Walsingham of prosperous gentry quite recently connected with the fish and wine trades. Walsingham invested in the voyages of exploration and depredation against the Spanish possessions in America; Mendoza's brother was Viceroy of Mexico. Mendoza—he was not yet forty, Walsingham ten years older—had just completed a brilliant career as commander of light cavalry in the foremost army of the day. He had served in Italy, Africa and the Low Countries. His hero was the Duke of Alva, with whom Englishmen had once been proud to serve, but whose name had by now become diabolic; and he had already made himself a reputation as a military historian of Alva's campaigns. Walsingham had never even trailed a pike in the raw bands of England. His literary output had been confined chiefly, and effectively, to dispatches; during the battle of the Armada Lord Henry Seymour wrote to him from aboard the *Rainbow* that he had contributed more towards the victory with his pen than many there had contributed with their swords.

Mendoza was a Catholic of the most rigid kind, Walsingham far closer to the Puritans than anyone else on the Privy Council except Sir Francis Knollys,[58] and each saw a minister of anti-Christ in the other. Personal witness had embittered their convictions. The rebels against whom Mendoza had led his cavalry in the Low Countries had been financed with English gold; Walsingham, Ambassador in France on the night of St. Bartholomew, had been unable to prevent murdering gangs from dragging men he had given shelter out of the Embassy to be massacred, and the instigators of that massacre had been Mendoza's friends. The King who had now accredited Mendoza to London was the same whose rule in England had driven Walsingham to spend his youth in exile. He hated Philip, and Mendoza despised Elizabeth. It was said that he never went to an audience with her without being shriven.[59] She came of families considerably less noble than his own, and her blasphemous oaths, her public conduct and private reputation were such as a Spanish peasant woman would have found quite shameless. Indeed he, the great-nephew of the great Cardinal Jimenez de Cisneros, and envoy of the nation that for centuries had been the shield of Western Christendom against the infidels, found the entire English Court and people (apart from the persecuted Catholics) the incarnation of upstart and acquisitive vulgarity.

Yet enemies who occupy the same posts and are sworn to the same tasks often mirror one another. Each of these men, as he passes along the corridors of plot and counter-plot, leaves the grim grave chill of utter ruthlessness. Their dress is not to be imagined as anything but black, their complexion as any but a tired and icy pallor. They appear to have had little private life; Mendoza was never married, and Walsingham might almost not have been, for all that we know of Lady Walsingham. They wore themselves out to serve cautious and hesitant sovereigns, of whom they constantly despaired. Walsingham was often ill and died in 1590 of an agonizing disease, and when Mendoza arrived in London he was already half-blind.

The Spaniard turned to the Queen of Scots not merely out of compassion. He cared nothing for the non-Catholic population of England, so long as they refused to save their souls. To his way of thinking Mary was the only truly anointed sovereign in the realm, although hitherto only of France and Scotland, and the obvious alternative to Elizabeth. She was suffering for the true faith, his faith, and prison had restored to her the dignity she had impaired as Queen. They never met, but between her guarded mansions and his watched Embassy there passed not only a highly conspiratorial and unscrupulous correspondence, but also a strong current of mutual respect and trust, and one of her last letters from Fotheringhay was addressed to him as 'my dearest friend'.

Apart from Sir James Croft, Mendoza claimed Lord Henry Howard as his chief spy at Court. In later years he appeared also to claim Sir Edward Stafford, English Ambassador in Paris. Of Stafford there is some doubt,[60] of Lord Henry none. Ironically, Lord Henry was a younger brother of that Duke of Norfolk who had once accused Sir James of treason. Since his brother's execution he could find no favour with Elizabeth and his New Year's gift to her in 1579, 'a juell of gold, being a ded tre with mystiltow set at the rote', was a symbol of despair. At the end of 1581 his cousin the Earl of Oxford denounced him as a crypto-Catholic and, fearing arrest, he asked Mendoza for refuge. Mendoza hid him in the Embassy. The danger passed, but Mendoza reported to Philip that he was grateful, 'no small novelty in an Englishman', and willing to serve. He might be useful; he was able, and had power in the North and friends among the ladies of the Privy Chamber.

Within weeks Lord Henry had become the Ambassador's 'second personage' and soon took the place of the terrified Sir James. Leicester and Walsingham tried to discredit him, as they had tried with Sir James, or failing that to have him sent on a mission into Germany. In July Mendoza gave him 500 crowns. In November he would have lost him on the German mission 'if I had not cast myself at his feet and begged him not to leave Court', given him another 500 crowns, and promised him a yearly pension of 1,000. Lord Henry accepted both, and Mendoza could now describe him as 'extremely zealous and gives me twice a week the most confidential and minute account of all that happens'. He was also admitted into the ciphered correspondence with the Queen of Scots, though Mary asked that he should not be trusted with anything of importance.

Mendoza particularly desired intelligence about the progress homewards of Francis Drake. In 1577 Elizabeth had sworn that she would have the head of anyone who informed Philip about the fitting out of Drake, and she had a king's ransom of reasons to keep secret his return. Mendoza made use of merchants and others 'secretly staying in some of the western ports', and when Drake finally dropped anchor sent spies to discover details of the great voyage, which the crews had been forbidden to disclose on pain of death. His efforts to obtain intelligence about the expansion of English trade, and frustrate it, is a special study in itself. Like Walsingham and many more (including Hamlet), he was adept in breaking into other people's mail. It was perfectly simple, he wrote to Philip, to open the couriers' valises in the inns. 'I myself have often done this here . . . and in an hour, with a bone reproduction of the same seal, I make up the packet, closed in the same way, having seen all I want to see . . .'

The question to what extent priests were used as spies, particularly arises in connexion with Mendoza. Priests could lead him to secular sources of Intelligence by advising him which Englishmen had been truly reconciled. Priests advised him about Lord Henry Howard. There was also a certain Antony Poyntz, whom Elizabeth had wished to send abroad as a spy posing as a refugee. He came to Mendoza and offered to act as a double agent, and the Ambassador, who felt doubts of his sincerity, was reassured by a Jesuit whom Poyntz had hidden for six months in his house. Some priests, however, fulfilled secret political functions far more direct than this, of which one example will suffice 'at perhaps the most critical moment in the whole reign'.[61]

*

In June 1581 King James VI of Scotland caused Elizabeth's ally the Regent Earl of Morton to be flung from power and beheaded, and soon afterwards there arrived from France a fascinating and ambitious cousin of the King's, Esmé Stuart, sieur d'Aubigny. Although for convenience's sake he paid lip-service to the powerful Ministers of the Scottish Church, every Court in Europe knew him for a Catholic and a friend of Duke Henri de Guise, son of the murdered François. Within a short while his charm, Parisian manners, and experience—he was forty—had completely won over the fifteen-year-old King, bored and bullied by his Calvinist tutors. He was made Duke of Lennox and given charge of one of the gateways into Scotland, Dumbarton Castle. His ascendancy at once suggested itself as a possible instrument to recover the British islands for the Holy See.

Early in September Mendoza got in touch with six leading English Catholic noblemen, all unnamed, who agreed secretly to convey into Scotland a priest also unnamed. The priest was to discover from Lennox what chance there might be of the King's conversion. Once James had been brought back into the fold and, as Mendoza wrote to Philip, had entered England with his armies, the Catholic noblemen would raise the North, declare him heir to Elizabeth, release Mary, and, if Elizabeth would not consent to the conversion of England, it was quite likely she would be deposed.

The priest returned next month. By then all six lords were in prison, and Mendoza felt 'obliged to conduct the business myself'. He was not reluctant; it gave new zest to his work in hateful London and might, if successful, bring the arrest and execution of his fellow-Catholics to an end. The priest, who had been wary with Lennox because of his French connexions, had gone much further with Lord Seton. Lord Seton would raise the matter next time he went hunting with the King; and Lord Seton inclined to think that the lure of a Spanish alliance and of two more crowns, the English and the Irish, would greatly help to win James back to Catholicism, 'in addition to its being the true road to salvation'. Mendoza sent this heartening report to Father Robert Persons, who had by now escaped to Rouen, and also to Dr. William Allen, who forwarded it to Pope Gregory. That winter the priest had a conversation with the King himself. Caution had been necessary, since James was extremely wary. Surrounded by ferocious courtiers, and constantly in danger of his life, James could not afford to be anything else; a pistol had been pointed at him even in the womb.

Before leaving England Father Persons had himself sent two priests to reconnoitre Scotland. One was William Watts, a Secular, and very probably the same who had also gone on behalf of Mendoza and the six lords. The other was a Jesuit, Father William Holt. If Persons happened to be away from London on his return, Holt was to visit a priest in hiding there, who would tell him to whom to report instead.

Another Jesuit had gone to Scotland from France, bearing impressive credentials. This was the Scotsman, Father William Crichton (or Creighton). During the previous year he had addressed a meeting of the Society of Jesus in Rome on the possibilities of reconciling Scotland. The Father General of the Jesuits had ordered him to repeat the address to the Pope, who had been so impressed that he instructed his Nuncio in Paris to help Crichton's journey home, and the Father General told him to report to Father Persons on the way. Persons took him to see the Duke de Guise and they all conferred together about 'the advancement of the Catholic cause in both realms of England and Scotland and the delivery of the Queen of Scots'. Once home, Crichton had secret conversations with Lennox, which Father Holt joined, bringing credentials from Mendoza.

Holt was back in London in February. He visited the priest appointed, who took him, somewhat to his dismay, to the Spanish Ambassador, and Mendoza kept him two days hidden in the Embassy in order to hear what Lennox and other Scots lords had to suggest. They suggested, Holt told him, that if the King would not come quietly into the Church he must be forced, provided always that his mother consented; he might for example be transported abroad, or deposed until Mary could arrive. They asked for 2,000 soldiers, preferably Italians, who could be embarked in Friesland and land at Eyemouth. Mendoza gave the penniless priest money to return at once to Scotland, taking with him assurances that the King of Spain would not fail to help them 'as in detail the bearer would verbally make known'. To Philip Mendoza listed the pros and cons of intervention, which must of course depend upon 'the position of Your Majesty's dominions elsewhere', and asked pardon for his boldness in having gone so far.

Some rather extravagant and presumptuous messages now began

to reach the south. Mendoza's original emissary arrived in London at the end of March disguised as a tooth-drawer, with his papers concealed in the back of a looking-glass. He was tired and footsore, having walked three hundred miles of the way, and brought two requests from Fathers Holt and Crichton. First, would the Ambassador go at once to Rouen to meet them, and the sooner the better, since they had already arranged for a ship to bring them back? Second, would he ask the Queen of Scots to make her Ambassador in Paris (the Archbishop of Glasgow) draw up two sets of credentials for Lord Seton's two young sons, one addressed to the Pope, the other to the King of Spain? And Mary herself received a letter from Lennox, from which it appeared that Father Crichton had led him to expect a Papal army of 15,000 men in order to 'reestablish religion in this island', free Mary and preserve her right to the English crown. Lennox asked that James should continue to be recognized as King; meanwhile nothing need be told him. If all these conditions were fulfilled 'and the English Catholics keep their word', Lennox would either rescue her or die in the attempt. 'Courage then, Your Majesty!'

'It is the first I have heard of such a thing,' Mary wrote to Mendoza about the 15,000 soldiers. The project was indeed 'highly desirable', but first she wanted to know whether the Pope and the King of Spain approved and would assist it; if they did and would, she could still do much even from prison to prepare the ground in Scotland. Mendoza had no intention of leaving his post to meet the two priests, and sent a message to detain them. It arrived too late. By the end of April Father Crichton was in France, and a number of secret top-level conferences took place between the Papal Nuncio, the Archbishop of Glasgow, the Provincial General of the Jesuits, (Father Robert Mathieu), the Spanish Ambassador (Don Juan Battista de Tassis), the Duke de Guise, Dr. William Allen, and Fathers Crichton and Persons.

By the end of May they had all agreed, given the means, on doing something. There was to be an invasion; how, was far from clear. Lennox now asked for 20,000 men by the autumn and 20,000 crowns at once. De Guise thought 8,000 foreigners would be ample. He had set his heart on taking part himself and would make a simultaneous descent on the English coast opposite Normandy, but since he was already being stigmatized as 'completely Spanish', he did not wish Philip to contribute more than money. The expedition should consist of Germans and Italians, should sail for Gibraltar in the Pope's name, and appear to have been sent against Barbary. The priests, on the other hand, thought that the King of Spain should manage it and the Pope supply the money. In their view it could assemble either in Portugal or else in the northern ports of Europe 'where very good vessels are to be found and easily equipped'. With suggestions of this kind Father Crichton set forth for Rome in high hopes to persuade the Pope, and Father Persons for Madrid in high hopes to persuade the King of Spain. Father Holt returned to Scotland to inform Lennox and continue with the evangelization of King James.

The grandiose project, if effected, would have plunged England into war and civil war and caused the deaths of thousands. But it never went beyond these early stages. While it was being hatched, Mendoza's tooth-drawer had been stopped on the Border and the papers behind his looking-glass found; Walsingham had them during June. The pro-English Earl of Gowrie kidnapped James during September, and Lennox's enemies tortured and obtained a confession from one of his envoys to France, which they also forwarded to Walsingham. A letter of Mary's was intercepted and deciphered in London by the same John Somer who had done her mother a similar disservice twenty years earlier. Elizabeth's spies in Scotland brought about the capture of Father Holt in May 1583; he was taken in disguise when about to board a ship at Leith, and admitted the generalities of the plot. According to Walsingham Elizabeth twice demanded that he should be tortured, but James allowed him to escape. And in June the Duke of Lennox died. 'We have lost the foundation of Scotland,' the Papal Nuncio lamented, 'and we must now prepare some new design.'[62]

The old one lingered for a year like a cobweb in the minds of some of the principals, but in September 1584 Father Crichton was captured on board ship in mid-Channel. The foolish man had on him an extremely detailed version of the whole plan. According to one account he tore it into pieces and threw the pieces into the sea, but the wind blew them back and they were put together; if so, it would not be the first time in the history of Intelligence that such a thing has happened. He was taken to the Tower and confessed everything. According to the English record of his confession, 'The enterprise failed by the deathe of the Duke of Lennox. He supposeth the intention remainethe.' This particular manifestation of the intention gradually evaporated, to be supplanted four years later by the Armada.

Walsingham pursued his at first slender clues from Scotland for at least two years. The climax is a familiar story: how he was led to the French Ambassador, then bribed his secretary M. de Cherelles; how Cherelles led him to Francis Throckmorton; how Throckmorton was shadowed for six months and finally gave away the Duke de Guise's plan to invade England, the connivance of the Queen of Scots, and the over-all direction of Mendoza. On January 19, 1584 the Privy Council summoned Mendoza and, speaking through Walsingham, who had spent his exile in Italy and knew Italian best, ordered him to leave the country within fifteen days. He told Philip that he had denied everything, but the Councillors' insults had made the soldier in him lose his temper and he had warned them that, having failed to satisfy their Queen in peace, 'she would in future force me to try to satisfy her in war'.

These events cannot be put into any arrangement which will show the priests involved as men concerned solely with the salvation of souls. They were not innocent couriers, nor were they masked Ambassadors. They carried masses of Intelligence into Scotland and brought or sent masses back, on the basis of which the captains and the kings discussed invasions, peered into their treasure-chests, and looked about for fleets and soldiers; and in so doing they became willy-nilly spies for the Pope, the King of Spain and Duke Henri de Guise. The comments of which the great personages delivered themselves at the time make clear that, whatever the priests themselves may have felt, the intention of their masters was to use them in a political as well as a religious role, and make clear also the limits of their use. Father Crichton's blithe promises and proposals exasperated Mendoza; 'the good man,' he wrote to Philip, 'has made them entirely on his own initiative.' The priests, 'though ardently zealous as regards religion, cannot be trusted with matters of State unless they are taught word for word what they have to say'. It was quite unnecessary for them to leave Scotland; 'on the contrary, they should stay where they are, and endeavour as gently as possible to convert . . . gaining souls, and giving me notice of what the Scots want. I say also that it is not necessary for them to take to the road themselves, as their profession is not that of arranging warlike matters, which must be done by other ministers, their function being to act as intermediaries, for which they are better fitted than any others.'

iv. Exiles Again: Walsingham and the Factions

In pursuit of clues to the ease with which Walsingham obtained intelligence against the Catholics, it is necessary to look once again at the human weaknesses and special political disputes which ever-lastingly bedevil exile, and caused the Catholics abroad to quarrel among themselves at least as much as the Protestants had done. It needs to be remembered that a great number of those who entered the English seminaries abroad intending to return secretly as missionaries were extremely young; twenty-four was considered quite a mature age. It was unavoidable that they should include youths ill-suited to the discomfort of exile, let alone the tensions of the mission or the final terrors of imprisonment and martyrdom. Among them were people merely adrift in the religious, social and economic uncertainties of the age, 'poor serving men, soldiers, and wanderers', together with sons of the gentry, 'almost boys', come abroad more out of obedience to their parents than any strong love to religion, and yet others who were simply on the run. Letters exchanged between those in charge of Catholic education abound in expressions of anxiety about a restless minority of students, who took ill to discipline and wanted to go home or send for friends and kinsmen regardless whether or not they were suitable for such a training; and such youths became material for spies.

There was also the problem of the over-eager. When Father Holt wrote to Persons from his hiding-place in Scotland about young men he was constantly encountering 'whose feet itch to run to racks', misgiving mingled with the pride. The fantasy of martyrdom is a common form of imaginative self-inflation, and those who imagine themselves as enduring most, are often (as in war) those who when brought to the test fail most poignantly. 'Divine Providence is far too surprising,' Dr. Barret wrote, 'to permit us to reprehend those who show less inclination [to go on the mission], or to retain those who are more eager, for I have known martyrs to arise from both categories; but I can name more from those who appeared fearful.' Sometimes it becomes clear that, like most teachers at some time or another, Fathers Allen, Barret and Agazzari did not know what to do, except their best, and hoped the best would follow.

Nearly all the exiles were, like Antony Tyrrell's father, desperately poor; Sir Thomas Markenfield actually died in the Low Countries of starvation. Philip's pensions to the seminaries arrived irregularly and the forced move to Rheims nearly ruined Douai. Perpetual harmony, which is not found even among the most mature communities, could not be expected among hot-headed young Elizabethans, not all sure of their heroic vocation, or even where their next meal was coming from. Unhappily tiffs about the quality of bed and board, servants, pocket money, favouritism and so on, quickly merged into an infinitely deeper and more destructive breach. Two groups appeared among the exiles: a Welsh faction against an English and then, more lasting, more important, Secular priests against Jesuits, each with their supporting laymen.

At the root this notorious conflict was one about authority over the whole government and administration of English Catholicism, and over the policy to be adopted towards the Government at home. Sternly disciplined, schooled in Rome, well placed and trained to influence Curia and Courts, the Jesuits, headed by Father Robert Persons, saw no hope of effective progress towards the conversion of England without active assistance from the King of Spain. The Seculars had, in general, less cohesion and less power and were less businesslike. They charged the Jesuits with entangling the faithful in interminable plots, of which they told no one save their own following, and which achieved nothing except fiercer persecution. The Seculars were ready to come to terms with their heretic motherland; the Jesuits were not. In the sense most relevant today the conflict prolonged, under terror and from exile, the old pre-Reformation conflict between Curia and countries, between the desire for national ('Gallican') liberties and the authority claimed by an internationalism centralized in Rome; it is relevant today, not only because a conflict similar in essence has produced a new crisis within Catholicism, but also because another very like it has emerged within world Communism.

By the middle 1580s then, wherever there were exiles, there was faction, in Rome, in Paris, Rouen, Rheims, in the colleges, in the Netherlands, everywhere in the Western Catholic world except perhaps in Spain. Each side gave to God its dedicated men, its scholars and its martyrs, and each spoke and wrote against the other in language of extraordinary violence. The English Government soon learnt of this disastrous breach and took advantage; many of the chief spies upon the Queen of Scots and the Catholics at home can be shown to have had connexions with it.

At the end of July 1585 a priest was captured named Barber, also known as Edward Strancham. With him there happened to be a layman called Nicholas Berden, also known as Thomas Rogers, who got away. Berden arrived at Rouen in August with papers and tokens from Father Barber as credentials, which at least one group of exiles recognized and accepted. In fact he was a spy. Posing as a Catholic, he had for some months, perhaps longer, been reporting to Walsingham on Catholic activities in England. He had won enough confidence to sup in secret with the experienced Jesuit Father William Weston (alias Edmonds), who had recently landed, and learnt from him the names of eleven priests and the houses they resorted to. He was able to reveal means by which Catholics in the Tower and other prisons communicated with one another and the outside world. A friendship struck up with William Allen's servant, then secretly in England, gave him intelligence of how Catholic books were being brought in and distributed, how funds were raised, where priests were being put ashore, in what disguises, and by whom received, all of which had gone straight to Walsingham. It was one of his chief tasks to trap Father Weston; it was another to report on those in touch with the Earl of Arundel in the Tower. Arundel, Norfolk's son, had been captured at sea sailing to France to put himself at the head of all the exiles; it is more than likely that the authorities had been led to him by Berden. In May Berden informed Walsingham that the exiles needed a London agent, and a priest called Ithell, for whom he had found lodgings, had offered 'to give me credit for the post. But I must have your Honour's pleasure first'.

Once in France, reinforced with his Honour's pleasure and the exiles' trust, he reported back to Walsingham and Sir Horatio Pallavicino and sent intelligence for several months. What he found out about the Guise plans to liberate Mary and invade was somewhat out of date, but (as Father Crichton had confessed) 'the intention remainethe'; and his shrewd account of the Pope's difficulty in financing the seminaries, of the two factions, and the rival Catholic personalities, had great use. On the one side, he wrote, were Father Persons and most of the Jesuits, on the other the Scottish Bishop of Ross, Lord Paget's brother Charles, and the Welshman Thomas Morgan, cipher-clerk to the Archbishop of Glasgow and one of Mary's most copious and trusted correspondents. William Allen 'playeth on both hands'. We know from other sources that Paget and Morgan had greatly resented not being invited to the Duke of

Guise's conference with the Jesuit fathers in 1582 to discuss the invasion. They thought such matters the business of laymen, not of priests, and their exclusion still rankled bitterly.

Among the refugees on whom Berden reported were, unknown to him, men already in Walsingham's employment. He thus did his master the service fairly common in that world of becoming unwittingly a spy on fellow-spies. He managed to warn Walsingham that two English spies he did personally know of, Solomon Aldred and M. de Cherelles, had been discovered. His letters[63] were directed to Thomas Phelippes. He claimed, like Phelippes, to be able to write many hands and usually corresponded in invisible ink.

After a year or so of this he thought it time to return as London agent for the exiles. So many of the Catholics in France had grown to trust him so completely that he promised Walsingham he would become central post office for them all. He had put out a story about having been compelled to flee because of certain papers found on him. The exiles had made a counter-check in London, as a result of which they assured themselves that the English authorities had not thought these papers dangerous; and since Berden was known to have a Protestant father and influential friends, the ease with which he could return home roused no suspicion.

He arrived in May 1586. Walsingham, who had given him no instructions to return, was extremely busy with the Babington plot and did not see him, if he ever saw him at all. Phelippes took charge and used him to watch Ballard and the rest. In August he had a stroke of luck. Father Weston (Edmonds) had been summoned urgently to a house in London. Francis Mills, one of Walsingham's secretaries, reported what happened. 'One thing this afternoon, about five of the clock is fallen out beside our expectation. Berd.[en] and Sheppard, the keeper of the Clink, being together here about Bishopsgate espied Edmonds the Jesuit, and he was presently apprehended by Sheppard alone, (Berd. not in any way appearing in the matter) his weapon taken from him, and he carried to the Clink, where he is to be kept in such sort as he may neither escape nor any friend of his know what has become of him . . .' Father Weston passed the next seventeen years in prison. He was banished from England two months after the Queen's death, after great sufferings and almost blind, and died in Spain.

Berden did not continue much longer as a spy. In February 1587 he anticipated Walsingham's instructions to Phelippes to send him after Antony Tyrrell. Perhaps the success of Tyrrell's flight to Hamburg discredited him. He seems, too, to have grown disinclined to such work. He was always asking for protection, especially', in May 1586, against the misplaced zeal of Mr. Justice Young. '. . . I was before like to have been discovered by his apprehending me, though he after set me free,' and again to Mills at the end of 1586, 'I beseeche your worshipp to be myndful of . . . warrantie for my saffetie to be sett doune in as large wordes as maye be, for that I am most ferfull of my securitie.' 'My nature is timorous . . .' he wrote. 'Though I am a spie (which is a profession odious though necessary) I prosecute the same not for gayne, but for the safety of my native country.'

All the same, his gains were not always negligible. There was quite a thriving trade in the lives and liberties of captured Catholics, as existed a generation ago for Jews in Nazi Germany and has always existed in such circumstances. They were a rare commodity. People like Berden, and even more Phelippes, who had a kind of monopoly of this commodity, could (as it were) sell them back to themselves; or could sell them to avaricious jailers, if they were not thought too precious for the authorities to release or too dangerous to keep alive, and had money for their maintenance. Gray, keeper of Wisbech Castle, procured some of his prisoners in this way. Thomas Fitzherbert signed bonds to give Richard Topcliffe £5,000 if Topcliffe would persecute his father and uncle to death, so that he could inherit. Berden merely asked leave to liberate on bail two priests, who would be worth the large sum of £50 to him. In remunerating himself in this way he felt he was doing the State a service. It grieved him 'to have to draw on his Honour's treasure, and if he will yield to some suits now and then at my request, I might be served out of the store of those traytors . . .' However, for his wife's 'near kinsman' John Lister in the Marshalsea, he merely begged favour and did not mention money.

In his small way he acquired power. In the last resort it rested with the Queen and Council, usually on Walsingham's recommendation, to decide what should be done with captive priests. But the Secretary could not be expected to know all of them. He depended on Phelippes and Phelippes, also fully occupied at the time, depended on Berden. So we find Berden sent a list of names from Walsingham's office with a request to write against each the fate he thought most suitable. Against some he wrote prison, or 'any place you like', or banishment; against others 'meet for the gallows or the gallies'; against Ithell, who had recommended him to the Catholics in France, he wrote 'Hang him'.

Berden several times expressed a wish to come into the open. He would give up spying, he told Phelippes in summer 1586, 'whensoever you shall think it meet, in such sort as I shall make all the papists in England to blush . . .' That winter he explained to Walsingham how hateful he found it to have won the Catholics' trust and copious offers of reward, 'as even at this instant when my credyth is greatest with them all, i will be hartely glad to pronounce my self ther persecutor (yf yt shall so please your honor)'. He had his wish in the New Year. One of the exiles in Paris denounced him as a spy. Instructed by Walsingham to 'forbere my service for some tyme', he wrote that he had resolved 'to enter a more publique course of lyffe'. He applied for and obtained the lucrative post of Purveyor of Poultry to the Queen's Household, a department in which he had formerly been an employee. His previous role thus became general knowledge, and in 1591 Father Robert Southwell wrote of him to Verstegan as one of those who 'have pretended themselves to be Catholikes, and that by the warrantise and advise of their superiors. They have heard Masse, confessed and received, only of purpose to discover Catholikes and to entrappe them'.

Berden was one of many whose career as a spy can be traced back to the emigration; among these there were some who, apart from spying, did their utmost to widen the breach between the factions. Some made reports of which only little survives, like Samuel Postinget and his companions, who arrived at the English College in Rome garbed as poor scholars, were admitted as pilgrims for six weeks, and while receiving religious instruction took elaborate notes of everyone there, which they sent back to Walsingham. Some played a principal part and can be followed for several years, like the tailor Solomon Aldred, or the infamous priest Gilbert Gifford, who reopened the last series of Mary Stuart's correspondence on Walsingham's instructions, or the priest Edward Grateley. Robert Alfield caused much trouble to Father Persons, in whose service he had crossed to France without Persons knowing that his father was a Protestant minister. For a time he became a soldier in the Pope's guard at the Castle of St. Angelo. It is said that he betrayed his brother Thomas, a priest who returned home and was martyred. Charles Stedd, or Slade, had been servant to Dr. Nicholas Morton,

English Penitentiary at St. Peter's at Rome in 1580. He accompanied Campion's group of priests home and betrayed at least four to their death. He was a 'witness' at Campion's trial and accused Father Luke Kirby of plots and insults in Rome against the Queen. Kirby replied: 'As I hope to be saved at the last doom, there is not one word of this deposition that concerneth me either true or credible.'

Two points about these spies on the Catholic emigration take one's attention. Several became propagandists after ceasing to be spies, as the spies Philby and Molody-Lonsdale have become in our own day under the guise of writing their memoirs. The priest Thomas Bell, and John Nichols, formerly of the English College at Rome, who had denounced Antony Tyrrell, published books against the Catholic Church, as have Philby and Molody-Lonsdale against the English society they penetrated.

Secondly, like Tyrrell, some of them were tormented by their consciences and recanted. The priest William Atkinson, apostate by 1595, suggested to William Cecil that he should travel to Ireland disguised as a Franciscan friar and murder the Earl of Tyrone with a poisoned Host. He wanted a good reward because 'I have lost millions of Catholic friends who maintained me before, by adhering to my honour'. In 1601 he recognized Father Thomas Tichbourne, whom he had known in Rome, in the London streets and denounced him. The ensuing martyrdom of Father Tichbourne was reported by the Jesuit Father Antony Rivers to have brought Atkinson to remorse but 'it is said he hath been in like penitent humour once before'; a little later he was blackmailing Catholics for what money he could get and 'hath gone by the Chief Justice's footcloth, openly in the streets bareheaded, the said Justice secretly talking with him and laying his hand upon his head'. The following month Father Rivers reported that the Lord Chief Justice had thrown Atkinson into Newgate prison for retracting evidence against a suspected Jesuit. He was penitent again and 'dangerously sick', but if he recovered his mood might change once more. Sooner or later, change it did. Father Bickley, whom Berden had once recommended in vain as a stool-pigeon, was banished in 1603 and returned on the mission. In 1617 Atkinson recognized him, promised to let him go in return for £20, and then denounced him. There may be many such stories, though only a few more which concern ordained priests; martyrs and steadfast ones far outnumber spies.

A large question mark rests against the names of Charles Paget and the Welshman Thomas Morgan. Jesuits suspected them almost from their first coming to Paris. Non-Jesuit historians have tended to accept Morgan as a true Catholic and loyal servant of the Queen of Scots, and so he appears in Professor Conyers Read's *Mr. Secretary Walsingham* and the *Dictionary of National Biography*. During recent years the Jesuit scholar Father Leo Hicks has brought a somewhat damning case against him.[64] Here we may leave his reputation open, like that of Sir Edward Stafford. Nothing in the story of Espionage astonishes, and for that reason things that astonish should not be immediately accepted. But if the charges made over the centuries are true, then we must recognize that, as the Spanish Armada sailed along the Channel, the English Ambassador in Paris was a Spanish spy; and that the man who wrote the Queen of Scots scores of long devoted letters of advice, whom she allowed to guide much of her secret correspondence in preference to her own Ambassador in Paris, and who controlled her ciphers and had a large measure of control over her money, had been a spy of Walsingham's for years.

Walsingham and those who followed him in office always commanded extensive sources of secret Intelligence against Catholics, quite apart from the official vigilance of J.P.s, constables, pursuivants and the rest; what with spies at the ports, Thomas Randolph's control over the Post, spies installed in Channel ships, spies representing themselves as Catholics in most of the prisons, and spies observing the demeanour of crowds at Catholic executions, the network stretched from Rome throughout Europe and England, across the Border, and in London did not weary even round the grim terminus at Tyburn. One last example may be given. No student of Elizabethan espionage can miss the name of Antony Munday.

*

Antony Munday, actor, playwright, balladist, translator, pursuivant, journalist, propagandist and spy, author of some fifty published works, had been born in 1553, the son of a London draper. At twenty-three he was apprenticed to a printer, probably after a brief appearance on the stage. After compiling a *Defence of Povertie* he decided that he had a surplus of wild oats, which 'required to be furrowed in foreign ground', and set out in the winter of 1578–9 for Europe accompanied by eighteen-year-old Thomas Nowell. Anything he would pick up about the lives of renegade Englishmen abroad was sure to find a market either openly as a book or secretly as Intelligence.

He claimed that soon after landing in France Nowell and he were robbed by wandering soldiers. But by feigning Catholic sympathies they obtained help from émigrés and managed to make their way to Rome, where they arrived at the beginning of February. On the strength of their letters of recommendation Morys Clenog, then Rector of the English College, admitted them as students. Munday made himself out to be the son of an English Catholic, deceiving even a priest who had been on the mission and said Mass at his 'father's' house. Nowell passed for a relative of the homonymous Dean of St. Paul's, and was much courted as a desirable convert who one day 'shoulde stande and preache against his kinsman'.

Munday assisted at Mass and observed the College's normal discipline, although he drew the line at self-flagellation. In the first furious debate between the English and Welsh he helped to foment the English against the Welsh Rector and was made to sleep in a cupboard in disgrace. In the summer he returned by way of the College at Rheims; there he spent a few days, and left for home at the end of July with a fine harvest of intelligence. Only a few months later the mission of Fathers Campion and Persons assembled at Rome, and long afterwards Persons was sadly to admit that God 'permitted that diverse ill-disposed persons at ye very same instant repaired . . . to be spyes in England, as Munday, Sledd, John Nichols and others'. When the fathers reached St. Omer they were warned that the searchers at the English ports had full descriptions of them, and though they assumed disguises and false names Father Cottam was arrested on landing from a description supplied by Sledd.

A certain George Eliot betrayed Campion in Berkshire, and within four days of Campion's arrival at the Tower Munday the journalist had issued a version of his capture, although he had not witnessed it. This scoop took all the credit from Eliot and roused him to fury. He had a special need to justify himself, being an apostate Catholic who had only recently submitted to the Government and received an appointment as a Yeoman of the Chamber and a commission to hunt down priests. Campion's capture had been a lucky break for him, and later in the year he issued his own eyewitness account, calling Munday's as 'contrary to truth as an egg is contrary in likeness to an oyster'.

There can be little doubt that the witness which Munday and Sledd contributed to the trial of Campion and his colleagues was false. Eliot visited Campion in his cell and declared that he would never have betrayed him, had he known the penalty would be death, and John Nichols offered to give fresh evidence which would clear Father Kirby. No such remorse troubled Munday. He compiled a summary of Campion's 'treason', which was read on the scaffold, himself attended the executions, took notes, and two months later published a popular account. On May 28 and 29 next year seven more priests were executed. This time Munday managed to get his story out next day, containing a vivid description of his own patriotic exhortations and arguments with the condemned men even while they had the noose about their necks and the executioner was chopping up those already hanged. He rounded off his piece with an advance puff for his account of life in the English College at Rome, 'which as soon as it can be printed shall be set foorth'. It came out three weeks later and still makes excellent reading, once the part its author had been playing is forgotten.

One of the first Catholic pamphlets on Campion's martyrdom stated that Munday had returned to the stage and been hissed off, had then ('O constant youth!') joined the campaign against the theatre, and 'now beginnes againe to ruffle upon the stage'. After attributing to Munday a mistress in the Barbican, where he certainly lived, the pamphlet accused Eliot of having turned spy in order to escape a charge of murder. Eliot rushed to consult Munday. They were now friends, and Munday, more experienced with the pen, incorporated Eliot's denial in his defence of his own behaviour.

Although during 1583 Munday found leisure to issue a translation of a comedy and a 'Fancye' entitled *The Sweete Sobbes and Amorous Complaints of Sheppardes and Nymphes*, he could also have been observed escorting to prison three priests and three Catholic gentlemen who had sheltered them. By the year of the Armada he had to his credit two more translations of chivalric romances, a *Banquet of Daintie Conceits* 'to delight their mindes who take pleasure in Musique', and an order of family prayers. He could now style himself 'One of the Messengers of Her Majesties Chamber' and in this role of pursuivant began to spy upon the Puritans, who did not yet know him as he was.

So when he was sent to bring Giles Wigginton to Archbishop Whitgift in December 1588, Wigginton did not suspect him. Munday posed as an admirer of Martin Marprelate, and Wigginton, swearing him to secrecy, talked to him about Martin's tracts as they were being rowed across to Lambeth Palace. Munday at once passed on these confidences to the Archbishop. If Wigginton did not thereupon put the Puritans on their guard against him, Marprelate soon did, and in print. In the passage quoted in the last chapter, where he mocks Whitgift's orders to the pursuivants, he wrote bitingly: 'I thank you Master Munday you are a good gentleman of your word. Ah thou Judas thou that hast already betrayed the Papists I think meanest to betray us also. . . . Didst thou not assure me, without all doubt, that thou wouldest bring me in Penry Newman Waldegrave press letters and all . . .' It is more than possible that Munday, like Thomas Nashe and John Lyly, joined that squad of witty authors whom Bancroft enlisted to answer Martin Marprelate in his own satiric vein; and one cannot but wonder if he was among the spies who stole the secret Puritan correspondence.

Avarice sometimes marred his religious and patriotic zeal. About 1590 one of Walsingham's men complained that he had got them a bad name by robbing a widow of £40 on the pretext of a search for Catholic objects of devotion, and two years later he had taken up with the nauseating Topcliffe, who praised him as 'a man who wants no wit'. The wit in later life became directed mainly to the arts. He appears several times in Henslowe's *Diary* as a playwright collaborating with such great ones as Drayton, Dekker and Webster. In 1598 he was given a limited preference over the greatest of all; Francis Meres, listing 'the best for Comedy amongst us' in his review of the contemporary stage, ended his catalogue with '. . . Greene, Shakespeare, Thomas Nashe; Thomas Heywood, Anthony Munday, our best plotter . . .' But nothing of his that has survived supports such praise.

Munday added a number of chapters to John Stow's *Survey of London*, and died in 1633 at the age of eighty. Fifty years earlier he had helped to betray at least twelve men to death. His epitaph referred only to his work as a topographer.[65]

*

The climax to the conflict between Jesuits and Seculars at the end of the reign and century affords a further glimpse of Richard Bancroft as a spy-master.

After the execution of the Queen of Scots the Jesuits followed

Father Persons in supporting the Infanta Isabella as Elizabeth's heir; the Seculars, like most of the Privy Council, supported James VI of Scotland. The death of Cardinal Allen in 1594 had removed the only mediator whom both sides respected, and Persons's book widened the breach between the Catholic rivals and drew the Seculars closer towards the Protestant enemy. By the late nineties the ludicrous and tragic extension of the quarrel to the group of priests comfortably imprisoned in Wisbech Castle had become known to the English Catholic laity and thoroughly disquieted them. In 1599 the Secular priest William Watson accused the Jesuits to the Attorney-General of high treason for supporting a Spanish-Catholic heir, while in Paris Charles Paget gave the English Ambassador a dossier of intelligence he had collected against them. To Bancroft, now Bishop of London, such rifts between godly men were an old story, and he knew how to use them in the interests of Established Church and State.

In the summer of 1601 he examined Thomas Bluet, seventy years old and one of the Secular leaders, and secretly permitted the publication of a series of violent Secular pamphlets as part of a campaign to turn the English laws against Catholics into laws against Jesuits only. The Seculars put forward the argument that there could be no peace in England, and no full acceptance of James by English Catholicism, until the Jesuits had been expelled, and let it be thought that this might be achieved by a mission to Rome. They undertook unequivocally to acknowledge the Queen's sovereignty in all temporal affairs, to oppose any invasion aimed at enforcing her excommunication, and to reveal all plots against her. Bluet, a priest named John Cecil, and two others were given passports to leave for Rome, and an extremely large sum was collected from the Catholic community, not without intimidation, to pay their expenses.

It would be pleasant to record that this extraordinary little delegation of men all legally open to sentence of death consisted of pure souls dedicated only to their Catholic faith. This was not so. Father Bluet, a prisoner for the last twenty years, had acquired a reputation for heavy drinking and violence; he had frequently struck fellow-prisoners, and only just been restrained from assaulting one of them with a stone mug. Father Cecil, under the alias of Snowden, had for some years been a Government spy. Nonetheless their aims contained an element of nobility and were far ahead of the times. This quixotic quartet trekked hopefully across war-torn Europe, believing they could persuade the Pope and the Cardinals, who had given them no encouragement, to recognize a heretic State, and the heretic State, whose Queen would put nothing into writing, to recognize the Catholic religion; they were brave if rather disreputable pleaders for freedom of conscience.

They failed in Rome. When they returned, Bancroft, still operating behind the scenes, permitted the release of further anti-Jesuit pamphlets. He had now collected a vast dossier on the entire dispute and become an expert on Catholicism.[66] Father Bluet visited him so frequently that Bancroft himself became suspect of Popery and prudently secured a document from the Privy Council authorizing him to conduct these secret negotiations with traitors. But having come home without any decree from the Pope to expel the Jesuits, the Seculars failed to obtain a decree of religious toleration in London, if—as is most doubtful—the Queen had ever even considered granting one. She pronounced in November 1602. All Jesuits were instructed to leave the country at once; the Seculars, to whom her Proclamation referred with slightly but not much less harshness, were given until February. On the day before their time-limit expired, thirteen Secular priests subscribed a total submission to the temporal power of the Protestant State, while retaining their spiritual allegiance to the Pope. Bancroft was not satisfied with the wording of this surrender, by a tiny minority, of everything over which English Catholics had disputed, suffered, and died since the Reformation, and the Jesuits considered that their refusal to compromise had been vindicated.

Whatever might have come of it, the submission fell literally upon deaf ears. It was offered to someone at last called upon to make another submission of her own. In the early morning of March 24, Elizabeth died.

Epilogue

QUESTIONS ANSWERED

'IN THIS CHANGE...' 1945–

i. Motives of Spies: Ideals

It will be seen from this account of a few years during the reign of Queen Elizabeth how many stones have been left unturned, how many angels or toads remain to be exposed. The mind quails at the project, which may yet be attempted by someone some day who has a generation or so to spend, of undertaking the chronicle and analysis of all Intelligence at all times everywhere; perhaps it is best left to that leisured day when Intelligence will be no more needed.

If in this vast and little-worked field the Elizabethan mine alone were to be fully explored, it would be found to contain at least a dozen separate shafts that would keep students busy for months. One or two have been suggested. It might also be useful to examine the financing of the secret service; or the vulnerability of that crowded scrambling Court; or the intelligence against the Armada; or the whole of Walsingham's network, of which only a very small part has been narrated here; or the counter-intelligence of the Roman Catholics; or the evolution of the informer; or the story of some single notorious spy such as William Herlle or Antony Standen or Château-Martin. It would be interesting to consider why, apart from the crowned heads, women played so small a part in Intelligence and espionage; and the query persists for that as for every age, to what extent—if at all—spies managed to affect the major course of history.[67]

This book has had a very limited and fairly simple purpose; to examine motive. I undertook throughout to commit Professor Elton's 'cardinal error' of studying the past for the light it throws upon the present. Erroneous or not, it can now be switched full on. Similarities between that epoch and our own will surely be conceded. 16th-century Europe was divided across as well as along frontiers, as the whole world is today, and the battle was and is one between spiritual and intellectual beliefs as well as for material power. It may also be allowed that the conspiracy and war in Scotland in 1559–60 offer an example of intervention in another country's affairs, which has been

followed over and over again since, and is being followed now. Huge
transformations, germinating for many years, received a kind of
ceremonial pause and tableau at the conference of Cateau-Cambrésis
in 1559. Huge transformations, germinating for many years, were
recognized to have occurred at the end of the Second World War,
and some statesman setting out for the Potsdam conference in 1945
might equally have jotted down that tiny and eloquent 'memo' of
William Cecil's 'in this change'. Both these years marked 'not so
much the closing of a period as an opening on the future'.[68]

In these pages we have met many kinds of spy, domestic and
international, anonymous and named. Some, like William Maitland,
James Melville and Sir John Leigh, spied only for a short time.
Maitland is known as a statesman, Melville as Ambassador and
memoirist, Sir Thomas Gresham as a financier, Kirkcaldy as a fine
soldier, and he and the lairds of Ormiston and Brunstane as sincere
devout Reformers. Obviously these men inhabited an air far removed
from that of Berden or Munday, or Sandy Pringle or Patrick
Graeme, or those countless anonymous ones whom we know only
from descriptions of their jerkins, their complexions or their beards.
Biographers of Bancroft and Gresham, Kirkcaldy and Maitland,
pass by their involvement in secret service with embarrassed regret,
if they mention it at all. One of Maitland's biographers denies that
he betrayed Marie de Guise, since she herself had already betrayed
Scotland.[69] We do not have to accept Buchanan's savage contemporary picture of Maitland as the Chameleon. We can if we choose
accept him as a Scottish patriot, and he has been compared to
Talleyrand. But to have accompanied Marie into Leith 'to summe
goode purpose', and then to have slipped out and betrayed all that he
learnt there and knew before, was the 'summe goode purpose' of a
spy. It was the act of a spy for James Melville, while employed by
France, to have made himself the secret messenger of Maitland's
defection to the English. While definition remains the aim, questions
whether a man was good or bad, or 'justified by events' or not, or
spied only for a short time, or was paid or not paid, are all beside the
point.

An analogy cannot be drawn between all spies in one age and all
spies in another, however similar. Nor can all spies in any single age
be classed together. While it is obviously necessary to separate men
like Gresham and Maitland from Berden and Munday, it is a grave
mistake to leave them out. Once a separation has been made within a

single period, analogies may be put forward with similar classifi-
cations in another period. It does however appear that many men of
all sorts, who spied, had this much in common: they believed and
desired others to believe that they were servants of some uplifting
cause. During the 16th century these causes were twofold, one
religious, the other patriotic, one a conception of God, whether
Catholic, Lutheran, or Calvinist, the other a conception of their
country. These objects of devotion, whose gigantic palanquins have
served to glorify pretty well every human virtue and conceal pretty
well every human vice, might coalesce into a single image or at least
become, like Siamese twins, conjoined. A Spanish Catholic, for
example, or an English Protestant, could give himself simultaneously
to both God and country; dedication to one need put him in no
doubt of equal dedication to the other. The God of certain though
by no means all English Roman Catholics, however, appeared to
demand the overthrow of Queen Elizabeth, the God of many Scottish
Calvinists the overthrow of Marie de Guise and later of her daughter.
This conflict between religion and patriotism spies managed in their
own minds to resolve by the argument that the wrong God was
temporarily in power in their countries, and true patriotism lay in
putting the right one in His place.

Time has relaxed the hold of all Churches upon national affairs in
most of Western Europe and separated religion from patriotism to an
extent unthinkable four hundred years ago. Spies in more recent
times have tended either to work for nation against nation, considering patriotism enough without spiritual overtones, or else for
secular conceptions of liberty, democracy, peace, class, law and
order, international brotherhood, and so on, such as were excited by
the American, French and Russian Revolutions, or put forward by
counter-revolutionary movements to oppose them.

Yet in instances where the admired ideal was being preached and
thought to be in practice in another country, many spies have
remained under some inner pressure to justify themselves in patriotic
terms. Many Communists, whether spies or not, have seen in
Communism not merely an idea and form of government established
in Russia, which they would like to simulate at home, but the fulfilment of something described in such words as their own country's
'destiny' or 'logical' or 'inevitable development'. To such people, as
to many Scottish Reformer and English Catholic sympathizers and
spies during the 16th century, it was not they, but their compatriots

in power, who were the traitors. Colonel Oleg Penkovsky claimed that he spied for the Americans and British against the Khrushchev government for the sake of the Russian people. Kim Philby, while announcing to journalists in Moscow that he had 'come home', still seems at moments to be claiming that he is a loyal Britisher. George Blake, the British diplomat in the Near East, and Richard Sorge, the German diplomat in Japan, appear too cosmopolitan in origin and outlook to have cared greatly for any motherland or fatherland. But other courageous Germans living at home, of all political parties or none, risked and lost their lives for passing Nazi secrets to the Allies, because they believed that Hitler had betrayed Germany; and most people would by now agree that they were the better Germans.

The power of national sentiment, of the people, society, and habits of thought and life which surround a man, is one of those exterior influences which rapidly become rooted in his being and remain enormous. Even during the late 16th century, while it was still in its adolescence and the power of religious sentiment had not yet lost its domination, the battle between God and country proved more than many men could stand, and for many country won the day. While continuing to believe in, and when possible practise, a form of worship enshrined in somebody else's country and forbidden in their own, they declined to commit armed insurrection, conspiracy or espionage for its sake. They saw no reason why, by making a few concessions to the government unfortunately established, and by winning a few for their persecuted religion in return, they should not manage to lead a life which would be both patriotic and devout; and they fell out with their co-religionists prepared to go to any lengths.

The great rift between Jesuits and Seculars would have divided Catholic England, even had the Armada been successful. The forces they expressed, ultramontane on the one hand, patriotic and insular on the other, were too strong, the difference between them too profound, for any military victory to eradicate or erase; indeed, it would probably have embittered them. A comparable rift has emerged in our own time under an ideological alias. Every political journalist familiar with Eastern Europe knew by the late 1940s that trouble could not fail to arise between the so-called 'national Communists', who had mostly fought in the Resistance or spent their exile in the West, and the so-called 'Muscovites', most of whom had come home from Russia. In 1949 Jugoslavia, who alone of these countries had liberated herself from the Nazis as much by her own effort as by those of Russia and the West, left the Cominform. Elaborate elucidations were put forward, connected with details of economics, foreign policy, personalities, past history, and so forth. All doubtless had played their part. But I happened to be summoned a few days afterwards to a private interview with a senior Jugoslav Minister, who provided the simple and, I think, correct generalization, that his country had had enough of Russian dictation and intended to develop Communism her own way.

Professor George Lukacs, the doyen of Marxist literary critics, told me later in Budapest that he found the Jugoslav schism incredible, although a little knowledge of human nature and the 16th century might have prepared him. Madame Anna Pauker, then Romanian Foreign Minister, remarked of Marshal Tito's defection that either he must be brought to heel or, darkly, '*il faudra finir avec lui* (we must get rid of him)'. But it is Madame Pauker who has been got rid of, and Marshal Tito who remains. The non-Cominformist conscience is with us to stay, like the Dissenters. We have no more heard the last of national Communism than Father Bluet's motley little mission to Rome was the last, or first, to be heard of national Catholicism. East of Russia it means at present something more primitive and fiercer, and something less fierce and more flexible to Czechoslovakia and the West.

People will continue to exist who prefer that the great idea, whatever it happens to be, should be enforced by the armed services of a mighty foreign country, and put war or the consequent sufferings of their nation second. Some Hungarians hoped this of America in 1950; a few Czechs may hope it of Russia now. In Scotland during the 1540s the laird of Brunstane did not think the English victory at Pinkie enough; he was prepared, apparently, to accept further massacres of his fellow-countrymen and a wider wilderness laid waste, in order to admit Protector Somerset and his 'cartloads of Bibles'. But other Scots of like religious faith drew back. English help against the Papist sovereign might be solicited and taken, English domination never. And in France, soon after the Treaty of Edinburgh, Sir Nicholas Throckmorton made the calamitous miscalculation that French Huguenots would prefer English Protestants to their own Catholic compatriots. Acting in part on his advice, the Queen gave orders to occupy Le Havre; whereupon the French stopped fighting and spying on one another, and together drove the English into the sea, as they themselves had been driven into the sea at Leith.

To the outsider, attempting as much dispassion as he can, the faith to which a traitor spy dedicates himself often appears to have been itself ill-served by the nation representing it, or the country, to which a patriot spy gives his life, so wickedly misled that it was not worth spying for. It may not seem so to the spy himself, of either kind. Perhaps it must not seem so. So many hostages have been given, he has so completely burnt his boats, that the secret certainty within which he has isolated himself cannot possibly be admitted to be fantasy. He dare confront such a thought as little as a lover dare consider that the woman he has set on a pinnacle of purity may be a harlot. It may be hopeless for him to withdraw. He may not care. Above all, he may have had other reasons for embarking on espionage than those elevated ones he offers to his employers and himself and later, if he is lucky enough to survive, to the world. He may simply enjoy spying. One motive seldom if ever makes a spy. Gleaming ideas are frequently conjured to cloak drab impulses, and we should reflect what separate and entirely selfish inducements have been in play, modifying the high-mindedness or displacing it entirely.

ii. Self-seeking Motives

The most obvious inducement of this kind is greed for money, or things only to be acquired with money.

Here we should try to distinguish between those spies who spied for the money alone, and those who needed it to cover their expenses or even for livelihood; but the line between them is sometimes blurred. Spies are often people who have had trouble with an Establishment. As a result they have lost status and, with status, money. They may be prepared for this and spy in the hope that one day the Establishment will be changed; or they may repent and try to work their way back into its favour. In either event they have to be supported. All the English exiles in France during Mary Tudor's reign were penniless; if the King of France could not relieve them, then they must wangle pardons by espionage for the Queen of England. Sir Peter Carew got his by betraying Sir John Cheke. Others went to Dean Wotton and on his instructions spied either on one another or the French.

William Kirkcaldy, 'humble, gentill and meak lyk a lamb in the house' (to quote James Melville), 'but lyk a lyon in the fieldis', fought gallantly for France against the Emperor, and also brought Dean Wotton intelligence against the French. What he did, he did not for England, but for Scotland. He was one of those many who have used the squabbles between two foreign nations in the interest of their own; like the Egyptians and Israelis who spied in Cairo during the last war for England against Germany, but turned once the war was over to their true causes, the independence of Egypt and of Israel. Pardoned by Marie de Guise, Kirkcaldy returned home, and went on working secretly for England. He had to have money, since she owed him eighteen months' wages. So the English paid him out of those coins Cecil and Sadler smuggled across the Border; 'The man is poor,' Sir James Croft explained. To have accepted such rewards need not be taken to mean that he or several other Scots had money as their aim.

A decade before the Armada the Privy Council employed one Edward Rawes of Fowey 'in a small barke for the discovery of the King of Spain's intent in preparing of a great navye'. He was caught, imprisoned by the Inquisition, and died in Spain; in recompense and 'for the relief of Their Lordships' promise', his widow was awarded a lucrative licence to export corn from Devon and Cornwall. Robert Cecil obtained £40 a year for John Daniell, who had reported on the Queen's enemies overseas. Daniell had betrayed his cousin and 'would not have spared him', so he said, 'if he had been my brother. I am for Her Majesty's service without respect of persons'.[70] Nicholas Berden probably retired from spying with the Purveyorship of Poultry to the Queen's Household. He had helped the slender secret service budget in two instances at least by getting his reward from his victims. Another of Walsingham's men called David Jones denounced a Catholic woman who had saved him from starvation; he asked to be paid out of her goods forfeited by statute, 'even if it be but the chain she wears'.

It was the law under many of the Tudor statutes, economic as well as religious and political, that part of the fines obtained from a convicted person should go to the person who had informed against him. The anti-Catholic Act of 1581 enabled payment to anyone whose information led to the capture of a Jesuit or seminary priest of 'such sum of money as shall be an honourable due reward for so good service'. Forfeitures, which included 100 marks from anyone hearing Mass and £10 a month from anyone maintaining an

unlicensed schoolmaster, as well as the £20 a month from all who refused to attend Church, went as a third each to the Queen, the poor,
and the informer. Between 1581 and 1601 John Towneley, head of the
Lancashire Catholic family, paid in all some £5,000 for refusing to
attend a Protestant service; if a third of this went to informers,
some people in Lancashire were doing very well out of him. Had
Catholicism triumphed, the system would not have altered, though
the victims would have been different.

We read of the Earl of Huntingdon asking the Privy Council to
send a 'wise and faithful' spy up north; presumably the man was on
some sort of establishment, and was paid. People offered themselves.
Thomas Churchyard, the soldier-versifier, nearly always broke and
at this particular moment out of favour, asked if intelligence would
be acceptable against the goings-on of Catholic Sir Robert South-
worth at Bath. The Governor of Berwick and the Wardens of the
Marches drew allowances for spies, some of whom were on a regular
pay-roll, some paid lump sums for odd jobs, some working for both
sides. Money is still a great alchemist on frontiers, and in Elizabethan
days the corruption of the searchers at the ports was as great a
headache to the directors of foreign policy as to the defrauded
Exchequer. Some of the priests contrived to slip ashore on lonely
beaches, but many, disguised, were put down at the ports, and it
was from the ports that agents left with intelligence for France and
Spain; officers who could be bribed to overlook illegal merchandise
might also be tempted to leave loopholes for human contraband.
Many names connected with the customs will also be found connected with Intelligence.[71]

As Sir Thomas Challoner wrote, spies 'look to be well feed'.
During the 16th century not many of them were. Like Ambassadors,
they were always asking for money. Spy-masters had so many out-
goings; whether it was a great noble like Mendoza, with a penurious
Howard in disgrace or a needy country gentleman and Court official
like Sir James Croft on his list; or a de Noailles with his two informers near the Queen; or Chapuys, that shrewd bourgeois accredited
to Henry VIII, who apprenticed young men in the craft of Intelligence and suborned one of Anne Boleyn's waiting-women; or
Sadler with brave William Kirkcaldy and See-no-sin Alexander
Whitelaw; or the exquisite Bishop of Montpellier with his '*bons
serviteurs du roi*'; or Cardinal Granvelle with those he entertained
'out of myne own purse'. Soon things in England would become

more regular. Robert Cecil would receive £1,400 a year for intelligence, and the Great Game would move on to Oliver Cromwell and Secretary Thurlow with tens of thousands to spend, and their Mr. Dorislaus opening the mail in his study at the Post Office, and Richelieu and Père Joseph, and Napoleon's Fouché, and Pitt, and finally our recent and present rigmarole of Secret Service Estimates, Ochranas, Ogpus, K.G.B.'s, G.R.U.'s, M.I.5, M.I.6. Deuxième Bureau, S.O.E., S.I.S., C.I.A. Things are more streamlined now. Spies are recruited now, scouted for, trained for a career; a young one is an investment, a middle-aged one a windfall.

Avarice, luckily for Intelligence services, in undying. Sir Thomas Gresham may have hoped that Jasper Schetz, with his lordships and his influence on the Bourse and his poetry and his brothers in their gold and silver suits, would have given his secrets to the Reformed cause for nothing; but King Philip's Treasurer still had to have his chain and thousand crowns. Beyond these great ones there crowds a shadowy farrago of ruffling adventurers, rolling stones, Debatable Landsmen, in-between people, fringe-men; somebody inward with someone inward with the Guises, somebody with a map of Calais, people with tall stories, people with stories to plant, professional Nosy Parkers, down-at-heel Irishmen who attached themselves to priests, then sold them, seedy hangers-on in faded brocade and drooping plumes, a man who drops in on Throckmorton 'to see how I am accompanied', a man who delivered Merano to the Emperor, a man 'great with all the secretaries at Court' going for fifty crowns, someone in the Venetian Embassy going for two hundred ducats or a benefice, suppliers of any or all sides in the commodity of real or phoney secrets. For what? It is often claimed for a spy that he or she 'changed the course of history'; the only one of whom this is true on a vast scale, Judas Iscariot, did it, so far as we know, for money.

*

Next comes the negative motive of fear through blackmail. Antony Tyrrell was blackmailed. Intimidation is easy for a spy-master who has found something out against somebody and can threaten to reveal it. George Eliot, who betrayed Campion, appears to have turned spy to escape attachment for murder. John Payne, another of those he betrayed to death, charged him also with rape, breach of contract, and cheating Lady Petre of Ingatestone, whose servant he had been. Other spies had fallen into debt and feared the confiscation of their property and the beggary of their wives and children. The Elizabethan Bernard Maude is an example of a private blackmailer who was found out and thereupon himself blackmailed by the State. He, Sir Robert Stapleton, and the keeper of the Bull Inn at Doncaster, played an old trick on Dr. Edwin Sandys, Archbishop of York, from whose household Maude had been dismissed and against whom Stapleton had a grudge. The old gentleman was spending a night at the Bull. They waited till he was in bed, then sent the innkeeper's wife in to him, burst in upon them, and accused him of trying to seduce her. Panic-stricken, the Archbishop disgorged a large sum as hush-money, but later took heart and wrote to Cecil. An inquiry followed and Maude was sent to prison for three years. He served one, and was let out as spy and agent-provocateur for Walsingham.

Cardinal Allen described how the seminaries at Douai and Rome had been infiltrated by 'young fellowes, fugitives from their maisters . . . being deprehended in divers cosinages, counterfeyting of letters, and plaine theftes, joyning to them others of ill disposition, that sometimes thrust themselves into such companies living together, as we do, to take and give notice of men's doings and demeanour, which men commonly call spies or intelligencers—we, by the Scripture, would name them false brethren'. Rather more than two centuries later, Napoleon's Minister of Police, Fouché, and his assistants 'chose as spies those unfortunates who had committed crimes for which they were yet unpunished; or . . . organized matters so that the men they chose who started with clean records should be trapped into committing a felony', and blackmailed them into spying. Half a century later still Wilhelm Stieber, fifty years a supreme spy for Bismarck and the King of Prussia, organized his 'house of vice' in Berlin, whose frequenters he threatened into serving him.[72] And so this immemorial intimidation of agents has gone on, goes on today, and will go on as long as the devil of power needs them.

Fear, though it embroils in espionage men who are trapped, also holds back from spying men who are still free and masters of their choice. Fear of the known perils and punishments deters potential patriot spy and potential traitor spy alike; they await the patriot in a foreign country, and the traitor in his own. But is not fear of the unknown even greater, of that going alone into places where none of the ordinary protections avail, where no Embassy will assist the patriot and his real employers are too far away to help the traitor?

A man, shall we say, employed in secret work, is approached by an acquaintance who has been sizing him up for months, and now invites him to spy for such or such a country. A new world opens, not into the light, but into darkness and half-darkness. Who is this man? He may be working for the recruit's own side, an agent-provocateur come to test his loyalty. And if the recruit consents, will he ever come to know his new masters, or have a friendly human communication with them? And will they go on wanting him and not always be ready to throw him aside for some invisible and greater gain? And will they themselves, whoever they are, continue in power? May they not one day lose it to others of a different kind, who will find his true name decoded in some secret file and hand him over to those he has been betraying? Early or late, any hour, he may himself be betrayed by some older hand, totally unknown to him, perhaps on the other side of the world, who has grown disillusioned, changed sides, and given away the story of his recruitment. Thoughts like these, apart from all scruples about love or loyalty or friendship, or all the subsequent strain of espionage work, are enough to daunt anybody invited to become a spy.

*

And then there is the positive motive of revenge. Perhaps it does not last long, or passes into some other motive. But revenge assuredly helped to make spies of several in these pages, especially among the blood-feuding Scots. Patrick Kincaid rushed off in an avenging fury to act the spy for the English and deliver them Edinburgh Castle. This is different from the smouldering revenge of the Melvilles, the Kirkcaldys, and Henry Balnaves. How many of that host of servants who spied on their masters were impelled by revenge for some real or fancied slight? When the worm turns, he becomes a serpent. The Swedish Colonel Wennerstrom, who later became a Soviet spy, was passed over for promotion and blamed a superior who happened to be working for the American Secret Service. After he had been caught he thought back on this episode and told his interrogators: 'In such a situation one soon feels distinctly that one has been slighted . . . out of the game and made an exception of. One no longer has any influence and hardly anyone pays attention to the views one expresses.' Many people might have felt pique or bitterness; Wennerstrom sought and took revenge.

It is said that revenge against a society that rules him an outcast, and blackmail, are the compulsions that make the homosexual spy. A great deal has been written about this of late, because of recent instances. Looking for Renaissance equivalents, the eye goes at once to the throne; for if to be queer is to be untrustworthy, then the two greatest security risks in the late 16th century were the King of France, and the King of Scotland and later of England. Nobody ever trusted Henri III of Valois, and of James VI and I it was said that he gave his money to his favourites and the secrets of the State to everyone.

The Earl of Essex, who tried to create a secret service for himself, has had homosexual interests attributed to him. So, more convincingly, has Francis Bacon, who for a time helped him to organize his secret service. So has Christopher Marlowe, whom Walsingham employed. So has Antonio Perez, the most dazzling and vengeful defector of the age, who first fascinated and then wearied the Courts of London and Paris with the secrets of his former master in Madrid. So has Lord Henry Howard, Mendoza's informant. Dr. Rowse has declared that Lord Henry was a crypto-queer.[73] I suppose that the evidence for a crypto-anything would be the absence of evidence; but there is something to suggest that Lord Henry's weakness was fairly well known. He, like Dr. Abbott, who succeeded Bancroft as Archbishop of Canterbury, and other cynics at Court, not only placed handsome youths in the path of King James. His letters to the favourite Robert Ker, produced at Ker's trial for the murder of Sir Thomas Overbury, were so obscenely fulsome that the judge refused to go on reading them.

But it would be far-fetched to pretend that homosexual tendencies had much to do with Lord Henry Howard's willingness to spy at Court for Mendoza, or with Bacon's or Perez's or Marlowe's involvement in secret service (though people may like to see an incarnate symbol of a spy's double life in the Chevalier d'Eon, who dressed sometimes as a man and sometimes as a woman, and whom Louis XV of France employed for a number of years in secret Intelligence). The special sexual disturbance of even undoubtedly and totally queer spies like the Austrian Colonel Redl, or in our own day John Vassall and Guy Burgess, has been given excessive prominence over a more general frustration, which these men shared with spies not homosexual at all. They have suffered from a frustration of power, which their abnormality, and with Redl the additional fact of being a Jew, enhanced and perhaps embittered, but did not entirely cause.

Lord Henry felt the same disappointment of a splendid position as his brother the Duke of Norfolk. Upstarts, much cleverer than the Howards, like the Cecils, or more attractive, like Lord Robert Dudley, pushed them aside. Lord Henry, implicated in his brother's silly attempt to marry himself to the Queen of Scots and later considered as a candidate himself, went to prison for a while after his brother went to the scaffold. He turned naturally to those nocturnal meetings with a Spanish Ambassador. Catholicism apart, the Howards had a pro-Spanish tradition, and the Drakes, Hawkinses, and Raleighs, those militant Protestant provincials and buccaneers, were not his sort. It was not always certain that they were the Queen's. One day she might change, or might even die, and there might be peace with Spain, and then would be his chance.

It never came during her lifetime. He once wrote to her that his only ambitions were 'a merry quiet and a contented poor estate with favour of my sovereign'. Merry quiet, contentment, favour —doubtless; poor estate—no. He yearned for office, and for luxury and wealth, the sweets of office. What Lord Cowper said of Robert Harley, one of the busiest of our great island spy-masters, and employer of Daniel Defoe, might have been said of Lord Henry: '. . . he loved tricks, even when not necessary, but from an inward need of applauding his own cunning.' But as long as Elizabeth was still there, Lord Henry stayed poor. Towards the end of the reign, when most of her near-contemporaries and old friends were dead, we read of this jealous pair, who had never trusted one another, talking together for a long time.[74] A reconciliation? Perhaps. But by then Lord Henry was busy intriguing with the King of Scotland, shrewd enough to ally himself with Robert Cecil behind the old lady's back, so that the crown would pass with the least possible disturbance to England and the greatest possible benefit to himself. And then she died, and for the decade or so he survived her he reaped a harvest as rich as it was belated; Howard was home at last, with favour, friendship with favourites, office, power, money, a huge patent for starch, a great house, a splendid artistic collection, the earldom of Northampton. Everything did change. There was indeed peace with Spain, and a Spanish Ambassador returned to London, beginning to rule the roost again as Feria had once done and Mendoza longed to do. Lord Henry was close

to him, and close to the King, and could let everyone know what a
terrible time he had had to suffer in the old days, and what a
dangerous old fool the Queen had been.

If he had once been a spy, it was not because he was homosexual,
crypto- or otherwise. It was because he had been disappointed of
public power and sought it in secret. The same, I think, was true in
our own day of Guy Burgess. He too had the mania for intrigue, and
told some visitor to Moscow that what he missed there most was
gossip; that quite influential, witty, knowing gossip of certain very
clever dons, journalists, and Members of Parliament. Howard saw
himself as someone who deserved power by virtue of his birth, but
had been balked by parvenus; Guy Burgess thought it his due by
virtue of his brains, and saw himself blocked by intellectual medio-
crities. One staked the future on Spain, the other on Russia. Russia's
size fascinated Guy Burgess; he liked to tell people during the war
that the Russians were talking about Britain as their 'gallant little
ally', as the British had talked about Belgium in 1914. Victorian
England, stuffy yet spacious, might have found room for him somewhere. But he knew all that was over. Power must pass to America
and Russia. Having lost what faith he had ever possessed in 'bourgeois democracy' and 'the liberal tradition', he could detect in
America only all that was stalest and most dangerous in Europe,
second-hand at that, plus a vulgarity and ignorance all its own, and
never troubled to look for anything else. So he turned to Mother
Russia, land of the Titan novelists, etcetera, but above all huge and
Messianic, and possessed of the same huge and Messianic idea of
which he himself had been possessed at Cambridge.

He felt that his abilities deserved to make some kind of mark.
Perhaps he left England because he was afraid of being nabbed
sooner or later for homosexuality, which particular martyr's crown
had been appropriated once and for all by Oscar Wilde; it was no
longer worth much. Besides, Guy Burgess was immensely political.
If he was to become martyred or notorious at all, it must be for
something not merely personal, involving a fine or a short spell in
jail, followed by odd jobs on the B.B.C. and occasional reviewing
for the *New Statesman* for the rest of his life. It must have to do with
great historical conflicts and *Weltanschauungen*, and be as upsetting
to as many people in authority as possible. This, after a fashion, he
achieved.

And so this once brilliant grubby renegade of the Imperial sunset finished up as an embarrassing adjunct to the sunrise in the East, posing for journalists from home, endlessly drinking, and at last deposited in a Moscow cemetery, orated over by Donald Maclean. It seems a sad, lonely and rather paltry end. He had more insight and was far better read than most journalists or politicians and, kept away from the bottle, could have become a useful adviser to Russians about England and to Englishmen about Russia. It was a pity that he insisted on blaring in public so many things best kept to himself, and secreting in his private treachery so much he might have said lucidily and vividly in the open. Still, after a fashion, and if only by thoroughly bedevilling Anglo-American relations, he attained power; and this was one of the things he wanted.

*

Desire for power is one of the things that have made spies of a number of men. In order to enjoy power, it is not necessary for the world to know that you are enjoying it. Those spies, whom power allures, stand in relationship to it as the miser does to money, secretly relishing what others with the same passion advertise and parade. The acquiring of highly confidential information imparts a sense of self-importance and of superiority over the multitude, who only know what they read in the newspapers. Such an ambition may take people harmlessly no further than the Civil or Diplomatic Service; but once there, to cheat others who share such knowledge, and pass it on to an enemy, gives a very special sense of being somebody very special indeed. A spy can put up with all manner of condescension, even of cruelty, if all the while he is successfully duping his humiliators; his is the real power and his, he hopes, will be the last laugh. As for the good-natured, the trusting, they can merely be thought of as fools, like those quondam colleagues in British Intelligence whom Kim Philby and Donald Maclean used to spend merry hours ridiculing in Moscow. This is a form of power.

Often, though far from always, spies have known the purpose of the intelligence they were providing, and been aware of or even witnessed its results. Nicholas Berden was able to recommend which of his victims should be butchered, which exiled, and which kept in prison. Eliot and Munday were present on the scaffold to mock at Father Campion. Gilbert Gifford assiduously carried the correspondence of Mary Queen of Scots to and fro between London and Chartley, knowing it would all be copied. Robert Poley, Antony

Babington's best friend, was allowed to read Mary's fatal letter to Babington and at once reported it to Walsingham. Both Gifford and Poley survived her execution and could feel they had had something to do with it.

The spy who stole John Penry's scraps of notes from his room at Edinburgh had the satisfaction of knowing that they were used to condemn him to death. Spies have led soldiers into ambushes, and watched them destroyed, and during the last war guided bombers on to convoys rounding Cape Wrath or reaching Liverpool. Kim Philby betrayed a paradrop of a hundred or two Albanians and sent to his death a Russian turncoat called Volkov, who might otherwise have sent him to his own; how many British and American agents he and George Blake gave away to the Russians, we do not yet know. Yefko Azev, posing as a Social-Revolutionary, helped to arrange the murders of Viatscheslav Plehve, the Tsar's Minister of the Interior, and the Grand Duke Serge, and at the same time betrayed the assassins' organization to the Tsarist police. Judas, posing as an apostle, not only betrayed Christ, but saw Him led away. If a man wants power over other men, and is content to possess it in secret, espionage will probably sooner or later give it to him, and continue to give it so long as he remains undetected.

But people have also become spies, because they have believed that espionage would give power over the course of history. In Elizabethan times men had far less control than now over the sea, the soil, the air, distance, disease, and so on. But seldom has there been less assurance of mastery over the general direction of mankind than there is today. This profound sense of impotence is chiefly felt among the populations most likely to be annihilated, inhabiting an area which stretches across most of Russia, the whole of Europe and the British Isles, and the whole of North America. It appears in the people's ever-widening separation from, and cynical indifference towards their rulers, and in demands for devolution and participation in countless fields. It shows itself in the clamour of youth, expressed louder in some countries than in others, against most of the old or middle-aged men who dominate the world they have inherited. It shows in certain works of certain artists, in some places banned and they themselves imprisoned, and in demonstrations everywhere against the war in Vietnam, apartheid, or the occupation of Czechoslovakia. It shows in the idolization of entertainers, who have never before provided so many and such seductive tunnels of escape; and of hermit heroes of adventure, who sail alone round the world and impose upon the elements a human will which it seems almost impossible to bring home to Governments. It shows in an ever-hardening cement of conformism, and insistence on conformism, among all leaders from Pope to President to Politburo, in a huge turning of official backs on libertarian experiment, and in a subjugation of inventiveness to the primary purpose of the consolidation of authority. It shows among the western world in the spread of drugs, and in styles of coiffure and dress, making their exotic assertions of individual independence against vast power-complexes and Goliath bureaucracies which, although manned by humans, take on more and more the aspect of machines that nobody can argue with or stop. Never before, in all these countries, has war been so much loathed, or the creative opportunities seemed so dazzling; never before have their citizens felt so helpless to avert the one, or make a real beginning with the other.

Each nation has gone stately on, mouthing the same trite obloquies against other nations; and from time to time somebody gets himself caught, who has struck his personal blow against impotence by betraying the secrets of the nation that employed him to the one officially its enemy. Several of these men have come from among scientists, or groups familiar with military-scientific work, which has made them more aware than most, and sooner than most, and more regularly than most, of the ghastly possibilities of destruction.

This may, it has been suggested, have been a motive of Sir James Croft in 1560 and 1588. Klaus Emil Fuchs was arrested on February 2, 1950; he was a German refugee who became a British citizen and head of the theoretical physics division of the Atomic Energy Establishment at Harwell, and for years he had been delivering secrets of atomic research to the Russians. Colonel Oleg Vladimirovich Penkovsky was arrested on October 22, 1962 in Moscow. He was an officer of the Chief Intelligence Directorate of the Soviet General Staff and, to give him his full title, deputy chief of the Foreign Section of the State Committee for the Coordination of Scientific Research; and he passed valuable Russian secrets to the American and British Intelligence services. Fuchs was a Communist of long standing. In the statement he made to his interrogators he said: 'The idea which gripped me most, was the belief that in the past man has been unable to understand his own history and the forces which lead to the future development of human society; that now for the first time man understands the forces of history, and he is able to control them and that therefore for the first time he will be really free . . .'[75]

Communists are not unique in thinking that it is for them to decide which way the world shall go, although they are unique in believing themselves possessed of a science, which tells them the way it cannot help going. Catholic and Protestant spies, mere patriot spies, spies attracted to ideals which have been neither Communist nor religious, have also sought to give their special lone-wolf direction to events. Wennerstrom felt pleased, as he said, to have his national loyalty to Sweden 'subordinated to larger international questions, i.e. Russia and the United States and world peace'. Penkovsky was a Communist who had become disgusted with what he saw made of Communism at home. In the papers he left to the West, and which the Russians have proclaimed a forgery, he wrote: 'To tell the truth about this system is the goal of my life'; and elsewhere, 'Khrushchev and his regime are demagogues and liars, who are proclaiming their love of peace as a pretence. I consider it my duty and purpose in life to be a humble soldier for the cause of truth and freedom.' Fuchs was a cold fish who had worked out his mission years ago. Penkovsky presents himself, or is presented, as an impulsive man desperate to cram it all into a year or two. They were the shadows who had somehow got on to the bridge and, merging unsuspected into the night, set out to steer the ship where they and not the captain wished to take her. Everybody else was the crew, the passengers, the herd, obeying orders. They alone were individuals, and had made a choice. The mere illusion of such power is sufficient for some people as a motive.

Perhaps this helps to account for the vanity and sense of self-importance which, though common to most men, strikes one as a specially blatant characteristic of so many spies. Few have had the blind complacence of Gustav Steinhauer, head of the German ring in Britain in 1914, who, having managed to get his entire personnel captured at the beginning of the First World War, wrote a book at the end styling himself 'the Kaiser's master-spy'. In some vanity has acquired the form of a perilous self-confidence. The lady called Cynthia seems never to have felt the slightest doubt about her ability to nobble a man. She was most attractive and, though also most intelligent, evidently had no truck with subtlety. Her approach was blunt and businesslike. Ever ready to yield herself if she had to, she simply demanded the French and Italian ciphers, yielded, and got them. Once, it is true, she yielded and did not get them, landing herself instead in a mess which ought to have been disastrous.

Oleg Penkovsky's almost manic assurance and need to give away everything he could caused him to go on trying to pass messages and keep sheaves of hopelessly damning notes even after he knew he was under observation. One must treat with reserve anything said at his trial; but one witness, a friend of his, called him 'very vain . . . he always wanted to express his own opinion and reacted strongly to those who did not agree with him . . . he loved to pose, there was much of the histrionic about him'. Mrs. Philby shows us the vanity of Donald Maclean in Moscow, of which there had been plenty of evidence in the West before. She was on the point of leaving for a holiday in America. 'Don't go,' he said, 'but if you must, don't say anything about what I'm doing.' This happened years after he had defected. She did not in fact know what he was doing, 'but I did not think it was anything very important. Maclean had a vision of himself as a statesman and a diplomat whose life had been dictated by his convictions'.

Nearly all those mentioned in these pages who spied in Elizabethan days appear to have been immensely pleased with what they were doing; both Berden and Munday, for example, were extravagantly vain. In our own day, again, Richard Sorge gave the Russians immensely valuable information about Japanese intentions towards Russia in 1941, and after his arrest could not believe the Japanese would not exchange him for important Japanese held by the Russians; he saw himself as an indispensable intermediary. He attracted women, but in secret service his attitude towards them shows a dogmatic superciliousness bordering on the idiotic: 'Women are absolutely unfit for espionage work. They have no understanding of political and other affairs, and I have never received satisfactory information from them,' and again, 'upper-class women have no comprehension of what has been said by their husbands'. It is just possible that the kind of woman who might have given Sorge 'satisfactory information' was the kind to whom his coarseness made no appeal. This particular remark comes oddly from so intelligent and observant a man, a compatriot incidentally of the ruthless and highly successful Elizabeth Schragmuller, who helped to organize the Antwerp school of Intelligence for the German Army during the First World War.[76]

What in the German is arrogance, in the book by the English spy Kim Philby becomes mere smugness. Philby has a sense of humour, which after a first reading makes the smugness worse. He is adept at damning with faint praise. To start with, you feel he wants to be fair to his former colleagues, even though it had been his unfortunate duty to betray them; after all, they were human beings too and did their best in their poor misguided way. What you begin to notice, after you have read enough of the excitement, the office scandal, and the jokes, is that hardly any of them seems to have been, in the author's opinion, anything like as clever as the author. Knowing some of them, you then begin to wonder if they may not have taken him in just a little. You wonder if it was not excessive vanity about his own ability to deceive that caused him to have Guy Burgess to stay with him in America and set off the trail that led to his discovery. When his wife told him that the British had known him as a Russian spy for seven years, 'he made me repeat it several times, looking very serious and reflective. Somehow this disclosure seemed to disturb him deeply. . . . Finally, he said quietly, but with more than a touch of pride, "I've been working for the Russians for *thirty* years, not just for seven years." '

This vanity so marked in spies is in part the schoolboy vanity of 'scoring off' people. The banana-skin has been adroitly placed, and the victim has duly slipped on it. The dressing-up has worked; what fun, that not even your wife, not even your closest friends saw through it! That 'inward need of applauding their own cunning', which Lord Cowper remarked in Robert Harley, and which appears regularly in Lord Henry Howard, is bound to surface if the cunning one has been caught and begins to talk and write about himself. Klaus Emil Fuchs was so full of self-importance, he could hardly stop telling his questioner how and why he had done it all, and what sort of a person he was. Any good case-officer must know how to flatter the spy allotted to him. The Pole Zygniew Stypulkowski has related how, during days of questioning, his Russian interrogator went to work. 'At four a.m. one day . . . he tried to soothe me, and succeeded. He took my arm and looked into my eyes' and said that the Russian Government had no wish to harm him. 'On the contrary, we need you because Russia's historical task is to rule over Europe.' Spies long for praise and need to be reassured that the sacrifice of truth, loyalty, and above all peace of mind has been worth while. Mrs. Philby has described Philby's hunger for Russian appreciation, and he himself—and we need not doubt him—of their tact, patience, and ultimately gratitude.

Wennerstrom seems almost to have fallen in love with his Russian case-officer. He was designated a Soviet Major-General, which made it possible, or so he believed, 'to go over the heads of certain persons in Soviet Intelligence . . . I was left with the very strong sense of having accomplished something and of having reached a high level of prestige'. He 'experienced a deep inner satisfaction with the results'. The case-officer, known to him as 'the General', shrewdly gave to this man, who had missed promotion in the Swedish Air Force because of his indifferent flying, the soul-boosting code-name of 'Eagle'. He was told that his work had given rise to special memoranda of appreciation and that he could draw sums of money at will. It is not difficult to create someone a Major-General, or even a Field-Marshal, who is not going to wear the uniform, or entitle him to unlimited expense accounts on which for the moment it is imprudent to draw, or to tap out the most glowing references for nobody's benefit but his own. Like Fuchs with his English interrogator Skardon, like Antony Tyrrell with Justice Richard Young, Wennerstrom wrote his General pages about his life. When circumstances prevented them meeting, he was 'an addict in need of a fix . . . he had to write to his case-officer in order to keep going'. Spies' case-officers and, later, after they are caught, their interrogators, play upon these egocentric oscillations. Vanity craves an audience, and in psychiatric jargon spies make a transference. All Intelligence services of any standing expect to find this characteristic in a spy, and are educated to exploit it.

Of power and secret Intelligence it may lastly be remarked that William Cecil, Richard Bancroft, and Francis Walsingham all had public careers in which they reached and remained at the top. The darkest corridors often come out just behind the throne. At the beginning of the reign Cecil gathered into his own hands the threads of the conspiracy in Scotland; Walsingham gathered into his the threads of the Catholic conspiracy; Bancroft those of the conspiracy he attributed to the Puritans. Like Richelieu in the next century, like Harley and Pitt in the next, like Metternich and Fouché in the next, they rose in part on their aptitude for Intelligence. We should be warned. Knowledge is power. Secret knowledge is secret power. Power tends to corrupt, and secret power tends to corrupt in secret. A man who manages to monopolize secret knowledge can build his

own walls round the State, and his own fortress in its midst. All the
dossiers, all the files are his; he can blackmail almost at will. His are
the agents-provocateurs, whom he can use to provoke and encourage
any plot he likes, in order later to suppress it and appear as the
saviour of his country. If he turns traitor, he can go a long way to
destroy it. Colonel Alfred Redl, all but head of the Austro-Hungarian
Empire's Secret Service from 1900 to 1905, was a spy for Tsarist
Russia. He prevented Russian secrets from reaching his own General
Staff, and sold the Russians the Imperial blueprint for the conquest
of Serbia; when in 1914 the Imperial armies finally launched their
attack, it failed hideously and tens of thousands of their soldiers were
slaughtered. The disaster has been put down to Redl, who had long
since committed suicide. Perhaps it came about for other reasons.
Perhaps it was chiefly his doing; in any event, he had willed it.[77]

   In the crucial hour of his career Richelieu won back the King of
France from the Queen-Mother, thanks to a back door she had
forgotten to lock. Metaphorically Intelligence is the key to the back
door. A contemporary writer, listing ambition among the motives for
associating with secret operations, quotes 'the pressures and influence'
which the American C.I.A. has brought to bear on foreign policy
and 'in the private sectors of the American scene'. He says also that
'prior to the Second World War' the professionals of the secret war
'were men who performed valuable services for their governments,
but their influence was by and large limited'. This may have been
true of the United States. It was not true in earlier centuries in
Europe, nor was it true of Elizabethan England.

*

A longing for adventure must always have been among the motives
that have tempted men to spy. Life then as now had its vast arteries
of boredom, and it will be a long while yet before a spy's life ceases to
seem exciting, glamorous, romantic. Dumas is immortal and though
it was the 17th century he wrote about it might as well have been the
16th. A clatter of hooves in the inn or *auberge* yard, a mud-stained
and exhausted rider drops from a sweat-soaked steed . . . the
dispatches! Swift hands seize them from his satchel, a fresh courier
leaps into a fresh saddle, by dawn they are with tow-haired Mr.
Phelippes, by midday on Mr. Secretary's desk . . . these must to the
Queen! Or else a drugged posset and, as the rider slumbers, deft
fingers break the seal, copy the secrets, put them back, remake the

seal and by midday Mendoza's half-blind eyes are poring over them and a courier waiting in the courtyard of the Embassy . . . these must to King Philip! Thomas Randolph, styled Barnaby, prowls under the walls of Leith, the Earl of Arran crouches in the woods on the way to the Swiss frontier, breakfasting on acorns with a kingdom or two at stake. Ormiston escapes over the walls of Edinburgh Castle, M. Devisat over the walls of Calais. Patrick Graeme sneaks into Marie de Guise's Mass and mutters in Glencairn's ear. And then those searches of the country houses, the spy leading J.P.s and pursuivants to the hollow places, the tally-ho as they run the foxy Jesuit to earth!

Spy-master Sir Ralph Sadler was fired on, Randolph was fired on, Sir Nicholas Throckmorton in Paris feared for his life, the Queen herself, so she said, fifteen times escaped assassination. And at the heart of every web was always the Queen of Scots, Andromeda of the Renaissance. Mary and Gloriana, one in her stately prisons, the other on her throne, the North and South Poles of all conspiracies; no wonder so many young men were willing to spy and die for them. They did not know, did not care, that Gloriana was painted thick and had black teeth, or that Mary had grown stout, or that both were going bald. Dumas does not bring home to us the tedium of those cross-country rides, or those dreadful cross-Channel journeys in emetic little boats, subject to 'horrible vomitings', or becalmed for days. How boring, how uncomfortable, must have been those weeks that Walsingham's stool-pigeons spent in the infested jails, hoping to get on the track of a conspiracy. The idea of a spy's life could nevertheless excite, and still excites. The schoolboy thrills go on, Kim Philby tells his wife to chalk a date on a wall and British Intelligence chalk it there instead, Greville Wynne builds a false bottom for his caravan, passwords go on, disguises, dressing-up, and all the juvenilia. During the early thirties Wennerstrom ventured into Soviet territory from Riga with the encouragement of the British Secret Service, and related that 'it had an adventurously seductive effect'. He began to spy for Russia and 'became fascinated with the whole thing'.

Here and there some but not much evidence of private villas put at spies' disposals, cornucopia entertainment allowances, and subsidized junketings in the *dolce vita*, suggests that a spy's life has been and still might be a gay one while it lasted, for a few. Somewhere, doubtless, intelligent sympathetic men and women hold salons at the financial expense of one great Power and the political expense of others; all over the place, doubtless, people are buying alcohol on the secret service budget. Hardly anybody, except those who know, remembers the long periods when there is no drinking, no dressing-up, no danger, even no deceit, and nothing happens.

Perhaps the intellectual excitement attracts even more than the physical. The mind of important spies is fully stretched and the heads and staffs of the Intelligence services who send them out wage against one another a perpetual battle of wits, with the added fascination of knowing, more than likely, exactly who their adversaries are; as Walsingham knew Mendoza, and Throckmorton the Cardinal of Lorraine, and Americans, Russians, French and British nowadays know and meet one another. Now and then one gets from the long dry dispatches a whiff of the pursuer's exhilaration, as surmise hardens into certainty or the quarry nears the trap.

Mendoza came to suspect that Don Antonio, Prior of Crato and pretender to the throne of Portugal, had come to England and was being secretly entertained by Queen Elizabeth. Philip II had just employed his armies to make good a rather insubstantial claim to Portugal. A successful attempt by the Queen to set up a rival claimant, backed by English arms, would give her a most inconvenient ally at the gates of Spain and on the flank of any northward-sailing Spanish Fleet. Mendoza had his spies out for weeks. Suddenly: 'He is here!' The note of triumph rings from the page. For weeks Thomas Phelippes and Sir Amyas Paulet, Mary Stuart's last jailer, had been busy intercepting—it is too weak a word, controlling—the captive Queen's highly conspiratorial mail. The notorious brewer of Burton took it in and brought it out in his beer-barrels. Walsingham watched every move and reported it to Elizabeth. At last Babington sent his fatal letter telling Mary of the plans for the invasion of England and her rescue, and above all for the six gentlemen who had sworn to kill Elizabeth. What would Mary reply? It was towards such a climax that the whole trail had been laid and, as Phelippes sent off Babington's letter, he wrote exultantly to Walsingham: 'We shall have her heart with the next.'

Deceit and detection of deceit are a constant challenge to ingenuity. Employees numbered now by thousands search restlessly for fresh tricks, swifter methods of warning, or of getting warnings, and practical jokes that will introduce death in quite new ways. Detached scholars are swept from their colleges to analyse, probe, and magnetize the needle of truth out of the giant haystack of rumours, plants, and wishful thinking. Ciphers and cryptology have absorbed many first-class minds. The great inventor and architect Leo Battista Alberti occupied spare time in breaking codes which had remained in use since the days of Julius Caesar. Franciscus Vieta, 'father of modern algebra', broke the Spanish codes for Henry of Navarre in 1589, and Philip II complained to the Pope that he was a sorcerer. John Wallis, the great mathematician, deciphered intercepted papers of Charles I for the Parliamentarians. In the 19th century Sir Charles Wheatstone, physicist and founder of modern telegraphy, invented a cryptographic machine and deciphered manuscripts hitherto thought unbreakable in the British Museum. Giovanni della Porta, to whom is attributed invention of the *camera oscura*, wrote books on cryptography. There are many such examples.

The problem of swift and secret communication remains a perpetual and fundamental challenge. In the old days no news could travel faster than a horse, and secrecy was limited to ciphers, invisible ink, insertions between the lines in onion juice and lemon juice, and so on; nowadays, one-time pads, micro-dots, cameras hidden in a button, microphones hidden in a badge, odd noises on the wireless, stratospheric photography, U.2s, satellites . . . the catalogue is endless. Somebody has to invent, manufacture, operate all this necessary and childish rubbish, fascinating alike to a genius or a twelve-year-old.

Intellectual challenge, then; hope of adventure; pursuit of secret power now or public power later, over people or over the course of great events; revolt against mere impotence; vengefulness; fear, either present and physical or induced by blackmail; love of intrigue; avarice, or simply a need for money; these are among the private tempters that drive, cajole, or drag a man into espionage, and dilute the unselfish purity of the patriotic, religious, or ideological motive. Sometimes the dilution seems so thorough, that no sign of dedication is to be traced at all, unless in the spy's own self-justifying apologia.

Motives are mixed; there is nothing new in that. The gay and generous Cynthia evidently could not do without excitement. She liked men and men liked her, and she could also truly say at the sad end to her life: 'I hope and believe I was a patriot.' Antony Munday and Nicholas Berden and their like claimed to be patriots and faithful servants of the Queen. Surely they were sadists and squalid mercenaries first, and not to be thought of with the patriot-spies of

the European Resistance in the Second World War, or the French-
women who spied on the Germans in the First. Great causes have
had to use and been disgraced by shoddy agents, and also have had
to use and been ennobled by true heroines and heroes. Yet if spies
have had any value at all, then Berden and Munday must be placed
somewhere below Cecil and Walsingham, Drake and Bishop Hooker,
among the defenders of Protestant England, as those who spied for
the Popes and King Philip must also be placed somewhere below St.
Ignatius Loyola, Torquemada, Don Juan at Lepanto, and St. Carlo
Borromeo, among the defenders of Catholicism; where exactly, and
what degree of nobility and unselfishness they possessed, readers
will determine for themselves.

Some of the spies in these pages had great courage, some had little
or none. The courage necessary to a spy is in proportion to the
inhumanity of those he spies on, and also to the degree to which they
have trusted him. Greater courage can hardly be possible than that of
the spy who risks hourly the tortures of a foreign occupier or a
native tyranny, unless it be the courage of the man who dares oppose
them in the open. Exactly to sub-divide motives would be Teutonic,
like bottling them and labelling the bottle 'so many grams avarice, so
many power, so many excitement, so many idealism'. In part, some
of them just spied because the time and the place and the man came
all together, and C or X or M happened to have had an eye on him.

iii. Ex-spies as Propagandists: Philby

Throughout the 16th century a few retired spies turned propagandist, among them Thomas Bell, John Nichols and Antony Munday.
Berden longed to throw off the mask and publicly release his loathing
for the Catholic communities he had entered in order to betray them.
In our own time Molody-Lonsdale and Philby have published their
books mocking the British society they penetrated, throve on and
betrayed. We are told that Philby edited Lonsdale's book. It is hard
to believe that he hoped to foist, even on the British, a lump of
falsehoods so stupid and transparent that they cast doubt even upon
the passages which might be true. His own book is more subtle and
calls for some attention.[78]

It is intended apparently as a preliminary version of his autobiography; more, so he tells us, is to follow. Mr. Graham Greene
introduced it as 'dignified and honest'. It is neither. Philby evades

telling us why he became a spy; although it was spying, and spying alone, that made him singular. Instead he gives an account of why he remained a Communist, an experience which he shared with thousands who did not become spies and which is of secondary importance. This account is vapid, fuddled, and has many gaps; yet it is useful, because through these gaps come glimpses of an answer to the primary question which he has ignored.

It seemed to him, he writes, 'when it became clear that much was going badly wrong in the Soviet Union, that I had three possible courses of action. First, I could give up politics entirely. This I knew to be quite impossible'.

This one can accept. He goes on: 'Second, I could continue political activity on a totally different basis. But where was I to go? The politics of the Baldwin-Chamberlain era struck me then, as they strike me now, as much more than the politics of folly. The folly was evil. I saw the road leading me into the political position of the querulous outcast, of the Koestler-Crankshaw-Muggeridge variety, railing at the movement that had let *me* down, at the God that failed *me*. This seemed a ghastly fate, however lucrative it might have been.'

The sentence about 'the politics of the Baldwin-Chamberlain era' is meaningless, since Philby does not make clear if by 'the politics' of this 'era' he means the policy of the Baldwin-Chamberlain party alone, or of all parties, Labour and Communist included. 'Where was I to go?' he asks, and like jesting Pilate does not stay for an answer. In fact there were several places, a good half-dozen alternatives, without reckoning espionage at all. He could have joined the British Communist Party and worked as an open member. He could have become a fellow-traveller. He could have worked for Maxton's I.L.P.; or for the rump of the Labour Party who would not follow Ramsay Macdonald into a National Government; or, if his meaning is that 'folly' and 'evil' were confined to the Baldwin-Chamberlain party, for any that opposed it, including official Labour; he could even have supported Churchill.

It was also open to him to remain outside parliamentary groups and actively express his fellow-feeling for the working-class in any working-class district in the country, living among them, learning from them, helping them. He could have gone into municipal politics and tried to do something about housing, education, health. A capable journalist, he could have written for one of the Left-wing newspapers. He could have become a militant trade unionist. He could have gone to Russia. The exclusive vision of a road 'leading me into the political position of the querulous outcast' implies in him great weakness either of belief or will. A desire not to resemble Mr. Koestler, Mr. Crankshaw, or Mr. Muggeridge, may or may not be something to commend. It is certainly not sufficient motive for becoming a spy, and Philby had no need to come to resemble any of them.

Thus plenty of possibilities were available to him, of which he mentions none. Instead . . . and you think he will now state frankly: 'I became a spy.' But what he does say is: 'The third course of action open to me was to stick it out, in the confident faith that the principles of the Revolution would outlive the aberrations of individuals, however enormous. It was the course I chose.' In fact it was only part of the course he chose, and the least important part. What is important about Philby is not the dreary old explanation why he remained a Communist, 'stuck it out', but that, with all the alternatives open to him, he became a spy.

Although others of his contemporaries, who shared his views, were invited to become spies, and consented, some must never have been made the offer at all; and some must have been made it who refused. Those who observed Philby from the start and finally recruited him concluded that he was the right material; there was something in him, apart from a mere talent for duplicity, which proved them quite correct.

We have a clear picture of a young man naturally ambitious for an influential and powerful career. Not for him the obscure arena of the slums, or the boredom of the trade union movement or the party cell. Not for him a life among the workers. He came from a distinguished family and public school. His feet were well set on the ladder reaching up into the great world, and he was no more going to let go, if he could hang on, than he was going to let go of Communism; letting go was not even a choice he thinks worth mentioning. Spying enabled him to retain his faith and not let go; more, it made it his duty to climb as high as he could get. And the kind of spying to which he was detailed fitted admirably his ambition, his family tradition and both the highly conventional and rebel side of his nature.

He had the lone-wolf adventurousness as well as the vanity of his father, the great explorer. His third wife tells us that he had friends

from many worlds. He became a war correspondent, a fairly adven-
turous profession, before he became a civil servant. But deep
entrenched in him appears always that other side: the administrator-
wallah, son of papa the erstwhile civil servant, grandson of a tea-
planter and a civil servant, nephew of a naval officer-administrator.
Sometimes his spying would take him to romantic outlandish places
like Mount Ararat, and then back he would come to that tidy, neat,
almost commuter spying, in Whitehall or in an Embassy, clearing his
own tray and snooping into his colleagues' trays and filing libraries
to clear theirs. He emerges in one aspect as an intensely conformist
person, anxious always to belong, scared of becoming an 'outcast'.
'Where was I to go?' He was fine, just staying where he was. His
'silent war', his secret mission, made him twice the bureaucrat; first
for the country he really served, second for the country he betrayed.
He had twice the power and prospects a rising civil servant normally
enjoys, since he belonged to two Establishments, and twice the
challenge to his gift as an administrator, with lots of important
Embassy and Whitehall work, sub-sections, sections, departments to
build up, the devotion of his juniors, the confidence of his superiors,
assurance of promotion, conviviality, secrets galore, and after hours,
or whenever he did it, the interesting problem of giving them away;
and was it so difficult, once he knew that he was trusted?

The talent scouts who spotted him must have recognized in him
someone fundamentally of the methodical, official, non-intellectual,
Geheimrat sort, yet with a strong originality, possessing an old-school-
tie loyalty and sense of service, most useful in a different school, and
determined to earn his O.B.E. and possibly a knighthood. This was
not one of those dismally sincere idealists, who would never be able
to organize anything and become disillusioned at the first big shock.
The secret ones could feel fairly sure of Philby. The calibre of his
devotion to them is shown by his blithe summary of the Second
World War: 'It is a sobering thought that, but for the power of the
Soviet Union and the Communist idea, the Old World, if not the
whole world, would now be ruled by Hitler and Hirohito.'

Battle of Britain . . . no importance. Desert campaigns . . .
invasion of Italy, Iwojima, Okinawa . . . insignificant. Americans in
the war . . . were they? D Day . . . what was that? Arms for Russia,
Murmansk convoys . . . trivial. Atom bomb . . . forget your guilt,
America; it was not that which made Hirohito sue for peace.
European resistance movements . . . all part of 'the Communist

idea'. Patriotic ideas . . . meaningless. If thoughts as glib as the above are enough to sober Kim Philby, he has nothing to fear from drink.

In his book and interviews Philby has in fact become himself the 'railer' he desires to scorn. The movement that let *him* down, the God that failed *him*, was England, and he is at least as sneering about it as his despised trio of intellectuals have been about Russia. The endurance which enabled him to 'stick it out' with Stalin failed him with England, and if 'the political position of the querulous outcast' belongs to anyone, it belongs to him.

iv. Conclusions: The Conspiratorial Necessity; Patriotism

Finally, why do people, if offered the opportunity to spy, refuse? When that approach was made to me in Vienna after the war, why did I reject it? Patriotism is too easy a word. It may be the right one, and the simplest. But people nowadays are more inquiring than they used to be, and want to put the old words, the old convictions, under microscopes, and to make up their own minds exactly what they mean.

What I myself mean, I can best clarify by referring to the story from Elizabethan days that has now been outlined. Indeed, this was why I set out to write about that period. It casts the present in a light which to me would be far less vivid without such a contrast.

An account has been given of certain conflicts, in which traitor spies participated, between England, Scotland, France, and Spain, between Roman Catholic, Protestant and Calvinist. We find that many English Catholics desired nothing more than freedom to practise their religion, while some went further and plotted the liberation of the Queen of Scots, the use of force to restore the old order, and even support for a Spanish invasion. Many Scottish Calvinists also desired nothing more than freedom to practise their religion and the expulsion of the French, while some also went further and sought the overthrow of Marie de Guise and a new order. Some English Catholics sent intelligence abroad. Some Scottish Calvinists brought intelligence into England. The point about all of them is, that they had no alternative. Conspiracy *was* their sole alternative, of which espionage inevitably became a part.

Four hundred years have elapsed, during which pathways of

public and non-violent opposition have been cut through this impasse and slowly and painfully enlarged to highways. They do not yet open, are very far from opening on to Elysian fields of ideal freedom. But in Britain they are there; and it is criminal, and rightly punished as a great crime, for any citizen to show them his back and return to the old dark tawdry corridors of the spy. It was not chauvinistic of Shakespeare, even at the end of the 16th century, to write of England as 'the envy of less happier lands', nor is it chauvinistic now. It was the simple truth then, apparent to a great poet, and is the simple truth again now, apparent to many millions. An Englishman still has abundant chance, and had it in the 1930s, to stand up against and confront great wrongs which do and did exist, and demand liberties which so far do not. Loyalty to his beliefs may compel him to forgo a successful career in a world with which he cannot agree. He may have to recognize that fulfilment must be deferred beyond his own lifetime. But none of these frustrations can be adduced to excuse or justify the spy.

Traitorous spying, in all countries where decisions about political control have moved out of the limits of conspiracy towards the open choice of the whole free people, and which contain the means and vitality to maintain that movement, becomes alien to those countries and pulls them backward towards a narrowness they have surmounted. To condone such spying in present-day England is to assume that the conspiratorial necessity still prevails, and totally to repudiate liberties fought for, worked for, won and conceded since those days. It is to permit any well-placed citizen, who happens at some particular failure or crisis to feel furious or fed up, to resort to a perfidious influencing of events which would undermine trust in proportion as it was discovered and inevitably provoke more counter-spying to resist it. Essentially we should be reverting to the sneaking smearing days of Nicholas Berden on the one hand and Richard Bancroft on the other, and of many others in more recent times. In this sense the traitor-spy in England is the arch-reactionary, dragging the community even deeper into the backwoods than the blimp who would like to ban trade unionism or bring back the pillory.

This is a political motive for rejecting spying, related to the political development of England. And just as the spy had his personal motives, so too do those who reject spying have theirs, which are also a common part of human nature. Something has already been said about fear of the known penalties and the unknown shadowy world into which spying leads. An even stronger deterrent is the abhorrence felt for people who spend years, and even a whole career or lifetime, feigning to be something they are not. Most men deceive at some time or another, politicians not the least. But in a passably free and critical society their deceit must soon be exposed, and public success cannot last long on such a foundation. In many societies, and in parts of England still, a homosexual may pretend that he is normal, whatever that means, or a Jew that he is not a Jew, or a half-caste that he is pure-blooded, whatever that means. That any such disguises should be thought necessary at all, reflects ill not on the person but on the society. Yet they are adopted as no more than a means of self-protection, of making life less difficult, and not as shields and masks behind which aggressively and continuously to betray. They are worlds apart from the sustained professional falsehood of the spy. During the last forty years an Englishman's word has been more than sufficiently devalued in the world at large. What kind of a life would be upon us, if it were to suffer a similar debasement at home, until no man could feel sure of his neighbour? This is the bitter slope we should begin to slide down, if we started to think well of traitor-spies.

And the spy, above all other kinds of men, is one who uses people. The more he can creep into their confidence, the more he can use them, and the more he will himself be used. Men and women have never ceased to use one another throughout the centuries, for their knowledge, for their influence, for their bodies, for their money, for their work. Sometimes the use is shameful. Slave-owners in the more distant, employers in the recent past, and in many places still, have used the energy of human beings by the million, paying them inadequately or not at all and casting them aside when it was drained. Sometimes the use is honourable. Several great servants of the State have described how Churchill used them. They expected it, knew what was at stake, and were proud. It was what they desired. The spy uses people for a purpose they do not desire, and of which they have no inkling. It is his necessary practice towards the company closest to him, towards whom he outwardly displays the most intimate loyalty, towards those who trust him. Friends are possible, a wife possible. But the spy must ask himself whether the friends can supply intelligence, and whether the wife is an impediment. If they can, they must be subtly milked. If she is, and cannot be used as a cover or façade, she must be discarded. A Christian who behaves in such a manner daily contradicts the respect for the individual which dwells at the heart of Christianity; a Communist descends to the most archaic and degraded habits of the capitalism he professes to despise.

In a novel love alone (apart from fear) traditionally has power to disturb the hardened spy. We have seen lately that this has been true in life. We shall not often be given a pair of stories that star so unforgettably the chasm between a spy's deceit and the simplicity of love, as the two books written by Philby and his third wife Eleanor. She describes how she rejoined and remained with him for some while after she knew him to be a spy; and the most cruel of many cruel thoughts that came to her was not that he had found another woman, but that he might originally have married her on orders (she was American and shared none of his real political beliefs), and that their years together had been primarily of use to him as a cover.

Something else she wrote about him stays in the mind. She called him sentimental. It does not surprise. Sentimentality at its worst is the compensation of people who have killed their hearts, yet go on feeling that they must feel something about someone, and no example sickens more profoundly than the sentimentality, turgid with self-pity, of the deceiver towards the ones he has deceived. Philby betrayed everyone who trusted him without turning a hair, but drank himself unconscious over the death of a tame vixen. About Sir Stewart Menzies, head of the Secret Service and the man he had cheated most, he wrote: 'Of the Chief I think with enduring affection and respect.' And when his wife finally cannot stand him any longer and leaves Moscow, he gives her a farewell note in which she is 'the best friend I have ever had or ever will have'. She cries. He cries too, the crocodile; and perhaps we are all supposed to cry.

The tear-soaked remorse which Antony Tyrrell poured out to those against whom he had borne false witness, was sentimental. And there is that closing scene in the short life of the Irish patriot Robert Emmet.[79] He was tried in Dublin for his leadership of a rising against England, which William Pitt quite possibly had instigated, and was sentenced to death. The Irish barrister Leonard MacNally acted for him. It was MacNally who had betrayed him to the English. After Emmet had ended that speech in his own defence, which every Irishman used to learn at school by heart, MacNally leaned across the dock and kissed him. No instance of sentimentality, in literature or in life, can be more odious than this one; the kiss of Judas Iscariot was at least a signal.

*

And if you were asked to spy not against, but for, your country, is that all right? Assume that you can get over the fear, the strangeness, the dislike of deceiving even national enemies—since it is patriotic spying, do you then accept?

Taken as absolutes, arguments against becoming a spy already presented apply as much to the patriot as the traitor. He too must often wear a double face, and pretend he is what he is not, and exploit those closest to him, if he is going to succeed. Spying is morally as wrong for everyone as is war, and other activities which for the sake of expediency we permit and subsidize. Yet suppose that a fellow-countryman well known to you becomes suspect of spying on behalf of a foreign country, and that traps are prepared for him, which cannot be made to work without your aid as counter-spy. Though morally disapproving, do you, in the name of expediency, accept?

It depends. It depends, all purely personal inducements to spy omitted, on the kind of cause you admire and the kind of cause which your Government represents. If you are a pacifist, and your Government militarist, or the other way round, you may sympathize with a suspected spy. You will not presumably wish to spy against him, nor presumably will you be asked.

But at what point precisely are your opinions going to be so affronted by your own Government, that you feel yourself unable to undertake the positive deceit and hazards of espionage, international or domestic, on its behalf? What is patriotic spying? What is patriotism? It would be disastrous for the British Intelligence Service if its members were prone to resign whenever the Government reintroduced prescription charges or cut the Naval Estimates, and to withdraw their resignations whenever such directives were reversed. Patriotic incentives to spy might be seriously abraded if a Prime Minister tried to raise a tax for the enlistment of a private army, or made judicial decisions subject to Cabinet approval. Such moves would be opposed. But what if the liberty to oppose itself had disappeared?

An Englishman who had accepted the risks of patriotic Intelligence either at home or abroad, taking for granted an England of Parliamentary institutions, the common law, considerable freedom of speech, and about half a dozen other major heirlooms, and believing in the need and duty to extend them, would be in something of a fix if even a few were to be abolished. It could happen suddenly by violence, as in Athens the other day, though this is unlikely. It could happen over a few years, as the fragile fabric of the Weimar Republic was first splintered, then smashed by Hindenburg and Hitler. Or it could happen gradually over a longer period, through an almost imperceptible whittling and paring down, completed by an outwardly quite urbane, but essentially ruthless, coup *à l'anglaise*. The coup would be carrried out either by the extreme Left or extreme Right. History suggests over and over again that, when a nation reaches a razor-edge, either side may go over. Which of them does, may be merely a question of an accident, the weather, or a message received or not received. The path to the razor-edge has been prepared for years by both sides, each governing more and more by administrative decree rather than by popular sharing and consent, but without the mass of the people realizing or even perhaps caring what was happening.

This is the likeliest manner in which revolution or reaction might take over the control of England. Espionage multiplies in all such periods. Those who have successfully committed the decisive violence need spies in order to hold power, those who have failed in order to overthrow it. The patriot who first entered the Intelligence services in calmer times will now begin to have a far worse dilemma forced upon him. Some latter-day Cecil or Walsingham or Bancroft may seek his help in the surveillance of the population. Mere refusal may not be sufficient for him. The other side may now approach him; and he may be so outraged at what is happening as to feel inclined to turn completely. If the coup is of the Right, and his sympathies nearest the Left, he may (even now) consider an approach from Russia; if the coup is of the Left, and his sympathies of the Right, from the United States. At the disposal of all will now surge up those reservoirs of human spite and jealousy which were at Bancroft's and Walsingham's disposal and would once again, as in all violent times and places, be harnessed in the name of patriotism. Economic snooping, over income, rewards for work, and so on, vastly extended during the preceding years, would be given the final stretch to cover men's opinions, as happened in Elizabethan times. We have seen that the role of the informer was first introduced into economic Statutes and then in 1581 incorporated into one primarily political.

Four centuries are not long enough to ensure that there could be no recurrence.

Such a prospect, although horrifying, is by no means fantasy. It would face different citizens from different sides. But many would be compelled to choose between two increasingly fanatical extremes, one shakily in power, the other in part underground; as many Englishmen have often felt compelled, in a leisurely distant way, to choose about foreign countries, but not for some time about our own. Some would lose heart and go into exile. Some would rebel openly, and be robbed of their careers, sent to prison, perhaps killed. Others, still somehow remaining hopefully in important posts, would face that terrible crisis, when all chance of retaining justice and liberty appears gone and no means left to recover them, except by foreign intervention prepared for by espionage. In its political aspect the decision rests with what a man in such a quandary understands by England; and it is in this sense that a study of espionage, as suggested at the beginning of this book, confronts us with the true nature of our allegiances and of things we do not normally have to bring into the scales. Spies challenge us to declare what our attitude would be towards events which do not seem likely to happen yet, but could happen.

The immediate here-and-now answer is that every man has to do all he can to stop them happening. Patriotism surely includes the resort to all measures and support of all institutions which lead away from such a crisis. In this narrative we have watched three great forces in semi-barbaric conflict. Stated in religious terms they have been a Protestant Ascendancy of recent growth struggling to install itself as an Establishment, Puritanism, and Catholicism. It was one of the great failures in a reign of many great achievements that the Queen and those who shared power with her were unable, or unwilling, to extend some measure of liberty to those movements on either side. One cannot reasonably argue that the whole temper of Europe was totally hostile to religious toleration the whole time. The Queen was old. Henri IV of France was many years younger when in 1599 he signed the great Edict of Nantes, and many generations were to pass before it was revoked. At the end of the 16th century France thus emerged from thirty years of civil war with, in law and theory at least, a degree of toleration that England, which had enjoyed peace, missed. In this sense God forbid that we should ever again have an Elizabethan Age.

Stated in present-day political (but not of course Parliamentary) terms, these three forces are Centre, Left and Right. The Centre is inhabited by men of both Left and Right shading outwards to the positions once occupied by Puritans and Catholics, one for ever seeking 'further Reformation', the other a recovery of things lost. In England of the second Elizabeth all these voices have freedom to make themselves heard and are heard. Those too who have ceased to hope anything from our political system, as the Separatists ceased to hope in the Elizabethan Church, have liberty to say so openly and say why. To believe in this inheritance constantly being begotten by time upon England is part of the nature of an English patriot, and worlds away from the hollow slogan of 'My country, right or wrong'. It is organic and capable of endless self-renewal, embodying desires that lie deep in human nature: the desire for settled government, the desire to alter what has been settled too long and become ossified, and the desire not to abandon ancient things merely because they are ancient. This trinity is inseparable. Anyone who is passively content with only the first, or who seeks a total overthrow either to go forward or go back, is out of the main creative current of our life and not in this sense a patriot. He does not have to be a patriot at all; then let him say so openly and tell us why not. But to my mind patriotism is not an opiate, but a goad.

The more openings citizens have to put right publicly what they consider wrong and publicly to oppose wrongs which cannot at once be righted, the less they will be driven secretly to conspire. Many countries are still not far removed from the conspiratorial necessities under which the Elizabethans were compelled to act. It is for us to shun reversion like the plague and to find and take up, within our crowded shores, challenges which they sought on far-off and empty ones. Even the Elizabethan settlement, for all its ruthlessness, was not totalitarian. An Englishman who spied for anything approaching a totalitarian England of the future, whose vital liberties had gone, would no longer be a patriot, nor would one be who watched them slip away without a fight: and an Englishman who spies against England even as she is today, with all her loss of blood and heart-attacks and other ailments, cannot be anything but a traitor.

Individuals for a long time to come will take to spying out of greed, or revenge, or because the open paths of opposition bore them, or do not suit their ambitions, or from a passion for intrigue, or from any other private motive. Not all the checks and locks and guards

so far devised can prevent them from beginning, and for a time
succeeding, if they are clever and have set their minds on it; they are
as unpredictable and, for a time, immune, as the person who has
secretly set his mind on murder. But since motive may be purely
personal as well as political, it is as well to recall that anyone who acts
with arrogance, unkindness, or injustice in a personal relationship
may be preparing the nativity of a spy; just as anyone who acts with
tolerance and charity may prevent it. Those who have been cruelly
mocked may one day want their own back; all life's Malvolios are
material for spies. Who knows that Colonel Redl was not lured
into spying by the intolerance of the Austro-Hungarian Empire
towards a homosexual and Jew? England has given up the legal
hounding of homosexuals and is working free of anti-Semitism.
Instead, still to surmount, we have the colour bar.

*

There would be no motive for internal spying in a Utopian State,
and no motive for international spying in a Utopian world, since
trust would reign within nations and between them. The Roman
Catholic Church endeavoured to hold all Europe within a single
spiritual allegiance transcending frontiers. She failed, and in her
contemporary task will fail again if, by preferring an order inherited
from the Roman Empire to a way of life bequeathed by Christ, she
continues the rending of Christ's coat. The first great rending was
the Reformation. Since then the Protestant spirit, with its stress upon
individual judgment concerning God, has marched to its inevitable
extreme and produced another centralized, hieratic, international
religion without God at all. Kremlin confronts Vatican across a gulf
of four hundred years.

The inability of the universal Church to reform from within, and
the counter-attack launched later in the 16th century against
Reformation from without, coincided with the rise of Western European nationalisms in England, France and Spain. The emergence
of a world-wide Godless faith during the 20th century coincides
today with signs of their decline, but has itself become identified
with nationalism in Russia, and the counter-attack with nationalism
in the United States. Neither of these is acceptable to Europe.
Their value to the Old World is not to provoke a late spurt of
countervailing nationalism of its own, for which the time has passed,
but a true and purified patriotism, which is nationalism without the

drums and claws, and which knows that no single nation can ever hold all the truth.

The effigies of Catholic Mary and Protestant Elizabeth have long been resting side by side in Westminster Abbey. Rome and Canterbury have at last met, under Michelangelo's great canopy, and asked forgiveness of one another for the past. Incomparably fewer people today can share the religious passions which once made enemies of two such noble and brave young men as John Penry and Edmund Campion, and of grave William Cecil the persecutor of them both. We see in those grim days an absurd and tragic waste of human energy, and pretend not to be able to understand it, while all around us similar waste continues under different names, and men otherwise good shout, fight and spy against one another no less fanatically than they did before. How many years are to pass, before President and Commissar also sicken of hatred, and the secular reconciliations are effected as the religious have begun to be, and a happier generation recognizes the hot and cold wars of this later age as the madness and disgrace they are?

Writers left free today have reason to be sad and proud, as well as grateful, when so many of their brothers are oppressed. Idealism and visions must matter a little, when so many governments seem to fear them. The vision of a world without spies, international or internal, is simply the eternal vision of one world, embracing the warm and brilliant diversity of nations, of Christian doctrine, of Marxist doctrine, of faiths not sprung from Western Europe or Mediterranean at all, together with the thought of those who believe in none of them, but put their trust in reason. We shall have made an advance the day we hear that somebody has spied for UNO.

Men wish constantly to strive outward, from home to neighbour, from neighbour to community, from community to nation, from nation to group of nations, from group of nations to the world. Countless previous motions of this sort have been corrupted by the greed and fear of nationalism and imperialism, which have halted them at so-called natural frontiers, given them spikes like porcupines and eyes like peacocks, and alternately treated all who lived beyond as enemies, allies against enemies, or fresh potential prey. Even the vision of one world could be eclipsed behind the fact of one dictatorship, spying on all mankind as separate governments have spied upon their peoples. Uncorrupted, the heartfelt need to trust will nonetheless continue to reach out from private life, in which it may find recompense, to envelop great societies, from which in fear it has recoiled. Such a consummation is easy to imagine, and necessary but difficult to believe in. Should it ever come, human beings will look back upon the spy as a dodo belonging to their adolescence, which was occasionally heroic, often exciting, but always racked with tensions, that restlessly offered their invitations to deceit.

Acknowledgments

I am most grateful for the courtesy and patience of the staff of the London Library, whose shelves contain nearly all the books I have needed for my purpose.

I wish also to thank:

Lord Croft, of Croft Castle, Herefordshire, for permission to reproduce the portrait of Sir James Croft, and *Country Life* for the loan of the print.

The National Portrait Gallery, for permission to reproduce portraits in its collection of William Cecil, Richard Bancroft, Sir Nicholas Throckmorton, and Sir Francis Walsingham, and for providing the print of the portrait of Sir Thomas Gresham, for which permission was kindly given by the Mercers' Company.

The Scottish National Portrait Gallery, for permission to reproduce its portrait of Marie de Guise.

The British Museum for permission to reproduce the portraits by Franz Huys of Antwerp (died 1562) of Queen Elizabeth and Mary Queen of Scots.

Granada Publishing Ltd., for permission to print extracts from H. A. R. Philby, *My Silent War*, published by Macgibbon and Kee Ltd.

M.B.

Books consulted and Notes

It has been made clear that this book is not, and is not intended as a work of research into original unpublished MSS. All the original works on which I have drawn have been printed. Those I have found most useful are listed below, together with secondary works and specific references as numbered in the text.

ABBREVIATIONS

D.N.B.	Dictionary of National Biography.
C.S.P.	Calendar of State Papers (Foreign, Spanish, Scotland, Domestic Elizabeth, etc.).
Am. Hist. Rev.	American Historical Review.
E.H.R.	English Historical Review.
Scot. Hist. Soc.	Scottish Historical Society.
Scot. Hist. Rev.	Scottish Historical Review.
C.R.S.	Catholic Records Society.
Trans. R.H.S.	Transactions of the Royal Historical Society.
E.E.T.S.	Early English Text Society.

PROLOGUE

Note 1. There are valuable references to secret intelligence during the Tudor period in Conyers Read; *Mr. Secretary Walsingham*, vol. ii, cps. 10, 11, in L. Stone; *Sir Horatio Pallavicino, an Elizabethan*, and in Richard Deacon; *John Dee, scientist, geographer, astrologer and secret agent to Elizabeth I*, cps. 6, 15, 16.

Mr. Deacon has lately published his *A History of the British Secret Service*. This is a most useful account of many of the principal figures during four centuries. But it makes little analysis of motive; and its account of the Tudor period (inevitably, in the space allotted) is cursory.

The quotation from General-Lieutenant Gorny is from *The Penkovsky Papers*, ed. F. Gibney, App. IV, p. 346.

Note 2. G. R. Elton; *The Practice of History*, p. 48.

Chapters I and II
'IN THIS CHANGE . . .' 1558–1559 and RETROSPECT

Cp. 2. Section i. Sir Nicholas and Sir James.
On their early life and situation at the death of Edward VI, see (apart from D.N.B., State Papers, etc.).
The Chronicle of Queen Jane, ed. J. G. Nichols, Camden Ser. R.H.S. 1850, no. 48.
Legend of Sir Nicholas Throckmorton, ed. J. G. Nichols, Roxburghe Club, 1874.
Diary of Henry Machyn, ed. J. G. Nichols, Camden Ser. R.H.S., 1848, no. 42.
Narratives of the Reformation, ed. J. G. Nichols, Camden Ser. R.H.S., 1859, no. 77, pp. 151, 163.
C.S.P. For. 1547–53, esp. p. 344, for Sir James on the Council of Boulogne.
State Trials, ed. Cobbett, vol. I, pp. 869–901, gives the trial of Sir Nicholas.
A. L. Rowse; *Raleigh and the Throckmortons*, pp. 1–56.
O. G. S. Croft; *The House of Croft of Croft Castle* (sometimes more filial than exact).

Note 3. S. T. Bindoff; *A Kingdom at Stake*. History To-day, 1953, pp. 642–8.
   Burghley Papers, ed. Haynes, 1542–70, p. 69.

Note 4. Thomas Heywood; England's Elizabeth, etc., 1631 edn., pp. 141–4.

Section ii. The Ambassador as Spy.
Alberico Gentili; de Legationibus. Classics of International Law, ed. J. B. Scott.
Philippe de Comines; Historical Memoirs. London, 1817.
V. E. Hrabar; De legatis et legationibus tractatus varii.
Abraham de Wicquefort; *L'Ambassadeur et ses Fonctions*. 2 vols.
Garrett Mattingly; *Renaissance Diplomacy*.
R. de Maulde la Claviere; *La Diplomatie au Temps de Machiavel*, 3 vols.
Ernest Nys; *L'Origine du Droit International*.
Jean Zeller; *La Diplomatie Française*. Letters of Guillaume Pellicier.

Note 5. For rewards at the English Court see Wallace T. MacCaffery; *Place and Patronage*, in *Elizabethan Government and Society* (essays for Sir John Neale), and J. E. Neale; British Academy Raleigh Lecture on History, 1948. *The Elizabethan Political Scene*.

Note 6. Mattingly, p. 232.

Note 7. B. Behrens; *Treatises on the Ambassador written in the 15th and 16th centuries.* E.H.R. li, 1936, pp. 616 et seq.

Section iii. Spies in Exile.

C.S.P. Edward VI and Mary, ed. Turnbull.
     Venetian, ed. Rawdon Brown.

Messieurs de Noailles, ed. Vertot.
John Vowell, alias Hooker; *Sir Peter Carew,* ed. John Maclean.
P. F. Tytler; *England under the Reign of Edward VI and Mary,* 2 vols.
E. H. Harbison; *Rival Ambassadors at the Court of Queen Mary.*
A. B. Hinds; *The Making of the England of Elizabeth.*
Christina Garrett; *The Marian Exiles.*
D. M. Loades; *Two Tudor Conspiracies.*
Amos C. Miller; *Sir Henry Killigrew.*
E. Vaillé; *Histoire de la Poste Française.*

Note 8. Neale; E.H.R. Jan. 1950, vol. lxv, pp. 91–98.

Note 9. Neale; *Queen Elizabeth,* p. 319. (Randolph is there called Walsingham's brother-in-law. He married a cousin of Walsingham's; the degree of cousinship differs in the two biographies of Walsingham by Read and Stählin.)

Note 10. Collection of Letters from Original MSS, London, 1753, pp. 230–3, ed. L. Howard. For Thomas Randolph, see also Zurich Letters, ed. Parker Society; History of Pembroke College, by D. Macleane, Oxford Hist. Soc., and Melville, Bannatyne Club (see below), pp. 230–4.

Note 11. Garrett, p. 64.

Note 12. Sir John Harington; Nugae Antiquae, 2 vols., i. 380.

Section iv. Espionage on a Frontier.

C.S.P. Scotland, ed. J. Bain, 2 vols.
The Hamilton Papers, ed. J. Bain, 2 vols.
Register of Privy Seal of Scotland, vols. iv–vi, ed. Beveridge and Donaldson.
Accounts of Lord High Treasurer, ed. Dickson and Paul.
Complaynt of Scotland, ed. Murray, E.E.T.S. extra ser. xvii, xviii (1872).
Foreign Correspondence with Marie of Lorraine. Scot. Hist. Soc., 3rd ser., 1923–5, iv, vii.
Scottish Correspondence with Marie of Lorraine, ed. Cameron. Scot. Hist. Soc., 3rd ser., x, 1927.
State Papers and Letters of Sir Ralph Sadler, ed. Clifford, 3 vols.
Illustrations of British History, ed. Lodge, 3 vols.

P. F. Tytler; *History of Scotland.*
Gordon Donaldson; *The Edinburgh History of Scotland*, vol. III, 1965.
M. H. Merriman; *The Assured Scots; Scottish Collaborators with England during the Rough Wooing.* Scot. Hist. Rev., vol. xlvii, no. 143, April 1968, pp. 10–34.
G. Ridpath; *The Border History.*
T. I. Rae; *The Administration of the Scottish Frontier.*
Rachel Reid; *The King's Council of the North.*
Sir Walter Scott; Poetical Works (notes).

Note 13. Complaynt, p. 108 and throughout.

Note 14. A. J. Slavin; *Politics and Profit. Sir Ralph Sadler*, p. 85.

Note 15. Register of Privy Seal.
Accts. Lord High Treasurer.

Note 16. Sir R. and H. A. Cockburn; *The Cockburn Family Records*, pp. 113–21.

Note 17. By a grant of February 1549. The revenue from the Duchy was 12,000 livres a year. See Complete Peerage, Cokayne & Gibbs, 1910 edn., vol. i, App. B.

Note 18.
There is something of a mystery about the laird of Brunstane's end. A letter from the Bishop of Ross in France to Marie de Guise dated 1554 asks favour for the bearer 'only son to the laird of Brunstane lately dead in the King's service, who asked me to ask you to help him'. The King here can only be the King of France. Perhaps, like other Scottish exiles (Leslie of Rothes, for example, and William Kirkcaldy) Brunstane enlisted perforce in the French army, and Marie had grown conciliatory by 1554. His son John Crichton received a charter under the Great Seal of Scotland in 1565.

Chapters III and IV

A GREAT CONSPIRACY and INTERVENTION AND ESCALATION

C.S.P.

Domestic Elizabeth.
Foreign Elizabeth.
Spanish.
A Full View of the Public Transactions of the reign of Elizabeth, ed. Patrick Forbes, 2 vols.
Relations Politiques de la France et de l'Espagne avec l'Ecosse, ed. A. Teulet, 5 vols.

Lettres et Memoires d'Estat, ed. G. Ribier, 2 vols.

Negotiations, etc., . . . relatives au règne de François II, ed. George Paris.

The Warrender Papers, vol. I, ed. Cameron and Rait.

Queen Elizabeth and her Times, ed. T. Wright, 2 vols.

Collection of State Papers, ed. Haynes-Murdin, 2 vols.

John Knox; History of the Reformation in Scotland, in his Works, ed. Laing, vols. i, ii, iv.

Sir James Melville of Halhill; Memoirs of his own Life, Bannatyne Club, vol. 17, 1827.

Louis A. Barbé; *Kirkcaldy of Grange.*

James Grant; *Memoirs and Adventures of Sir William Kirkcaldy.*

Gordon Donaldson; *The Scottish Reformation.*

William Forbes-Leith, S. J.; *The Scotsmen-at-Arms and Life-Guards in France.*

R. K. Hannay; *The Earl of Arran and Queen Mary.* Scot. Hist. Rev., xviii, 1920, pp. 258–77.

Francisque Michel; *Les Ecossais en France ; les Français en Ecosse.*

Charles Rogers, (for Henry Balnaves), Trans. R.H.S. iii, 1874, pp. 179–193; (for Ormiston and Brunstane), *Memoirs of George Wishart,* Trans. R.H.S., iv (1876), pp. 260 et seq.

J. W. Thompson; *The Wars of Religion in France.*

E. Russell; *Maitland of Lethington.*

H. M. Wallace; *Berwick in the reign of Queen Elizabeth,* E.H.R., xlvi (1931), pp. 79–88.

Note 19. Lodge, Sept. 1557, quotes earlier peace feelers 'from an espiall', and intelligence about the wish of Châtellerault and other nobles to 'restrain the Dowager' of her authority.

Note 20. Neale, E.H.R., op. cit., p. 98.

Note 21. As for example, Robert Norville, who appears to have been persecuted by his fellow men-at-arms for his Reformed opinions, see Michel, vol. i, p. 522.

Note 22. Melville, p. 257.

Note 23. Knox, Works, i, p. 393.

Note 24. C.S.P. Span. 1558–67, p. 540. April 6, 1566.

Note 25. Michel, p. 433 n; Sc. Hist. Soc. iv. 137; C.S.P. Scot.(ed. Thorpe), vol. i, p. 177, no. 99.

Note 26. George Buchanan; Chameleon. In Miscellanea Scottica, Glasgow, 1818.

Note 27. At the end of August. It is not clear who finally brought Arran out of Europe.

Note 28. For the Melvilles see Sir J. Balfour Paul, Scots Peerage, vol. vi.

Note 29. Tytler, *History of Scotland*, vol. vi, p. 146.

Note 30. See Donaldson, *History of Scotland*, pp. 66, 130.

Note 31. For the Privy Council meetings see various slightly conflicting accounts by various historians of the period.

Chapter V
VICTORY

Section i. The Financier as Spy.
Relations Politiques des Pays-Bas; ed. Kervyn de Lettenhove.
Cardinal Granvelle, Correspondance; ed. Gachard.
Marguerite d'Autriche, Duchesse de Parme, Correspondance; ed. Gachard.
Philippe II, Correspondance sur les affaires des Pays-Bas; ed. Gachard.
Guiccardini, Descrittione de tutti i paesi bassi; Fr. translation de Belle Forest.
J. W. Burgon; *Sir Thomas Gresham*, 2 vols.

Note 32. H. Buckley; *Sir Thomas Gresham and the Foreign Exchanges.* Econ. Journal, xxxiv (1924), pp. 589–601.

Note 33. Royall Tyler; *The Emperor Charles V*, p. 243.

Note 34. Harbison; *Rival Ambassadors*, p. 77.

Note 35. He continued to spy for Cecil in Madrid. See refs. in J. H. Pollen, S.J.; *English Catholics in the reign of Queen Elizabeth*, p. 90.

Note 36. References to spying by merchants for the English Government, though by men of less standing than Gresham, occur throughout the reign. The Government was in turn troubled by merchants spying against it for other Governments. See J. A. J. Housden, E.H.R., xxi (1906), pp. 739–42, *The Merchant Strangers' Post in the 16th century.* Tawney and Power, Tudor Economic Documents, ii, 224, quotes John Hales to the effect that they were 'no other but spies for foreign princes'. Sir Thomas Mildmay declared that 'under colour of merchandise . . . many intelligencers and spies adventured to come hither . . . and by riding from place to place and haven to haven they might understand the state of the same with all such landing-places as were meet for any enemy to land at'. (Housden).

Section ii. The Tightening of the Rings.
For the conspiracy of Amboise (p. 124) see article by N. M. Sutherland in E.H.R. 1966, vol. 81.

Note 37. C.S.P. Foreign 1559–60, no. 906; Teulet, i. 406, ii. 143–4.

Section iii. Sir James Croft; an Enigma?

For Lord Grey, see A Commentary, etc., of William Lord Grey of Wilton, K.G., by his son, ed. Egerton, Camden Soc., 1847, no. 40.

For Aconcio and the state of Berwick, see Iain Maciver; Antiquaries Journal, vol. xlv (1965), pp. 61–96; and Lynn White, jr.; *Jacopo Aconcio as an Engineer*, Am. Hist. Rev., lxxii (Jan. 1967), no. 2, pp. 425–44.

Conyers Read; *Mr. Secretary Walsingham*, 3 vols.

N. Williams; *Thomas Howard, fourth Duke of Norfolk*.

Note 38. *Jewels and Plate of Queen Elizabeth I*, ed. A. J. Collins, p. 130.

Note 39. Loades, op. cit., pp. 246–7. Leicester also played with the Spaniards for a time, and the financier Benedict Spinola even suggested that Philip should send him the Golden Fleece.

Note 40. Quoted in John Scott; *History of Berwick-upon-Tweed*, p. 161.

Note 41. Lettenhove, ii. 527.

Note 42. C.S.P. For. 1562, no. 1170.

Note 43. For Morris, see Conyers Read, iii, p. 148; also C.S.P. Dom. Eliz. 1581–90, clxvii, no. 58, p. 157, 'Morice servant to her Controller reports all proceedings of the Court and his master's secrets to the French Ambassador for money,' an echo of M. Louvel in 1560.

Note 44. Conyers Read, iii.

On Croft's death Sir Thomas Shirley asked William Cecil for the Comptrollership and 'my thankfulness to your Lordship shall be £500', quoted in Cheyney (see below), i, 53. C.S.P. Dom. Eliz. 1581–90.

Chapter VI

BANCROFT AND THE PURITANS

Richard Bancroft; A Sermon Preached at Paul's Cross, in Biblioteca Scriptorum Ecclesiae Anglicanae, ed. Hickes.

Early Tracts ascribed to Richard Bancroft, ed. A. Peel.

Dangerous Positions, ed. 1640.

A Survey of the Pretended Holy Discipline, ed. 1593.

'A Seconde Parte of a Register', ed. A. Peel, 2 vols (vol. i for examples on pp. 156–8).

Two Puritan Diaries, ed. M. M. Knappen.

The Presbyterian Movement (Minute book of the Dedham Classis), ed. R. G. Usher.

The Marprelate Tracts, ed. William Pierce.

An Introductory Sketch to the Marprelate Controversy, ed. Arber.
P. Collinson; *The Elizabethan Puritan Movement*.
M. M. Knappen; *Tudor Puritanism*.
R. G. Usher; *The Reconstruction of the English Church*, vol. i.
Benjamin Brook; *Lives of the Puritans*.
Daniel Neal; *History of the Puritans*.
William Pierce; *John Penry, his Life, Times and Writings*.
    Historical Introduction to the Marprelate Tracts.
G. Bonnard; *La Controverse de Martin Marprelate*.
J. Dover Wilson, The Library, 1907, on Sir Roger Williams as Marprelate.
P. M. Dawley; *John Whitgift and the Reformation*.
Owen Chadwick; *Richard Bancroft's Submission*. Journal of Ecclesiastical History, iii, pp. 58–73 (1952).
Gordon Donaldson; *Attitude of Whitgift and Bancroft to the Scottish Church*. Trans. R.H.S., 4th ser., xxiv (1942).
W. P. M. Kennedy; *Elizabethan Episcopal Administration*. 3 vols., Alcuin Club, no. xxvii (1925): and W. M. Frere; *Visitation Articles and Injunctions*, Alcuin Club, xiv, xv, 1910.
R. A. Marchant; *Puritans and Church in the Diocese of York*.
N. H. Nicholas; *Memoir . . . of Christopher Hatton, K.G.*
E. St. J. Brooks; *Sir Christopher Hatton*.
State Trials, ed. Cobbett, vol. i, pp. 1263–71, for the Knightley trial.
John Strype; *Life of Whitgift*.
    Life of Aylmer.
    Annals of the Reformation.

Note 45. For the use to which Thomas Randolph put his Mastership of the Posts see Housden, E.H.R., xviii (1903), xxi (1906). For Somers' will, C.S.P. Dom. Eliz. 1581–90, p. 585.

Note 46. Knappen; *Tudor Puritanism*, pp. 183–4.

Note 47. Collinson, p. 397.

Note 48. Kennedy; *Eliz. Epis. Admin.*, p. cxxxi.

Note 49. Knappen; *Two Puritan Diaries*, p. 60.

Note 50. S.P. Dom., clxxiv, 1581–90, no. 52, p. 181.
    It is more than likely that the Puritans, had they triumphed, would have employed a system similar in essence. For example, one of their complaints against the Bishops was that, if they had been the men they should have been 'it had been easie . . . to have trusted the ministers of every parish for the secret espialls . . .'. A Seconde Parte, vol. ii, p. 193.

Note 51. Marprelate Tracts. Just Censure and Reproofe, pp. 353–5.

Note 52. H. Trevor Roper; *The Philby Affair*, p. 66. See also Allison Ind; *History of Modern Espionage*, p. 133, 'most counter-intelligence is . . . a dull, incessant but essential grind.'

Note 53. See also Letters of Richard Verstegan (below), p. 170.

Note 54. Strype, *Life of Whitgift*, vol. 2, p. 385.

Chapter VII

SECRET SERVICE AGAINST THE CATHOLICS

C.S.P. Spanish (1580–6) for some of Mendoza's dispatches.
Statutes, ed. Prothero.
William Allen; 'Letters and Memorials', ed. T. G. Knox.
  Copie of a Letter (Stanley's surrender of Deventer), ed. Heywood, Chetham Soc., xxv (1851).
The Archpriest Controversy, ed. T. G. Law, Camden Soc., 1896, new series, no. 56 and Trans. R. Hist. Soc.
J. Morris; *Troubles of our Catholic Forefathers*, 3 vols.
Henry Foley; *Records of the English Province of the Society of Jesus*, 7 vols.
Publications of Catholic Record Society:
  Memoirs of Father Persons. vol. xxxix and Misc. iv, pp. 1–161.
  First and Second Douai Diaries.
  Tower Bills (Misc., iii, iv).
  Letters of Richard Verstegan, vol. lii, ed. Petti.
  Letters of Allen and Barret, vol. lviii, ed. Renold.
  The Stirs at Wisbech, vol. li.
  Misc., i, 47–71, ii, 219–88, xii, Prisoners.
  Philip Earl of Arundel, vol. xxi (includes several of Nicholas Berden's letters).
Richard Challoner; *Memoirs of Missionary Priests*.
A. Jessopp; *One Generation of a Norfolk House.*
Conyers Read; *Mr. Secretary Walsingham*, esp. vol. ii, cps. x, xi, and vol. iii, cp. xii.
E. P. Cheyney; *History of England from the defeat of the Armada to the death of Elizabeth*, 2 vols.
Karl Stählin; *Sir Francis Walsingham und seine Zeit*, Heidelberg, 1908.
Garrett Mattingly; *The Defeat of the Spanish Armada* (see especially for references to Mendoza).
A. Morel-Fatio; *Études sur l'Espagne*, ser. iv, cp. ix. Don Bernardino de Mendoza.
W. R. Scott; *Joint Stock Companies to 1702* (has references to Mendoza's intelligence about English trade).

T. G. Law; *Jesuits and Seculars.*

A. O. Meyer; trs. McKee, *England and the Catholic Church under Elizabeth.*

J. H. Pollen, S.J.; *English Catholics in the reign of Elizabeth.* Articles in 'The Month', 1902–4.

Leo Hicks, S.J.; *Thomas Morgan, an Elizabethan Problem.*

A. J. Loomie, S.J.; *The Spanish Elizabethans.*

Richard Simpson; *Edmund Campion.*

C. A. Beard; *Office of the Justice of the Peace.*

Philip Hughes, S.J.; *The Reformation in England*, vol. iii.

For Antony Munday, see:

    English Romayne Life, Harleian Miscellany, vol. vii, ed. 1808, pp. 447–60.

    George Elliott. A Very True Reporte (capture of Campion), ed. Arber, English Garner, viii, pp. 203–26.

    John a Kent and John a Cumber, ed. J. Payne Collier (includes biography, list of works and tracts of Munday), Shakespeare Society, 1851.

    Holinshed, Chronicles, ed. 1808, vol. iv, pp. 447–60.

    F. Meres; Palladis Tamia, ed. Arber, English Garner, vol. ii, pp. 99–100.

    J. Dover Wilson; Modern Language Review, iv, July (1908–9), pp. 484–90. *Antony Munday, Pamphleteer and Pursuivant.*

    Thomas Nashe, Works, ed. McKerrow, iii, 374, iv, 475, An Almond for a Parrat.

    A. Kenny; *Antony Munday in Rome*, Recusant History, vi, no. 4 (1962), p. 153.

    B. H. Thompson; *Antony Munday's Journey to Rome.* Durham University Journal, xxxiv, 1941.

A. Kenny; *Early Life of Antony Tyrrell.* Clergy Review, vol. xlii (1957).

C. Devlin; *An Unwilling Apostate* (Tyrrell). The Month, new ser. 6, July–Dec. 1951, p. 346.

W. F. Rea; *Self-Accusations of Political Prisoners* (Walpole). As above, p. 269.

Note 55. Hughes; *Reformation*, vol. iii, p. 379.
Letters of Allen's recently published prove an interest in active political intervention much earlier than the date hitherto assigned (see Letters of Allen and Barret, pp. 275–83, and notes at xv and 282–3).

Note 56. C.R.S. Misc., iv. Lord Burleigh's Map of Lancashire.

Note 57. For Huntingdon, see Morris, i, pp. 133–8. For another opinion of him as the 'good Earl', see Claire Cross; *The Puritan Earl.*

Note 58. Knollys seems to have approved of Topcliffe. Demanding greater care after the Babington affair that recusants should not come near the Queen, he wrote that 'such servitors in that behalf, by secret inquisition (as Mr. Topclif is), would be comforted'. (Strype, *Whitgift*, iii, 199). Topcliffe could argue against the banishment rather than execution of priests that a banished priest would prove a good spy for Spain 'and in any tyme of sudden invasion . . . is the best Guyde by night or daye'.

Note 59. C.S.P. Dom. 1581–90, p. 30.

Note 60. Conyers Read; Am. Hist. Rev., xx (1915), pp. 292–313. Pollard, E.H.R., xvi (1901), 572–7. Neale, E.H.R., xliv (1929), pp. 203–20. Conyers Read, Am. Hist. Rev., xxxv (1930), pp. 560–6.

Note 61. Conyers Read, ii, 369.

Note 62. Letters of William Allen, p. 415, no. cclvii.

Note 63. Berden is discussed in Conyers Read, ii, 330–5. For letters see C.R.S., xxi. Earl of Arundel.

Note 64. *Thomas Morgan, an Elizabethan Problem.*

Note 65. The traveller Fynes Morison did not, as Munday deliberately did, cross Europe as a spy. But in his fascinating and thrilling account he describes the diary he kept in cipher morning and evening of things observed, ranging from sauces and rare plants to harbours, armouries and armed forces. He advised other travellers to send such notes home every six months, but in some places they 'may be dangerous'. He skilfully avoided Mass in Catholic countries, but sometimes had to fast or 'negligently dip his hand' into holy water, in order to escape the notice of spies.

Note 66. Intelligence of landing-places, defences, etc., sent Bancroft in 1602 by a priest and a Catholic student are quoted in Foley, ii, p. 138.

EPILOGUE

Note 67. Loomie, chapter 3 on Richard Owen, and the introduction to the Verstegan letters, cover some of the Catholic counter-intelligence. As for women, Elizabeth herself expressed the age's attitude. Complimented on knowing so many languages, she replied (de Maisse's Journal, ed. Harrison and Jones, p. 40), that 'it were no marvel to teach a woman to talk; it were far harder to teach her to hold her tongue'. Yet the heroic wives of the Puritans and their helpers managed to hold theirs, e.g. Mistresses Waldegrave, Crane, Penry and Wigston.

Note 68. New Cambridge Modern History, ii, p. 358.

Note 69. Russell; *Maitland of Lethington*, p. 38. See also the references in W. L. Mathieson; *Politics and Religion*.

Note 70. Dasent, Acts of the Privy Council, xii, 1580–1, May 26, 1580. C.S.P. Dom., ccliii, 62, August 5, 1595.

Note 71. For smuggling, etc., see *The Smugglers Trade*, by G. D. Ramsay, Trans. R.H.S., 5th ser., ii (1952). A. P. Newton; *The Establishment of the Great Farm of the English Customs*, Trans. R.H.S., 4th ser., i (1918). Lipson; *Econ. Hist. of England*, vol. ii, 364. Cunningham; *The Mercantile System*, p. 89.

Note 72. For Stieber, see Ronald Seth; *Spies at Work*. For Maude, see E. St. J. Brooks; *Sir Christopher Hatton*.

Note 73. For Perez, see G. Maranon; *Antonio Perez*, Eng. trans. C. D. Ley, pp. 151–5, 338–9. Rowse, *Raleigh and the Throckmortons*, p. 101.

Note 74. Letters of Philip Gawdy, ed. Roxburghe Club (1906), Nov. 16, 1600.

Note 75. Rebecca West; *The Meaning of Treason*, Penguin edn., p. 217.

Note 76. For Schragmuller, see Seth, p. 104. Also quoted, Eleanor Philby; *The Spy I Loved*, p. 116. F. W. Deakin and G. R. Storry; *The Case of Richard Sorge*, p. 216.

Note 77. H. Montgomery Hyde; *Cynthia*, cp. 7 and p. 181. T. Whiteside; *An Agent in Place. The Wennerstrom Affair*, pp. 8, 27, 39, 102, 120. C. Felix; *The Spy and His Masters*, p. 49.

Note 78. Gordon Lonsdale; *Spy*. H. A. R. Philby; *My Silent War*, pp. xvii–xix (English edition).

Note 79. Leon O'Broin; *The Unfortunate Robert Emmet*, p. 164.

INDEX

Ambassadors are grouped together. Strong points on coasts or tidal rivers, harbours, etc., are grouped under PORTS. The great majority of those men marked as martyrs, of whatever denomination, were brought to their death through the denunciation of a spy.

Paulet, William, Marquis of Winchester, 109; Sir Amyas, 244
Payne, John, priest, 229; John, Puritan, 175; Richard, Gresham's servant, 117, 120–1
Penkovsky, Oleg, spy, 6, 237–9
Pensions, 27, 27 n.
Penry, John, Welsh separatist martyr, 159–60, 162–3, 166–9, 170, 171, 173, 176, 184; execution, 177; 259
Percy, Sir Henry, 8th Earl of Northumberland, 54–6, 71, 79–80, 88, 91, 138, 150; Thomas, 7th Earl, Blessed Thomas Percy, 54, 57, 88, 91, 93, 100, 150, 181, Table II
Perez, Antonio, 232
Persons, Robert, S.J., priest, 182, 201–3, 205, 206, 207, 210, 213, 216
Phelippes, Thomas, in charge of spies, 149, 189, 208–10, 242, 244
Philby, Mrs. Eleanor, 239, 240, 253; H.A.R. ('Kim') spy, 6, 8, 211, 235, 236, 240, 246–50, 253
Philip II, King of Spain, no longer King of England, 17; dilemma of, 18, 116–19, 121; decision, 111, 119; lack of money, 112, 121; allied with Guises, 150; *also* 13, 14, 21, 31, 32, 36, 58–61, 75, 80, 82–3, 107, 109, 114, 116, 118–19, 123, 127, 132, 142–4, 150, 181–2, 188, 197–204, 206, Table I
Pickering, Sir William, as spy, 36–7
Pitt, William, 229, 253
Pole, Reginal, Cardinal, 24, 113–14, 181, Table II
Poley, Robert, spy, 235–6
della Porta, Giovanni Battista, 245
PORTS: (coastal forts, etc.)
Amsterdam, 106, 117, 120
Antwerp, sympathy with Reformation, Gresham in, centre of news, etc., 105–23, 187
Berwick-upon-Tweed, vital to defence, 77–8; bad conditions, 54, 77–8, 133, 137; secret talks at, 89–90, 93–4; spies near or inside, 76, 88, 91; tardy fortification of,

133; allowance for spies at, 44, 140, 228; *also* 16, 24, 47, 54, 55, 87, 94, 102, 106, 136, 137; Treaty of Berwick, 135
Boulogne, plans betrayed, 32, 122, 129
Broughty Craig, money for spies at, 45; betrayed, 69
Caen, 36
Calais, 16, 20, 33; fall of, 38–9; 52, 58–9, 87, 118, 122, 243
Dieppe, 61, 86, 87, 120, 123, 129; Knox in, 61
Dover, 61, 144, 145
Dumbarton Castle, 15, 127, 200
Dunbar, 47, 85, 87, 124
Dundee, 124
Dunkirk, 41, 118, 122, 144
Emden, 83; Gresham shipping from, 110; 117
Eyemouth, fortified against Berwick, 16; 48, 54, 87, 90, 201
Fécamp, preparations at, 87
Gravelines, searchers bribed at, 110
Groningen, watch kept from, 117
Hamburg, 83, 110, 121, 193
King's Lynn, invasion suggested at, 117; 157
Le Havre de Grace, 92, 225
Leith, Marie de Guise fortifies, 95, 98; Maitland follows her there, 95; rides out, 99; critical point, 96; besieged, 134, 135, 138; assault fails, 136; *also* 48, 102, 104, 106, 111, 124, 127, 128, 140, 146, 226, 243
London, throughout; *see* Tower
Lübeck, 83
Middleburg, watch kept from, 117, 121
Montrose, 124
Newcastle, Duke of Norfolk at, 111, 128; priests caught near, 187; 128, 162, 169
Ostend, 144
Plymouth, 142
Portsmouth, 133
Rouen, preparations observed at,